The National Licensing Exam for
Marriage & Family Therapy

An Independent Study Guide

The National Licensing Exam for

Marriage & Family Therapy

An Independent Study Guide

Written by a Doctor of Marriage & Family Therapy
Lucas A. Volini, DMFT, LMFT

MFT
Licensing Exam

Publications

Publisher's Notice

Mention of specific companies, organizations or authorities in this book does not imply endorsement by the publisher or author, nor does mention of specific companies, organizations or authorities imply that they endorse this book, its author, or the publisher.

Published by: MFT Licensing Exam LLC
                       1082 Prairie View LN
                       Waconia, MN
                       www.mftlicensingexam.com

Cover design: Pixel Studios
                       www.fiverr.com

Edited by: Ann Marie Mazzuca
                       Busia's Quilting & Book Editing, Inc.

Printed in the United States of America

ISBN-13: 978-0-692-53711-4   MFT Licensing Exam LLC
ISBN-10: 0692537112

This book is dedicated to the past, present, and future members of the
Minnesota Association for Marriage & Family Therapy

It has been my exceptional privilege to share in a community of such passionate, imaginative, and generous individuals. Each day, the actions of our members faithfully demonstrate what it means to be a relational healer…

Anxiety is our best teacher…(S)He, therefore, who has learned rightly to be anxious has learned a most important thing…

-*Søren Kierkegaard*

An Open Letter to Recent Graduates,

Congratulations on your completion of a Master's Degree or Graduate Certificate in the study and practice of Marriage and Family Therapy. This is a time in your professional career filled with as much excitement as there is ambiguity. As so, there are likely many questions you have been asking yourself regarding next steps...

Where can I find a good job?

What am I qualified for as an unlicensed Mental Health Professional?

What hours count toward licensure?

Where can I find quality supervision?

AND Ultimately...

Where do I even begin to prepare for the National Licensing Exam!?

The purpose of this manual is to lessen the anxiety and overwhelming ambiguity associated with the National Licensing Exam, and in turn, learn to be rightly anxious. In preparing for the National Exam myself, I grew dissatisfied with the available study options. In my area, one option included paying an additional $300 to take a preparation course, putting it financially out of reach considering the steep costs already associated with the exam itself. The other option was a $185 study guide right around 800 pages. I again found myself having to consider another expense while finding time to review 800 pages of text covering the entire field of Marriage and Family Therapy. After consulting with many colleagues who took the exam, the most common feedback received found the exam to be far more *application based* than *knowledge based*. To me, this was incongruent with investing hours upon hours reviewing the particulars of each theory to family therapy.

As so, this independent study guide is not an exhaustive text of theory and detailed information; instead, it is a roadmap containing the bare essentials covered in the exam. It is more oriented toward *learning how to pass the exam* than it is with *relearning* everything you just covered throughout graduate school.

Over the past decade or so, the measures used by the National Licensing Exam have evolved. What was once an evaluation of basic knowledge (i.e. who is better at remembering which intervention belongs to which theory) is now a measure of your capacity to effectively apply the principles learned throughout graduate school in an ethical, systemically-informed manner. What was once the recommendation to take the exam fresh out of graduate school does not necessarily apply to the new format. Understanding that statutes vary from state to state regarding when the exam can be taken, if you happen to be in a state where you can count hours toward licensure prior to passing the National Licensing Exam, consider focusing on growing as a therapist as opposed to pressuring yourself to rush through the testing process.

I attribute the high score I received upon passing the exam far more exclusively to the experiences I gained while in the field than anything I learned from a textbook. I had taken the National Exam after completing well beyond the 4,000 required post-graduate hours of field experience including extensive MFT Supervision and clinical case consultations. During this time, I had worked as a school-based therapist, in-home therapist, outpatient therapist, day treatment therapist, and opened my own private practice. All the while, I was constantly engaged in ongoing supervision with various supervisors and participating in rich clinical case consultations through the agencies in which I was employed. These were the experiences that brought theory to life, bringing meaning to navigating systemic dynamics within families and grappling through tricky ethical dilemmas that the textbook could never prepare you for. As your practicum experiences will serve you well for those having to take the exam prior to counting hours toward licensure, for others, I recommend *slowing down* to soak in the supervision and fresh client experiences.

For everyone, allow yourself to learn and grow from your clients and colleagues. Find a supervisor that can walk you through the administrative nightmares of managed care and the requirements mandated by the Department of Human Services regarding how our files must be maintained. Find another supervisor that can nurture the deeply personal experience of evolving as a therapist, focusing on *Self of Therapist* work and passing down his or her wisdom onto you as it was once passed onto them. Find *another* supervisor that you can laugh with, modeling effective self-care and demonstrating how specific and ongoing ways of paying attention to ourselves is the only way to establish longevity in this field. Maybe this will all come from one person, or more likely from several. Be sure not to limit yourself as the richness of this field blossoms from the diversity of its members. One thing I can say is regardless of any financial struggles my family and I were going through, I do not regret even $1.00 spent on quality supervision. It is important to consider the long-term investment on the quality of foundation in which you will grow from.

This is only my advice based upon what worked for me. Keep in mind that the national exam is now highly oriented toward clinical vignettes, navigating through tricky client encounters, crisis situations and unforeseeable ethical dilemmas. This manual can serve as a resource to look through as you accumulate your hours and reviewed more intensely once the exam date approaches. This is meant to be the bare essentials of what is needed to know as far as the *context* of the exam; however, the *process* of the exam can only be acquired and fine tuned out in the field during your practicum and post-graduate experiences.

I encourage you to shoot me an email with any questions related to navigating the field of Marriage & Family Therapy, feedback about this study guide, recommendations for future editions, or to schedule a web-based tutoring session. Best of luck!

Your Colleague,

Dr. Lucas Volini, DMFT, LMFT
lucas@mftlicensingexam.com
www.mftlicensingexam.com

Table of Contents

Part I

Exam Overview, Test-Taking Strategies & Study Techniques

Exam Overview

The National Licensing Exam in the field of Marital & Family Therapy is developed and maintained by the Association of Marital & Family Therapy Regulatory Board's (AMFTRB) Advisory Committee and scored by the Professional Testing Corporation (PTC). For a complete review of the exam itself, I encourage you to spend some time reading through the website at **www.amftrb.com**.

The exam is comprised of *200 multiple-choice questions*, each of which containing *four potential correct answers*. You are encouraged to answer every question regardless of your confidence in the right answer as no penalties are given for incorrect answers. You will have *four-hours to complete the exam* which is facilitated at one of the many PSI professional testing centers across the nation. This leaves you with about one-minute and 20-seconds to answer each question—some may take more time, some may take less, which we will cover in test-taking tips and strategies later on in this manual.

Candidates will also be asked to fill out an additional application for PTC. Once the PTC application is completed and the examination fee of $350.00 has been received, candidates will receive an identification number and information concerning the testing centers. Candidates will be instructed to contact PSI directly to schedule their examination date and time.

Keep in mind that registration occurs the month prior to each exam. Meaning, if you wish to take the exam in January, you must register through PSI by December first. This means that your application has already been approved by your respective State Board of Marriage & Family Therapy. That process can take more than one month and precedes your eligibility to apply for the exam itself through PSI. So, if you plan to take the exam in January have your application sent to the Board of MFT no later than November first, knowing that October will more likely guarantee your eligibility to sit for the exam in January.

Please contact your state board with any questions concerning application deadlines and additional fees for licensure and application. Your state may have additional requirements that supersede the ones outlined above.

Also, keep in mind that many states accommodate you applying for the National Exam and the State Licensing Exam at the same time—this can save you a few months of waiting to take your Oral Exam on state statutes and laws. As soon as you pass the National, your scores will be sent to your State Board which will automatically qualify you to sit for the Oral Exam on the next available testing date.

*Note: Not all states require passing an Oral Exam prior to receiving licensure.

Test Specifications for the Examination in Marital and Family Therapy

The exam consists of six knowledge domains. The percentage listed signifies the amount of questions on the exam that fall within that domain. Half of the exam will measure your knowledge base and ability to *apply* such knowledge regarding *The Practice of Systemic Therapy* (Domain 1) and the *Designing and Conducting of Treatment* (Domain 3). Domain 5, *Managing Crisis Situations,* is a newer Domain (AMFTRB, 2015).

Domain 1
The Practice of Systemic Therapy (23.0%)

Tasks related to incorporating systemic theory and perspectives into practice activities, and establishing and maintaining ongoing therapeutic relationships with the client system.

Domain 2
Assessing, Hypothesizing, and Diagnosing (16.0%)

Tasks related to assessing the various dimensions of the client system, forming and reformulating hypotheses, and diagnosing the client system in order to guide therapeutic activities.

Domain 3
Designing and Conducting Treatment (23.0%)

Tasks related to developing and implementing interventions with the client system.

Domain 4
Evaluating Ongoing Process and Terminating Treatment (13.0%)

Tasks related to continuously evaluating the therapeutic process and incorporating feedback into the course of treatment, as well as planning for termination.

Domain 5
Managing Crisis Situations (10%)

Tasks related to assessing and managing emergency situations, and intervening when clinically indicated and/or legally mandated.

Domain 6
Maintaining Ethical, Legal, and Professional Standards (15%)

Tasks related to ongoing adherence to legal and ethical codes and treatment agreements, maintaining competency in the field, and professionalism.

*****Note:** The term client refers to the individual, couple, family, group, and other collaborative systems that are a part of treatment (AMFTRB, 2015).

This is a general description of each domain. By visiting **www.amftrb.org**, you can retrieve an exhaustive breakdown of what each domain covers in great detail. This is *highly recommended,* as it will provide you with much clarity as you begin preparing for the exam. The website will further identify how they set a passing score, how scores are verified, instructions on taking the practice exam (highly recommended, as we will discuss more), score reporting, and exam dates.

Next Steps

Visit the website **www.amftrb.org** to review the context of the exam and all relevant information. They provide a detailed overview of what each domain specifically covers, serving as a helpful roadmap as you structure your studies.

The AMFTRB Practice Exam

There is no better measure of your preparedness for the exam than taking the practice exam provided through **www.amftrb.org**. The test is comprised of recently retired questions from the actual exam. Many, MANY MFTs report that the score they received on the practice exam was within 1-2 points of their actual score. The passing score changes as each cohort completes the exam—it is based on a curve of how well that group of test takers performed and which questions were included in that exam (each question is individually weighted based on difficulty, so the more difficult questions included in the exam, the lower the passing score). Passing cut-off scores have often ranged between 64%-74%, depending on that cohort and particular makeup of the exam. Many, MANY test takers report failing by 1-2 questions, so knowing the particulars of the field of Marriage and Family Therapy will help to get those freebies as you navigate the more challenging vignette-based questions (e.g. an individual's capacity to balance thinking with feeling and belonging with individuality refers to Bowen's term of...*DIFFERENTIATION*...do not miss these questions).

Scoring within the low 70s is a good sign that you are right where you need to be. Scoring a 75 or higher means you are in good shape. Scoring above an 80 on the practice exam? Maintain exactly where you are. Go into the test feeling *rightly anxious*; meaning, enough anxiety to stay focused, motivated, and on your game but not *too much* anxiety to the point that it hinders performance. I could not think of a better measure preparing you to go into the exam confidently than passing the practice exam through AMFTRB with a score beyond 75%.

Keep in mind the practice exam will not provide you with answers you got wrong, but will show your score in each domain—just as the actual exam will. Do not let this discourage you. As other practice exams will tell you which answers you got wrong and provide an explanation of the right answer, know that these are not questions drafted by the actual test creators. Performance on the other practice exams will not transfer to the actual exam nearly as well as the AMFTRB practice exam.

Enough about the exam itself. Let's get into test-taking strategies and study techniques...

Test-Taking Strategies

Multiple-Choice Test Taking

When taking multiple-choice tests, keep in mind the basics of test taking—read each question carefully and have a systematic approach to the whole exam. Below are specific strategies for approaching multiple choice questions.

Recognize Qualifiers

Qualifiers are words that alter a statement. Words such as *always, next best, except,* or *never,* among many others, can have a dramatic impact on which potential answer is right and which potential answers are wrong. Remain mindful as you read through each question while clarifying what the question is asking. This is often done by recognizing qualifiers.

To beat qualifiers, you need to know the qualifier families:

- All, most, some, none (no)
- Always, usually, sometimes, never
- Great, much, little, no
- *Least* likely, *most* likely
- The *next* best step
- Except
- More, equal, less
- Good, bad
- Is, is not

Notice Negatives

Negatives can be words like no, not, none and never, or they can be prefixes like "il", as in illogical, "un", as in uninterested, or "im," as in impatient. Much like qualifiers, negatives have the potential to shift correct answers to incorrect answers. Do not expect intentional trick questions on the exam, but do expect some potential answers in the multiple-choice set to align with what you *may* think the question is asking in the case that you overlooked any *qualifiers* or *negatives*.

Choose the Best Response

On the exam, expect that multiple answers may technically be correct in relation to what the question is asking. In this case, be thoughtful in choosing which of the two right answers is *MORE RIGHT* than the other. Do not pressure yourself to be *certain* in which answer is more right—many of the questions will leave you with much uncertainty so expect that to be part of this test-taking process. The ambiguity will want to slow you down and lose confidence to the point that you may run out of time. As taught by our friend Rollo May, increasing our tolerance for ambiguity is a prominent sign of good mental health. It is okay to leave the test feeling very unsure about yourself—if anything, that is a sign that you gave each question a lot of thought.

Mark Only "Sure Things" First, Make Several "Passes" Through the Test

Some individuals will report "flagging" challenging questions with the intent of coming back to them at the end of the exam. In some cases, future questions may have a clue that triggers your memory on an answer you skipped. Remember, this is a long exam with 200 questions that must be answered within the timeframe of four hours. Although "flagging" *knowledge-based* questions may be helpful, many questions are *vignette based* and take time to read through effectively. Keep in mind that skipping those questions and having to read back through them may set you too far back against the clock.

So, "flagging" questions you are unsure about *may* or *may not* lend itself to the National Exam given the time constraints. You are better off "flagging" knowledge-based questions than vignette-based questions. If you find yourself keeping a good pace, allow more answers to be skipped as you are certain there will be extra time to further review them. This strategy will be dependent upon the pace in which you are able to maintain.

*Rule-Out Obvious Wrong Answers

This is a *VERY IMPORTANT* tip for the exam. On many questions, you should be able to quite easily rule out one or two questions right off the bat. This will increase your odds of choosing the correct answer to 50%. Remember, the two potential right answers left may both be right, so choosing the *MORE RIGHT* answer is not always cut and clear. Trust your gut and choose one while making sure to keep a good pace. This is when field experience from your practicum and post-graduate experience will serve you well as your intuition is more developed.

Taking the Exam

Several MFTs recommend familiarizing yourself with the testing center prior to the exam date. Take a drive to the location and know whether or not any detours or construction will add to drive time—remember, if you show up late, you forfeit your exam spot and must re-register for another date including paying an additional registration fee. Call the testing center and ask them the following questions:

- Do you allow food or drink in the exam room?

- Do you allow music or headphones in the exam room?

- Can I wear noise-canceling headphones if they are disconnected from an audio device?

- Will there be individuals taking an exam other than the National Licensing Exam in MFT?

- Anything else you are curious about regarding the testing environment.

It is important to walk into the exam with a sense of esteem in yourself as a therapist. Expect that you will get an 80% or better and take pride in your already proven abilities to work with clients from a systemic orientation (after focusing your time on practicum experience and professional development in the field).

Much like we tell our clients, take in every opportunity to track your breathing. Allow yourself a long, drawn-out deep breath or two every few questions. This will both manage anxiety and increase oxygen to your brain—enhancing cognitive functioning and keeping you sharp.

Track your pace. You have four hours to answer 200 questions. Set some milestones for every 50 questions. For example, if the exam starts at 2:00 and come 3:00 you have just answered question 50, you are on pace to finish *just* on time. This may be cutting it too close. If this is the case, you are likely *overthinking* each question so begin to rely more on what your gut is telling you. If you answer question 100 and notice it is only 3:40, you are ahead of the game. Treat yourself to a meditative walk down the hallway to stretch your legs and rest your mind in the present moment. You do not get any points for finishing early so keep your eye on the clock and permit yourself regular breaks as needed.

> *Note: You are not allowed to bring food or drink into most examination rooms, but you will likely be able to keep a water bottle and snack in the waiting area. I'd recommend calling your testing center prior to taking the exam to see what your options are.

Maintaining Perspective

Do not put too much pressure on yourself to pass the first time around. Many others in your situation fail their first attempt. If you end up missing the cut off, know that you are in good company. It is a challenging exam just as it should be in ensuring the integrity of our profession. The work we do as licensed professionals has the potential to be tragically harmful. Take pride in the fact that our profession goes to great lengths ensuring that only the highest qualified and capable healers are awarded the privilege to serve individuals, couples, and families under the title of Marriage and Family Therapist. One statistic I am sure of is *most* people who fail the exam on their first try eventually end up passing the exam. This suggests the importance of taking the practice exam found at **www.amftrb.org** as well as gaining field experience in your practicum and post-graduate work, as both will prepare you well for what to expect come test day.

Maintaining a Mindset Congruent to What the Exam is Measuring

When taking the exam, try to prevent yourself from viewing the questions through the lens of, "What would *I* do in this clinical situation?" If you have been practicing for some time by now, your approach has likely become a subjective integration of who you are as a therapist. As so, the test questions may not align with your clinical judgment—not to say that you are wrong, but that it may not be what the exam question architects are measuring.

What is a Congruent Mindset?

"What would a 65-year-old, Caucasian male, with a thick, white beard, wearing a tweed sport coat with suede elbow patches, trained in *systemic therapy*, do in this clinical situation?"

Answer these questions objectively per the textbook. Subjectively, you may likely disagree with the *correct answer*, or better yet, *your* correct answer of what *you* would do next likely will not be provided. This is okay, as the test is not meant to measure what *you* would do. Keep in mind that this is an objective measure and don't let yourself get frustrated. Instead, enjoy the experience of investigating what the question is asking and how the *textbook* would most likely answer.

ALWAYS BE THINKING SYSTEMICALLY!!!

Many of the questions will ask, "What would a *Family Therapist* do next?" For me, this question was frustrating. Years of education had taught me there is no such thing as a *Family Therapist*, that the experience and practice is subjective and deeply personal. I have 25 different theories I could rattle off of the top of my head, all of which would argue a different response to what a *Family Therapist* is. DO NOT LET YOURSELF GET CAUGHT UP IN THIS STRUGGLE. Fortunately for me, this frustrating experience came during the practice exam, allowing me to explore the concept of a *Family Therapist*. Expect that many vignettes will take this format. In Part III of this manual, *The Theory & Practice of Marriage & Family Therapy*, we will outline and explore *the universal concepts of a family therapist* in preparing you to confidently approach vignettes from this perspective. First, let us see where you are with a sample question…

Sample Question

The mother of a 12-year-old boy calls to request that her son be seen for therapy. She reports him being withdrawn at home and acting out inappropriately at school (school has reported disrespectful language toward teachers and peers and refusal to work on occasion). Mom and the school staff agree that this is only the 12-year-old son's problem, as his younger sibling (age eight) is flourishing across all environments. A Marital and Family Therapist would do all of the following except:

a. Validate mom's concerns and struggles that her son is acting out inappropriately.
b. Aim to determine how the son's inappropriate behavior is occurring independently from his brother and parents.
c. Work with the son individually to explore why he is engaging in inappropriate behaviors.
d. Invite the entire family in to expand the symptom to the system.

Answer **A** and answer **D** are two automatic rule-outs. Family Therapists will *always* validate the concerns and struggles of those coming to us for support (**answer a**), as well as make an effort toward expanding the symptoms of an individual to the larger system (**answer d**) (this is most easily done through having at least the primary family group in session for the initial assessment).

Although answer **C** may appear to contradict answer **D**, working with an individual while conceptualizing the *symptom* as a systemic problem is perhaps not ideal but nevertheless common practice. In comparison to answer **B**, a *Family Therapist* is likely to work with individuals but will *never* assess for an individual's behavior as occurring independently from the system as this ultimately contradicts systems theory.

If the correct answer was not obvious to you, that is okay! After all, you are just getting started. This independent study guide is specifically designed to prepare you in approaching each question with a clear understanding of what is expected as you investigate the *most correct* answer. As so, let's talk about effectively using this independent study guide to ensure you get the most out of your studying...

Study Techniques & Manual Overview

How to Use this Independent Study Guide

This manual is meant to serve as an independent study guide—that is, a structured approach to effectively preparing for the National Licensing Exam in Marital & Family Therapy. It contains the bare essentials of what is needed to know come test day; no more, no less. This manual will cover the following domains:

- **Part I:** Review of the Exam, Test-Taking Strategies, Study Tips, and Manual Overview
- **Part II:** The History of the Field of Marriage & Family Therapy
- **Part III:** The Theory & Practice of Marriage & Family Therapy
- **Part IV:** Other Clinical Considerations & Concepts
- **Part V:** Sample Test Questions
- References (recommended readings), Glossary (key terms & theory conceptualizations)

General Overview

When working through this manual, pay attention to text that is either in **Bold** or *Italicized.*

Bold Text: The last name of primary contributors and theorists will always be in **bold** text. When you recognize this, ask yourself whether or not you are familiar with this contributor via their associated theory and what role they played in its development. For instance, when you see Murray **Bowen,** you should think to yourself, "**Bowen,** okay, he developed **Bowen's** Multigenerational Family Systems Approach, which is most recognized for the *genogram* and his concept of *self-differentiation.* I should remember, that although the *genogram* is most connected with **Bowen,** it was actually his student, Phillip **Guerin,** that renamed **Bowen's** concept of a *Family Diagram* the *genogram*).

Italicized Text: Every key term, intervention, or relevant concept that will be covered on the exam will always be *italicized.* When you see text that is *italicized,* ask yourself a similar question as stated above for **bold** text. For instance, when a statement refers to *The MRI Group,* you should be able to tell yourself, "Oh, *The MRI Group,* that was **Bateson's** initial group in *Palo Alto* where they researched patterns of communication in families with a schizophrenic patient. It was eventually turned into the *Mental Research Institute* by Don **Jackson,** where they developed the *MRI Systemic Approach* to therapy, and was later renamed by Richard **Fisch** as the *Brief Therapy Center at MRI.*"

Visual Triggers

On the first chapter page of each theory, you will notice a square box in the upper right-hand corner. You may use this to create your own symbol to associate with each theory. This is a common study technique for visual learners. For instance, in the box for *Contextual Family Therapy,* you can draw in a gavel to remind you that **Nagy's** father was a judge and how that influenced the development of his theory. Feel free to draw in a gavel on each page for that theory as well as include them on your flashcards you may choose to make.

Outline of Major Theories

This manual is not meant to re-teach you the theories you already learned throughout graduate school—Instead, it is meant to review the major theories in a way that the exam will measure. As you will see, the review of each theory is outlined congruent to the domains of the exam, as follows:

THE PRACTICE OF SYSTEMIC THERAPY (Domain 1)
Primary Contributor
Class of Family Therapy
Historical Overview
Essential Themes of Therapy
Key Terms

ASSESSING, HYPOTHESIZING, & DIAGNOSING (Domain 2)
Assessment
Diagnosing

DESIGNING & CONDUCTING TREATMENT (Domain 3)
Who is Involved
Treatment Duration
Goals of Therapy
Primary Interventions and/or Techniques

EVALUATING ONGOING PROCESS & TERMINATING TREATMENT (Domain 4)
Early-Phase
Middle-Phase
Later-Phase
Termination

In Application to the Vignette

This is meant to familiarize you with what the exam will measure, shifting your mindset toward conceptualizing these theories through the lens of *application* and not *retention*. Although the exam will measure a basic knowledge base of key terms and definitions, the majority of the questions will take the form of a vignette.

For instance, a question about *differentiation* will either be a *straightforward* question (knowledge-based question) asking, "The concept associated with balancing thinking with feeling and togetherness with belonging is: *Self-Differentiation*".

Or, more likely, it will be an *application-based* question asking, "Based on the presenting problem, the therapist encouraged the emotionally-reactive husband to reduce his anxiety and use an I-Statement to help his partner better understand what he is wanting." Here, the therapist is helping the client work toward: *Self-Differentiation*.

Key Terms & Primary Interventions

As you will see, the major *terms* and *interventions* for each theory are left blank. This is intentional as it encourages you to use outside resources as you work through each theory. As I have outlined the major concepts of each theory—as relevant to what the exam will measure—you may wish to explore the theory more in depth. For instance, perhaps you are highly seasoned as a *Solution-Focused Therapist* and do not need to do a thorough review of the theory as you already grasp the major concepts, and more importantly, how they are *applied* to the here-and-now of the therapeutic encounter. Then you stumble upon *Object-Relations Theory* which is more unfamiliar. You may wish to pursue outside resources (provided in the resources and recommended readings section) to explore the approach more in depth and fill in the primary interventions and key terms accordingly.

The process of reading a term's definition and writing it out by hand is endorsed by research to enhance retention and make long-term memory storage more accessible to recall (Herbert, 2014; Mangen & Velay, 2011). Although it may be more time consuming—and, arguably an ancient study approach—it will contribute to more accessible retention in areas covered on the exam. At the end of this chapter, review the ***Note** outlining suggested resources to be used along with this independent study guide.

Challenge yourself to track down the definitions of each term through various resources, as they are a compilation of my notes throughout my Master's and Doctoral-level education mostly comprised of primary resources. As you find the definition of each key term, move beyond a general knowledge of what it means and challenge yourself to *apply* the intervention to the provided Becker Family Vignette. This will expand your comprehension of the key term or primary intervention and better prepare you for *application-based questions* on the exam.

> *__Note:__ There is a glossary included in the back of this manual that contains the definition of every term and concept left blank in Part III of this independent study guide. This may be useful for the theories you are familiar with, but it is encouraged that you explore the theories you are unfamiliar with more in depth—using outside sources—in preparing to *apply* the concepts to vignettes throughout the exam.

Flash Cards

This manual does not come with flash cards, nor are they provided as a supplemental resource at **www.mftlicensingexam.com**. This is intentional. The time spent for me to create flash cards would be minimal, and the cost to manufacture them would be a fraction of the selling price. I advise against investing additional money into this process for flash cards. Instead, it is recommended that you produce them yourself. The very process of creating the flash cards will contribute to retaining the information far more than reading through pre-printed definitions.

Audible Study Aids

Many individuals endorse being an auditory learner and several of us spend many hours a week in the car commuting to and from work. As so, I created an audio recording that reviews this manual, including each theory compared and contrasted with one another, as applied to the Becker Family vignette. This Disc Set is available for purchase at **www.mftlicensingexam.com**.

Mobile Phone / Tablet App (iOS/Android Compatible)

To accommodate the many conveniences afforded by our technological world, I created an App containing a general review of this information. This too can be purchased at **www.mftlicensingexam.com**.

The Vignette

Because this exam is heavily based upon *application* over *regurgitation,* it is important that you can demonstrate the capacity to *apply* these theories and concepts as you learn them. This program is based upon having the same family vignette follow us throughout each theory and approach to family therapy we review—demonstrating the similarities and differences while bringing the concepts to life through pragmatic application.

The outline of each theory—as stated above—will demonstrate the key themes of the theory, its primary goals, a list of interventions and techniques used throughout, and finally, the process in which therapy unfolds. You will be asked to apply each approach to the family vignette including how the theory will guide the early phase, middle phase, and later phase of therapy—eventually leading to termination. This will strengthen your skills for Domains 1-4 in relation to the particulars of each theory.

A glossary in the back of this manual will provide a brief narrative of the overall conceptualization of the Becker Family in relation to each particular theory; however, it will not provide a completed treatment plan. It is recommended that you draft a conceptualization of the Becker Family after reviewing each theory prior to comparing and contrasting it with the version provided in the glossary. Keep in mind that your conceptualization may likely vary from the one provided, not necessarily meaning it is wrong. Many of these theories lend themselves to creativity and no two therapists will ever conceptualize the family in the exact same manner (e.g. *Symbolic-Experiential*) whereas others are more structured and will look similar across several therapists trained in that approach (e.g. *Solution-Focused* or *Emotionally-Focused*).

If you are struggling to devise a treatment plan based upon a particular theory after reviewing the provided case conceptualization, take that as a sign to pursue other resources that will expound upon the theory in greater depth. You should walk into the exam feeling confident in your ability to effectively apply each theory to a family vignette congruent with the domains covered.

Let's meet the Becker Family that will walk us through each theory…

The Becker Family

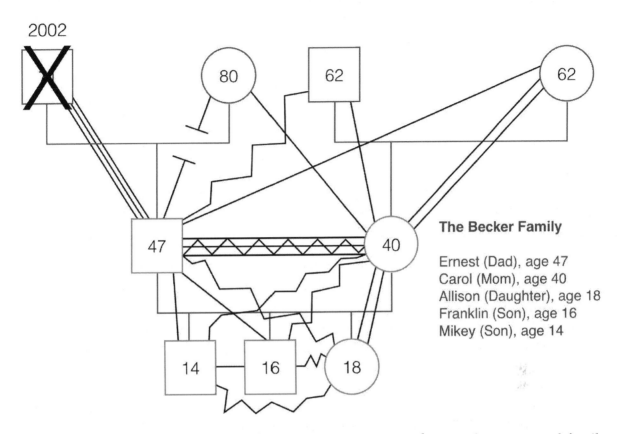

The Becker Family

Ernest (Dad), age 47
Carol (Mom), age 40
Allison (Daughter), age 18
Franklin (Son), age 16
Mikey (Son), age 14

The Beckers are a Caucasian, middle-class family pursuing therapy due to general family disconnection. Mom initiated the phone call stating that things are "out of control" and that "changes need to happen, and fast!" Mom further elaborated that she and her husband are very disconnected and have been for the past 11 years. She said he will work all day and come home to "decompress" in his workshop attached to the garage and spend most weekends with their two sons at various sporting activities and "guys-only outings." Mom reported that she and her husband have been sleeping in different bedrooms for the past three years. Mom said she will spend most days at her Mom's home—which is close in town—and as much time as she can with her daughter before she goes off to college in five months. Mom said she is very disconnected from her sons and her husband is very disconnected from his daughter. She reported the family being "split into two" and appeared quite desperate for change to occur. Mom requested that she, her husband, and her daughter come in as her two sons are refusing to attend family therapy.

> *Note: You will come to know this family quite well, so let yourself grow curious about the particulars and idiosyncrasies of each family member. It will be appropriate to let the family grow and evolve over time as you work with them through the various theories.

Study Tips

For those of you in states that do not require passing the exam prior to counting supervision hours, slow down, focus on your professional development, and take the exam closer to the end of your 3,000-4,000 pre-licensure hours. For others, your practicum experience will serve you well on the exam so remain mindful throughout your client encounters and supervision hours. Ask a million questions, every day (that is your job as an intern).

Next in line comes my encouragement to *enjoy this process*. Yes, I said it! *Enjoy studying for the National Licensing Exam*! This process does not need to be something approached with dread and fear; instead, it can be a valuable experience where you grow as a therapist. I imagine you will be surprised at how much you have retained from graduate school and experience a sense of expertise as you review many of these theories. You may also revisit some concepts that did not fit at the time you first learned them, but now, may be something you experiment with in your next client session.

When I look at my mentors who have lasted in this field for decades—maintaining a sense of vitality and passion that has grown throughout their careers—an emerging common factor is their intellectual fascination with the richness of the ideas and concepts flowing throughout our field. This helps to balance the emotional fatigue we will inevitably come to experience from time to time. The meaning we derive from our work cannot be dependent upon our clients getting better—which, is not always immediately gratifying—as this is a recipe for burnout. By remaining intellectually fascinated by our work, constantly challenging ourselves to grow as therapists through each new book we read or training we attend, we find that we also grow as individuals. Preparing for this licensing exam can be the first step toward developing an identify of a professional, life-long learner.

Many students ask about how much time should be spent studying for the exam, and some professionals (or, manuals) provide them with an answer. One of which that I have heard was 300 hours of studying over the span of 6 months. Please, do not feel like you have to do this! When it comes down to it, there is no way to objectively measure quantity over quality. I know people who surpassed those 300 hours and failed just as I know individuals who did not spend 1 hour of studying, walking into the exam with nothing but a Master's Degree and field experience and passed with an impressive score. This is a subjective process so study at a pace and rate that feels right for you. Some may work through this manual in a week while others take their time over the span of a year. Do not measure yourself against others— you should know the way you work by now so trust that process and have your study approach fit you, not the other way around.

Now, this has only been my personal advice based on what worked for me. To broaden your experience, I asked some members of the Minnesota Association for Marriage and Family Therapy who successfully passed the exam to weigh in and offer advice to their future colleagues…

Dear Colleagues,

One of my biggest barriers to taking the exam was anxiety around not passing. Although I had confidence in my abilities as a new therapist and was successful in my graduate program, I experienced significant self-doubt in my ability to pass the exam. So, the first step I took was to discuss the test-taking process with other professionals who already passed the exam. I learned about their preparation strategies, struggles with anxiety, and experiences of taking the exam in general. I also told several colleagues that I was planning to take the test soon, which created a level of accountability for registering and preparing for the exam (proceed with this step at your own risk!).

I also found it helpful to immerse myself in the theoretical literature of the field. For this, I drew from several texts that were utilized in my master's program, several primary sources in family therapy, and structured my review using a prior edition of the study guide you are reading now. Finally, I took advantage of opportunities to discuss the material I was studying with other professionals. This brought the material home and served to synthesize the theoretical knowledge. If you are able, it is also helpful to take advantage of opportunities to teach or train others in the theories of family therapy.

Looking back, I would have given myself more time to study. I rushed into the preparation process and, although this is congruent with my learning style, it added unneeded stress and anxiety. Because taking the exam is a necessary step in becoming a fully-licensed professional, it can be easy to feel that your ability to pass is representative of your ability or efficacy as a therapist. This is not the case. It is important to view the exam for what it is- a necessary measure that ensures you have an acceptable knowledge base to continue working towards independent licensure. You are not expected to be a master therapist before taking the exam. You are only expected to have a sufficient level of knowledge, which was given to you in your master's program. It only needs to be focused and refined for the purposes of this exam.

-Anthony Mielke, MA, Doctoral-Candidate, LMFT
Waconia, MN

Dear Colleagues,

When I prepared for the national exam, I combined several study methods. While I read and reviewed various study manuals, I incorporated visual and auditory learning modalities as well. For example, when I was driving, I listened to audible study aids. In addition, an iPhone app was an efficient use of time when I was waiting at an appointment, a passenger in a quiet vehicle, or had a few minutes of down time.

Knowing that I am a visual learner, I completed a visual study guide with images from the internet. I copied and pasted pictures of seminal theorists, book covers, or visual reminders of key concepts. As I was testing, I could recall images and consequently, recall the information. Finally, read the exam questions thoroughly and completely. You will have sufficient time to complete the exam.

-Dr. Rachelle Reinisch, DMFT, LAMFT
Rosemount, MN

Dear Colleagues,

Preparing for the national exam was mutually anxiety provoking as it was rewarding. I found that utilizing a variety of study methods was most effective. I began by forming a small group (two super-knowledgeable ladies) to study with. We set time aside to meet every other week and would pick specific theories to review. I found my two study partners to be great sounding boards as we would share the same worries, anxieties and frustrations throughout the process. Each week I would set aside two nights where I would study for 2-3 hours independently. During these studies, I focused on the theories we were going to review in our study group. This helped me stay on track and accountable for our group study dates. One other helpful method was picking a new place to study each week. New libraries, new coffee shops, or new parks. I know we all can struggle with feeling isolated and as if we have no life during this process, so going out to new spots gave me a sense that I was doing something exciting and fun each week. It gave me something other than studying to look forward to.

The author of this textbook asked me what I might do differently as I look back, and I answered, "Not be so anxious about my ability to pass the test!" The anxiety I felt surrounding the test is a feeling I can still vividly recall. Thankfully now, I am able to reflect on that anxiety and shake my head at myself (without the need of EMDR). You are more prepared than you know! Good luck and we are all excited to welcome you into the Marriage and Family Therapy World!

-Tracy Davis, MA, LMFT
Minneapolis, MN

Dear Colleagues,

Preparing for the National Exam can seem to be a daunting task - *"Who said that thing about 'psychotherapy of the absurd'?" "What exactly is differentiation of self again?".* I too had such questions. What can be helpful in times such as these is to do what we are asked to do in the therapeutic process and see the world through the other's eyes. In that way it becomes easier to contextualize, and therefore remember, each theory and their fundamental tenets. *Where did this theorist develop their theory and method, who else was with them, what did they contribute or take with them, what makes them stand out?*

My experience was like that of an investigator, attempting to make connections between schools of thought and differentiating theorists from one another and how they may have seen the world. When I let go of the anxiety and fear of failure, I was able to enjoy the exam by looking at the world through the eyes of each particular theorist.

-Steve Lochen, MA, LMFT
Kimball, MN

Dear Colleagues,

Many have asked for study suggestions when preparing for the National Exam. When I was ready to prepare, the first thing I did was grab my favorite study buddy (Brie Vortherms, you rock!) and we made a schedule to study weekly for about 3 months before the exam. Now, we weren't always diligent about following through on that (nobody's perfect, right?), but I can tell you having another person going through the same process at the same time, trying to remember the same info was HUGELY important. So grab your best study buddy and hit the books!

Other things that I found helpful were highlighters, colored note cards, and a really big drawing pad. I used different colored note cards to differentiate theories (purple), people (blue), and concepts/techniques (green). For the big drawing pad, I wrote out the comparisons between the theories.

Finally, I am a huge advocate of the practice test provided by the AMFTRB online. Yes, it costs $60, but it gave me the encouragement I needed (I passed on the first try!). It also gave me ideas of what I needed to study (it breaks down the domains and suggests which you need to study more).

In the end, I passed the first time (and screamed when I opened the letter on my front stoop by my mailbox) and have not looked back. You can too!

-Tamara Statz, MA, LAMFT
Minneapolis, MN

Dear Colleagues,

Studying for the national exam can be a daunting undertaking. To make it an enjoyable experience, I would recommend coming up with a plan before you begin to study. If you have a plan, the whole thing won't feel quite so overwhelming and you might even enjoy yourself! If possible, find some colleagues to study together, encourage each other and bond over the experience.

Everyone is different. Some people need to study more, some less. What made it a positive experience for me was putting myself on a weekly study schedule. I didn't want to worry every week about, "How much should I be studying?" I decided to devote 100 hours of my time over a 20-week period. That helped me relax into a routine of studying five hours per week. I formed a group with two colleagues and met with them for three hours every two weeks. A combination of individual and group study was the best for me. The time I spent preparing for the national exam not only helped me pass but also made me a more knowledgeable clinician after I passed.

-John Otsby, MA, LMFT
Minneapolis, MN

Review

Well, there you have it. Take some time to consider the advice from your colleagues as well as the tips on effectively using this independent study guide. Hopefully you have a better idea of structuring your test preparation in a way that suits your particular learning style.

Now, it is time to get into the bulk of the material that will be covered on the exam, beginning with a review of the History of the Field of Marital & Family Therapy, followed by an overview of the Theory & Practice of Marital & Family Therapy.

Best of luck as you dig in and remember referring to **www.mftlicensingexam.com** for additional study aides as well as an opportunity to receive live, web-based mentoring as you work through this study guide.

*Note: Primary resources were used throughout this manual to better reflect the essence of the theories through the written expression of their creators. This will be found in the references list toward the end of the manual, and will serve as a resource guide for further reading on each theory. Keep in mind, the following textbooks will nicely complement this manual and contain majority of the vocabulary terms' definitions while elaborating upon the major theories.

Nichols, M. P. (2012). *Family therapy: Concepts and methods* (10th ed.). Belmont, CA: Brooks & Cole.

Gehart, D. R., & Tuttle, A. R. (2003). *Theory-based treatment planning for marriage and family therapists.* Belmont, CA: Brooks & Cole.

Goldenberg, H. & Goldenberg, I. (2013). *Family therapy: An overview* (8th ed.). Belmont, CA: Brooks & Cole.

Piercy, F. P., Sprenkle, D. H., & Wetchler, J. L. (1996). *Family therapy sourcebook: Second edition.* New York, NY: The Guilford Press.

Part II

The History of the Field of Marriage & Family Therapy

History of the Field of Marriage & Family Therapy

The exam will expect a knowledge of our field's historic development. This may not always be covered in depth throughout the graduate program so take the time to appreciate the richness of our profession's history while honoring the pioneers that contributed to Marriage & Family Therapy's evolution into a distinct field of study and clinical practice...

Contributions from the Field of Psychotherapy

The Freudian Era

Although **Sigmund Freud** is often credited for developing psychotherapy from its bare roots, it was his mentor, Josef Breuer, that first treated the infamous "Anna O" with what *she* then deemed the *Talking Cure*. Breuer later referred to it as the *Cathartic Method*. Essentially, Breuer recognized that as Anna processed her physical ailments, feelings, and the impact it had on her day to day functioning, her symptoms either reduced or temporarily disappeared. As this laid the groundwork, Freud took this concept and expanded it into what we still refer to today as psychoanalysis (grounded through psychoanalytic theory). This concept brought psychotherapy into the 20th century, which Freud elaborated on up until his passing in 1939. During his time, he acquired many students and colleagues (most notably, Carl Jung, Otto Rank, Ludwig Binswanger, and Alfred Adler) to help better establish and elaborate upon this inventive new treatment modality. As Freud will always be considered the individual that brought force to the wave of psychotherapy, it required breaking away from his linear and individualized lens for the field of Family Therapy to prosper.

Alfred Adler

Due to a shift in philosophy and **Freud's** unwillingness to make room for **Adler's** growing insights, **Adler** left **Freud's** team of consultants in Vienna in the early 1900s and initiated the *Child Guidance Movement*. **Adler** believed that the individual was influenced by more than internal drives and instead identified the role that society—and, *others*—had on individual personality development and functioning. Some primary factors of **Adler's** new approach that impacted the development of the field of family therapy was his notion that pathology taking form in childhood suggests that therapy should focus on working with children (Rasheed, Rasheed, & Marley, 2011).

> ***Fun Fact!** When Adler broke away from Freud's psychoanalytic framework, Freud and Jung began writing letters to one another discussing the nature of Adler's obvious—and quite humorous—neuroses.

As **Adler** launched the *Child Guidance Movement* in Austria, it was brought to the United States by **Rudolph Dreikers** (one of the very first to practice *family therapy*). **Dreikers** founded *Family Counseling Centers* throughout the 1920s, maintaining the theoretical foundation of Adler's approach. Beyond **Dreikers'** expansion of Adler's approach, his most notable contribution found that symptoms experienced by young children are not the actual problem, but that family tension and the psychopathology of the parents lie in the root cause of the struggles (Rasheed et al., 2011). Despite this insight, the primary approach remained to treat parents—or, just the mother—separate from the children.

Adler's approach continued to take shape and left a lasting impact on the practice of therapy at large. Many consider *Adlerian Therapy* an approach to Family Therapy and can be found throughout much of the field's literature. His most notable contributions include the concepts of *overcompensation for felt inferiority, social interest, sibling birth order*, and working with families in therapy in front of a live audience comprised of their community members.

Group Therapy

Many working concepts of group therapy were found to similarly apply when working with families, primarily: Several people involved, greater degree of social and interactional complexity, and both simulating everyday social reality more so than individual therapy (Broderick & Schrader, 1981).

Kurt Lewin

Lewin was an influential researcher and developer of *field theory*, most notably bringing recognition to the concept that, "The whole of a group was greater than the sum of its individual members." **Lewin** also developed the *process of change*, which went as follows (Rasheed et al., 2011):

Stage 1:   *Unfreezing* (creating the motivation and readiness to change)

Stage 2:   *Changing* (helping the client to see, judge, feel, and react to things differently, based on a new point of view)

Stage 3:   *Refreezing* (helping the client to integrate the new point of view into the organization as well as the individual personality)

Wilfred Bion

Bion, out of *The Tavistock Institute* in England, studied groups in depth and found that predictable properties emerge out of the group's dynamics. Most notably, this brought awareness to the dynamic nature of *process vs. content*. Having a profound influence on the development of Family Therapy, it remains the primary contribution from the theory and practice of encounter groups (Rasheed et al., 2011).

Jacob Moreno

In the 1940s, **Moreno** created an approach to therapy called *Psychodrama*, an experiential exercise that combined working concepts of group therapy with theatrical techniques.

Peter Laqueur

In the 1950s, **Laquer** started *Multiple Family Group Therapy*, an approach comprised of seeing several families together in a large group using techniques from traditional therapy, psychodrama, and encounter groups (Rasheed et al., 2011). Co-therapists were often used with this approach.

As we applaud the many efforts of Alfred Adler as he demonstrated his concept of *daring to be imperfect* by breaking away from the dominant study and practice of psychoanalysis, unknowingly paving way for the development of Marriage & Family Therapy, let us shift to the pioneers and theories that had more of a direct impact on our profession's development—whether they had intended on it or not...

Research into the Causes of Schizophrenia

When reflecting upon the development of our profession, few events left more of a lasting impact than *The Race to Cure Schizophrenia*. A mental illness that was growing in recognition yet lacking any distinct sense of etiology, treatment, or prognosis, many thinkers alike focused on studying the illness in hopes of finding a cure.

Throughout the 1950s as several researchers observed and studied the causes of schizophrenia, three common factors tied together various findings to determine a monumental hypothesis (Forisha, 2013):

1. When the individual with schizophrenia got better, at least one other individual in the family got worse.
2. Despite reporting progress in symptom reduction while patients were in the hospital, quickly upon returning home, the intensity of symptoms reemerged in the patient.
3. Despite reporting progress in symptom reduction while patients were in the hospital, quickly upon returning home, significant disruptions within the home were reported.

A shared hypothesis among these findings concluded that *a change in one family member results in a change in the family system as a whole,* suggesting that individuals may be better served when treated within the context of his or her family system. These are two of the primary principles that inform the practice of family therapy and suggested the limitations of the then dominant linear models of thinking in reference to mental illness. What was one small step for the researchers of that era was one giant leap for the profession of Marital & Family Therapy.

The Early Pioneers of Marital & Family Therapy

Prior to the groundbreaking findings from the vast studies on schizophrenia, many contributors recognized the value of treating families through therapy and counseling. As some of the early pioneers worked directly with families in a clinical, clergy, or community-based setting, several notable contributors were developing theories in other fields of study, never intending for their findings to eventually be applied to the theory and practice of Marital & Family Therapy.

Bertrand Russell (1920s)

Russell's *Theory of Logical Types* defined systems, within definable systems, within definable systems. The main concept of this theory was to define hierarchies based on levels of abstraction (e.g. a class cannot be a member of itself nor can a member of a class be the class) (Broderick & Shrader, 1981). **Russell** was a philosopher, logician, mathematician, historian, writer, and social critic. His *Theory of Logical Types* eventually influenced Gregory Bateson's integrated approach to understanding communication within human systems.

Paul Popenoe (1930)

Founded the *American Institute of Family Relations* on the West Coast.

Emily Mudd (1932)

Founded the *Marriage Council of Philadelphia* which eventually grew into AAMFT in 1979 and continues to serve as our primary Professional Association.

Nathan Ackerman (1938-1950)

Ackerman was among the first to classify the family as a solitary unit of treatment (i.e. the family system as the client, as opposed to one individual) and was one of the first therapists on record to work with whole families.

Ackerman was trained in psychoanalysis, and through his understanding of the individual's expressed interplay between his or her conflicted id, ego, and superego, recognized that various correlations and alignments within families often conflict with one another in similar ways. Ackerman saw this dynamic play out either between dyads/triads within the nuclear family (e.g. mother and daughter vs. father and son) as well as across generations.

In **1957,** Ackerman founded a Family Treatment Center in New York, which became later known as *The Ackerman Institute* in **1971** following his death. At his treatment center, Ackerman would require all family members to be present at all meetings while endorsing open and honest expression of feelings. When working with families, Ackerman was always lively and open to the effective use of therapist self-disclosure while emphasizing the importance of paying attention to *non-verbal cues* as a means to understanding the hidden and unspoken aspects of family functioning (Rasheed et al., 2011).

Ackerman's most notable intervention was his notion of:

Tickling the Defenses: This denoted his famous phrase for teasing, provoking, and stimulating members of the family to open up and say what is really on their minds.

When reviewing the early contributions of Nathan **Ackerman**, we can see how his ideas and clinical concepts are present in the more elaborately developed approaches to the Transgenerational and Experiential Therapies. As so, Ackerman is often referred to as the *Father of Family Therapy*—a well-deserved title.

Ludwig von Bertalanffy (1940s)

Bertalanffy developed *General Systems Theory*. The primary principle of this theory states that the *parts of system are interrelated and that the whole is greater than the sum of its parts*. This concept was heavily advanced and made relevant by Kurt **Lewin** within his *Field Theory* (previously discussed) while also serving as the foundation for many approaches to Family Therapy. As discussed earlier in this manual, *General Systems Theory* was first applied to groups before recognizing the direct application to better understanding *family systems*.

Lyman Wynne (1940s)

Wynne applied psychoanalytic ideas to his work with families with severe mental and physical disorders. His primary contributions were his concepts of (Rasheed et al., 2011):

Pseudomutuality: Describes a systemic pretense of harmony and closeness that hides conflict and interferes with intimacy.

Pseudohostility: A volatile and intense way of disguising and distorting both affection and splits.

Rubber-Fence Boundary: The families are seemingly yielding, but are in fact nearly impermeable to information from outside systems.

David Levy (1943)

Levy coined the term *Maternal-Overprotectiveness* as a result of his studies on schizophrenia, which described mothers who were deprived of love when they were children, resulting in a characterological makeup defined by *dominance* and *indulgence*.

Frieda Fromm-Reichmann (1948)

Reichmann coined the term *Schizophrenogenic-Mother*, which described mothers characterized by domineering, aggressive, rejecting and insecure women that influenced the development of schizophrenia in children. She later shifted her emphasis from a pathological parent to a pathological relationship, making room for the possibility of family treatment.

John Bowlby (1949)

Bowlby was the founder of *Attachment Theory*, a theory at the core of many approaches to family therapy today. *Attachment Theory* suggests that children will develop a *secure* or *insecure* attachment style based upon the nature of the relationship with their mother or primary mother substitute—or, lack thereof—that will influence behaviors both throughout childhood and into adulthood. Since then, research has expanded into categorizing four different attachment styles (Bowlby, 1988):

Secure Attachment
Insecure Attachment (anxious-resistant type)
Insecure Attachment (anxious-avoidant type)
Disorganized/Disoriented Attachment

Theodore Lidz (1950s)

Lidz was a professor out of Yale University and invested much of his research into the causes of schizophrenia. He too viewed the etiology of the illness as occurring systemically within the family, and although disputed the idea that maternal reactions were the primary contributor of the illness, he shifted focus onto the harmful influences of the fathers. Regardless, he was interested in the dynamic between the married couple and the development of schizophrenia in a child. His lasting concepts from his research were (Rasheed et al., 2011):

Marital Schism: The parents are overly focused on their own problems which harms the marriage, the individuals, and the children.

Marital Skew: One parent dominates the family, and the other is dependent.

John Bell (1951)

Bell may have been the first to treat families. He did so in multiple family therapy groups and called his approach *family group therapy.*

His approach to therapy had three phases (Rasheed et al., 2011):

1. Child-centered phase
2. Parent-centered phase
3. Family-centered phase

Robert MacGregor (1950s)

MacGregor developed *Multiple Impact Therapy* as a way to have maximum impact on families who came from all over Texas to spend several days with a team of professionals.

Don Jackson (1959)

Jackson introduced the term *Conjoint Therapy,* describing marital therapy in which the spouses were seen together.

This brings us to the 1960s, an exciting time in the history of family therapy as the profession started to gain a reputable and exciting identity. Although still competing heavily with the dominant tradition of psychoanalytic thinking, in 1962, Don **Jackson** and Nathan **Ackerman** founded the peer-reviewed journal, *Family Process,* with **Jay Haley** as the first editor. This journal demonstrated the many contributions of systemic therapies to the academic community.

> ***Fun Fact!** When Marriage and Family Therapy first made its way into the University setting as an independent field of study, which department initially housed the program?*
> **Answer:** The Department of Home Economics!

Eventually came the formation of the **Mental Research Institute** (or, *The Palo Alto Group*), where all the magic really started to happen...

The Mental Research Institute (MRI)

Gregory Bateson
William Fry
Jay Haley

John Weakland
Don Jackson
Virginia Satir

How MRI Came to Be...

It all started with a man named **Gregory Bateson**, a brilliant cultural anthropologist with extraordinary vision and intellectual rigor. In the early 1940s—along with his wife, Margaret Meade—Bateson grew interested in studying the patterns, processes, and organizations within human communication.

When attending a conference, Bateson met **Milton Erickson,** a clinical hypnotist known for his use of paradoxical interventions when addressing clients' natural resistance to change (more on Erickson and his influence on the Systemic Schools later). Through his meetings with **Erickson, Bateson** was introduced to **Norbert Wiener's** theory of *Cybernetics.* Already a proponent of *General Systems Theory* (**Von Bertalanffy**), and learning that Norbert **Wiener** was a student of Bertrand **Russell** (*Theory of Logical Type*), the integrated theoretical basis for his interest in *Human Communication Processes* took form. In **1951,** Bateson published *Communication: The Social Matrix of Society* before founding a research group a year later to study…you guessed it, schizophrenia!

Eventually, members of **Bateson's** initial research group included Jay **Haley, John Weakland, William Fry,** and Don **Jackson**. In **1954, Bateson** received a two-year Grant from the Macy Foundation to study schizophrenia, and two years later in **1956**—along with his research team—published their landmark paper *Toward a Theory of Schizophrenia.* Through *Cybernetics* (Norbert **Wiener**), they applied the concept of *homeostasis* to *family systems* (compliments of Don **Jackson**). As their studies tracked and analyzed communication within families, they found that people in ongoing relationships develop *rule-determined repetitive patterns of interaction,* which they referred to as *behavioral redundancy.* Based on their findings, symptoms of schizophrenia resulted from a distinct pattern of communication, the **double bind,** in which one individual received *contradictory commands* from which there was *no escape.*

The term **double bind** is more complex than its often oversimplified misinterpretation of a contradictory message, and included six distinct phenomena that *must* be present in order for the interaction to meet criteria.

The *six characteristics* of a **double bind** are (Forisha, 2013):

1. The communication involves two or more people who are involved in an *important emotional relationship.*

2. The pattern of communication and the relationship is a *repeated experience.*

3. The communication involves a *primary negative injunction*—or, command *not to do* (some act) or *not to NOT do* (some act), either of which come with a threat of punishment.

4. A *second abstract injunction* is given that contradicts the primary injunction but at a more abstract level and is usually nonverbal. This also occurs under threat of punishment.

5. A *third negative injunction* both *demands a response* and *prevents escape,* effectively *binding* the recipient to the environment in which these patterns exist.

6. When the above double bind messages have been communicated enough times, the individual has become conditioned which no longer requires all of the above criteria to be present in order to elicit the same intensity of response (panic, rage, and what was then hypothesized, eventually *schizophrenia*).

For Example

Every day after Michael returns home from school, he goes to greet his mother with a hug, but when he actually hugs her, she tenses up and subtly pushes him away from her. When Michael then withdraws from the hug, his mother responds by stating, "You must not have missed your mother very much to give her such a rejecting hug." Michael reacts with a sad face which his mother further responded to by stating, "Now Michael, you must not be so emotional and easily offended…I expect an actual hug when you return home from school tomorrow." Michael is caught in a bind since not showing physical affection toward mom (*primary negative injunction*) is *threatened* to be *punished* and *attempting* to show affection to Mom (*second abstract injunction*) is *actually punished*. Mom stating that Michael is expected to continue and correct this pattern the next day (*third negative injunction*) creates *no escape* from the *interaction*, and his dependence on his parents creates *no escape* from the *environment*. For Michael, the meaning of communication becomes unclear, influencing what may turn out to be a *disordered style of communication* that is labeled *schizophrenia*.

Finally, in **1959** Don **Jackson** created a clinic to hold both the research and treatment work—still famously known today as *The Mental Research Institute*.

The research team of five brought in Virginia **Satir** to act as the clinic's *Training Director* followed a year later by **Paul Watzlawick** to join the group of clinicians and researchers. **Bateson** remained as the primary researcher of the group (never practicing therapy himself) while the rest applied the theoretical findings to the context of treating families.

From this research evolved *The MRI Systemic Approach, Strategic Family Therapy,* and *Milan Systemic Therapy* (Milan Systemic was heavily influenced by the work at MRI, but was not housed out of MRI). As these three theories were developed directly out of **Bateson's** research, you can still see the influences of **Bateson's** integration of *General Systems Theory, Cybernetics, Theory of Logical Types,* and **Erickson's** *Paradoxical Interventions* laced throughout several approaches to Family Therapy—both within the classical and post-modern movements.

As we can see, despite never actually working with families, Gregory **Bateson** was at the center of the Systemic Therapies Universe…

Bateson at the Center of the Systemic Therapies Universe

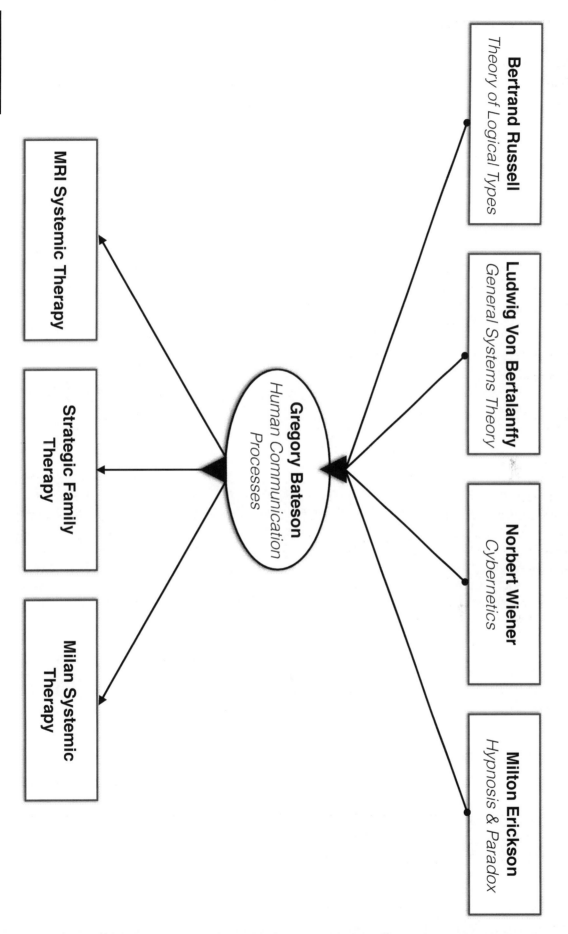

Figure 2.1

In **1962, Bateson's** research project disbanded but the *MRI Group* carried on as a prolific and innovative training center for *Systems-Oriented Therapies*. In **1966,** Richard **Fisch** founded the *Brief Therapy Center* as part of *MRI* (Rasheed et al., 2011). As some of the original members finished their careers in Palo Alto, others ventured on to new developments, creating new waves across different parts of the country. Before reviewing the later—and perhaps, more familiar—pioneers of our field, let's review the conceptual foundations of the MRI Group more in depth…

Conceptual Foundations of the MRI Group at Palo Alto

The MRI Group that continued paving way for the development of our field through groundbreaking research and daring clinical applications had its foundation in two independent but interrelated theoretical paradigms, *General Systems Theory* and *Cybernetics*.

General Systems Theory

Founded by **Ludwig von Bertalanffy,** *General Systems Theory* proposed that all living systems share universal characteristics. The idea that *the whole of system is more than the sum of its parts* is the fundamental principle of *General Systems Theory* and is essential to gaining an understanding of any living or organizational system. No system can be understood merely by examining its parts—it is the interdependent nature and dynamic, circular functioning between the parts that must be considered when understanding the system as a whole.

Cybernetics

Cybernetics was initially developed by Norbert **Wiener**, a mathematician out of MIT in an effort to resolve the problem of how to get antiaircraft guns to hit German planes moving so fast that it was impossible to calibrate settings rapidly enough for gunnery batteries to hit their targets (Bale, 1995). When **Bateson** met **Wiener** at a conference, the two hit it off, and Bateson later attributed **Wiener's** developing theory to family systems—particularly *Cybernetics'* concept of how control mechanisms provide feedback to the primary system. Basic cybernetic systems consist of frameworks which function according to the laws of recursiveness, feedback, and self-correction (more on these terms shortly) (Bale, 1995).

Note: Pretty cool, huh? A primary theory underlying the development of Marriage and Family Therapy was initially originated to shoot down German planes more effectively during WWII.

Key Concepts of Cybernetics
(Bale, 1995; Bateson, 1979; Watzlawick, Beavin, & Jackson, 1967)

Boundaries: These are theoretical lines of demarcation in a family that define a system as an entity and separate the subsystems from one another and the system from its environment.

Boundary Interface: Regions between each subsystem of the family and between the family and the suprasystem.

Familial Boundary: The term used to represent the concept of *Boundary Interface* mentioned above within the literature of family therapies.

Open Systems: Interact regularly with the environment with relatively no inhibition.

Closed Systems: Are more isolated and resistant to interactions with the environment.

Family Models/Maps: Individuals and the system at large will *consciously* or *unconsciously* use models or maps meant to manage their boundaries and make sense of their individual and shared realities.

Circular Causality: In determining the origins of problems, *General Systems Theory* departs radically from traditional, *linear causality*. This is different than *linear causality* and acknowledged that two things do, say, or feel mutually influence one another in a recursive, circular relationship.

Entropy: This refers to a system's tendency to break down which, over time, threatens the survival of the system.

Negative Entropy: A systemic state that emerges when a system is balanced between openness and closeness.

Equifinality: This is the idea that an organism or system can reach a certain end state from a variety of different sources, conditions, and means or from different initial states. For example, Generalized Anxiety Disorder may stem from a biological imbalance, trauma, or free-will.

Equipotentiality: This refers to the notion that different end states can occur from the same initial conditions. Similar events (e.g. natural disaster) can turn into depression or trauma as well as growth or happiness.

Homeostasis: This refers to the tendency of a system to resist change and maintain dynamic equilibrium or a steady state. This is maintained by negative feedback and input loops.
  *Note: Don Jackson introduced this to family therapy.

Feedback Loops: These are at the core of the cybernetics model. They are the self-correcting mechanisms which serve to govern families' attempts to adjust from customary patterns and maintain its organizational sameness (homeostasis).
    *Note: Feedback occurs from outside the system while Input occurs within the system.
Amplifying or Positive Feedback Loops: These increase change in a family's homeostasis (*morphogenesis*). They attempt to change these systems from its steady state to a new steady state or balance.

Attenuating or Negative Feedback Loops: These reduce change in an existing homeostasis.

Example of Homeostasis and Feedback Loops

Imagine a family of three—mother, father, and 8-year-old son. The family has created a desirable homeostasis. Dad and Mom work 9-5 jobs, and the son attends school and after-school programming until Mom is able to pick him up after work. They all gather at home, have dinner, do some homework, child goes to bed, and Mom and Dad spend some time together. Mom goes to bed, Dad stays up an hour or so later to read and watch the news. The system is balanced, it is working efficiently, and it is congruent with its environment. A few-years-later, the son reaches adolescence and things start to change (moving into the adolescent phase of life presents a **positive feedback loop** to the family system). Because Mom and Dad were settled into their routine which was working well for them, when their son asks to start going home with friends after school and needing rides after dinner time, Mom and Dad resist this presented change to maintain **homeostasis** (Mom and Dad resisting this change to maintain homeostasis is an example of a **negative feedback loop**). It was proposed by the *MRI Group*, and **Haley** in particular, that families must be able to adapt to change as it is presented—thereby, recognizing and responding to negative feedback loops and allowing homeostasis to shift. Families naturally resist this tendency, hence the use of paradox becoming a hallmark of strategic therapies (More on Strategic Family Therapy later).

Isomorphism: This is a phenomenon in which two or more systems or subsystems exhibit similar or parallel structures. For example, a therapist seeing a family that starts showing up late to sessions will similarly begin showing up late to supervision to discuss the case.

Metaphor: This is a symbolic representation that captures the basic and essential features of an object or event by using a description of a different category of objects or events.

Morphogenesis: Describes a system's tendency toward growth, creativity, change, and innovation.

Morphostasis: This describes a system's tendency towards stability and staying the same.

Process: This refers to dynamic aspects that are changing within the system. Often, family therapists make the distinction between process (how something is said) and content (what is being said)

Recursiveness: This refers to reciprocal or circular causality. Rather than viewing an element in a vacuum devoid of interactions between its environment and its own system's levels or subsystems, recursiveness speaks to the mutual interaction and influence that occurs between people, events, and their ecosystem.

Ripple Effect: This refers to how a change that occurs at one level of a system will result in changes across other levels of the system.

Structures: These are aspects of a system that are universal across systems, in that all systems have a structure to them. Structures can be adapted, changed, and influenced by a variety of events as well as intentionally through therapeutic intervention. Although all systems will have a structure, there is no one universal structure or set or measure of objective quality of structure. Structure is defined subjectively by the observer.

A System: A unit bounded by a set of interrelated elements and which exhibits coherent behaviors.

Communications Theory

This theory supports a model of sequential causality which can be understood through behavioral chains of behavior (Littlejohn, 2002). For example, child acts out undesirably, parent responds by scolding the child, the child thereby acts out even more. Therapists aimed to disrupt this pattern by focusing on interactions that perpetuate problems (observable and changeable) as opposed to hypothesizing and working through underlying causes (unobservable and unchangeable). Communications Theory conceptualized families as systems that resist change and demand structure. Communications Theory utilized the well-known metaphor of a thermostat to illustrate how systems function. A thermostat aims to maintain a set temperature (homeostasis). When the temperature in the space is at 71 degrees, the thermostat shuts off. When the environment presents a change to the thermostat (positive feedback loop), it starts back up (negative feedback loop) to readjust the temperature back to 71 degrees (maintaining homeostasis). Family systems run into trouble when negative feedback loops prevent them from changing in ways that would benefit the family. Healthy families are able to adjust to positive feedback loops accordingly, determining whether or not adjusting to change will benefit or harm the family. Unhealthy—or, dysfunctional families—remain stuck and resist healthy change. Therapist who practice from this theory conceptualize symptoms in individuals as a means to keep a system stuck.

Key Terms from Communications Theory
(Littlejohn, 2002; Watzlawick, Beavin, & Jackson, 1967)

Complementary Relationships: Based on differences that fit together.

Symmetrical Relationships: Based on equality; the behavior of one mirrors that of the other.

Types of Communication

Proxemics: spatial relations

Streptic Communication: Sounds (e.g. claps, whistles)

Haptic (or, symbolic) Communication: Includes touch.

Paralinguistic Communication: Includes tone, pace, and inflection.

Kinesthetic Communication: Refers to body motion

Communication may also be

Analogic: Has little structure, but is rich in content such as a child's kinetic family drawing.

-OR-

Digital: Verbal communication that is perceived and interpreted based on meaning.

Metacommunication: Communicating about communication—communication that modifies, qualifies or even disqualifies a communication (this is frequently occurring in family therapy). Essentially, this is referring to the nonverbals going on in the room that have a profound impact on what is being said at the auditory level. This is directly related to the emphasis of tracking content AND process in family therapy.

> ***Note:** The Group for the Advancement of Psychiatry (The Gap Report) published a report that showed the vast majority of therapists who worked with families identified *improved communication as their primary goal in treatment.*

Other Conceptual Foundations

Although these theories were not directly related to the *MRI Group*, they still have their roots in several notable theories throughout our field and may be covered on the exam...

Human Systems Theory

This theory identifies communication as the primary domain of human systems. Its primary principle states that all human behavior occurs through communication, and that one cannot escape communicating.

General Living Systems Theory (GLST)

James Miller is the pioneer of this theory. *GLST* synchronized common factors defining the elements of family systems within one framework. The theory's main principle is:

Isomorphism: This is a phenomenon in which two or more systems or subsystems exhibit similar or parallel structures. For example, a therapist seeing a family that starts showing up late to sessions will similarly begin showing up late to supervision to discuss the case.

Cognitive Maps

These are models created experientially as a means to interpret and make sense of incoming information from the environment, which eventually become tied to a corresponding répertoire of behavioral responses. For example, an individual who was physically abused in a relationship created a cognitive map of how to behaviorally respond when another individual raises his or her arm (in this case, covering his head and face). When this same individual is standing on the street corner, and another individual next to him raises his or her arm to flag down a taxi, he will naturally respond in similar ways and makes a motion to cover his head. Other similar terms include explanatory frameworks and the concept of mirror-neurons. This is a primary component to *Cognitive-Behavioral Family Therapy.*

The Later Pioneers of Marital & Family Therapy

Milton Erickson (1960s)

Erickson never became *directly* involved in the development of Family Therapy, but significantly influenced members of the original *MRI Group* after his thoughts and ideas were introduced by **Bateson**—particularly, **Haley** and **Weakland** who used many of his paradoxical techniques to address resistance to change. **Erickson** was a pioneer in the development and advancement of Clinical Hypnosis. He developed several brilliant—yet unconventional—techniques to produce change in relatively few sessions by engaging the unconscious mind of his clients. **Erickson's** therapy was, like **Haley's**, done *to—not with—* clients. He also emphasized brief therapies that were ahistoric and problem focused.

> ***Note:** These two principles were hallmarks of both the *MRI Systemic* and *Strategic* models of Family Therapy. It is also worth mentioning that the principle of having therapy be *done to* families as opposed to *with* families contrasts significantly with the more *Post-Modern* approaches to therapy (more on this later). This, along with the regular use of paradoxical interventions, ended up being a leading argument against these therapies and eventually dismantled them from the highest reigns of Marital & Family Therapy.

> ***Note:** If Bateson had not unintentionally met **Erickson** at a conference and hit it off in just the right way, **Erickson's** contributions to the developing theories of Family Therapy—and, psychotherapy in general—may have gone forever overlooked. The field as we know it may have developed in profoundly different ways...

Jay Haley (1950s-1990s)

Haley branched off of the *MRI Group* shortly after **Bateson** concluded his research. **Haley,** decidedly influenced by **Erickson,** developed his own brand of brief therapy characterized by using *directives* to get the families to change their behaviors and thereby break repetitive behavioral cycles. These were often *therapeutic paradoxes*, maneuvers designed to get patients to take responsibility for their choices and behaviors through unconventional therapeutic measures. **Haley** later worked with **Salvador Minuchin,** the founder of *Structural Family Therapy*, and became interested in *family coalitions*. Thus, **Haley's** *Strategic Family Therapy* Model bridged the *Systemic Schools* with **Minuchin's** *Structural Family Therapy* (more on this later).

Virginia Satir (1950s-1980s)

Satir always remained a therapist (social worker, as a matter of fact) and never identified as a theoretician. **Satir** remained interested in working with families and most notably expanded the significance of communication toward the equally significant measure of feelings and affect to her clinical work. Her work was characterized by her warmth and acceptance with families, her authentic use of touch, and her supernatural capacity to empathize with clients. **Satir** too left the MRI Group and became more associated with *Experiential Family Therapies* than the *Systemic Schools*. She eventually developed her *Human Validation Process Model* and coined other notable terms and concepts that continue to leave a lasting impression on the practice of Marital & Family Therapy today (more on Satir later).

Murray Bowen (1940s-1980s)

Bowen has arguably the most complex and thorough theory in all of Marital & Family Therapy. **Bowen**, like most pioneers, was psychoanalytically trained and applied these concepts to systems theory through his recognition of psychoanalytic concepts manifesting themselves within systems and reproducing themselves through generations. **Bowen** also contributed to the vast research on schizophrenia, which engaged his curiosity of expanding far beyond schizophrenia and into a comprehensive theory that understands all family interaction (more on Bowen later).

Carl Whitaker (1930s-1980s)

Whitaker had a unique and daring style that drew quite the crowd of students, clients, and other professionals from around the world. He too became fascinated by the study of schizophrenia before developing his own brand of Family Therapy. Although **Whitaker** remains as a leading figure in the development of *Symbolic-Experiential Family Therapy*, he declines any personal recognition and instead insists that he had no theory—he was nothing more than *himself.*

Whitaker took the concept of therapist as "blank slate" from the *psychoanalytic schools* and not only turned it upside down but exploded it into a trillion pieces. His work emphasized the therapeutic usefulness of self-disclosure and transparency, encouraging therapists to become less about theory and textbooks and more of themselves when in session. This led to his encouragement of working with *co-therapists,* which allowed him to be more daring and *crazy* while in session (more on Whitaker later).

Ivan Boszormenyi-Nagy (1950s-2000s)

Nagy was psychoanalytically trained and the son of a judge. Each of these experiences had a clear impact on his work. He developed *Contextual Family Therapy*. According to **Nagy**, family members are bound across generations by *loyalty* and *trust*. (more on Nagy and Contextual Family Therapy later).

Salvador Minuchin (1950s-1990s)

Minuchin started the *Philadelphia Child Guidance Clinic* where he was later joined by **Haley**. **Minuchin** developed *Structural Family Therapy* which remains as the most widely used approach by Marriage & Family Therapists (more on Minuchin and Structural Family Therapy later).

Fred and Bunny Duhl, along with David Kantor (1950s-1990s)

Kantor was the founder of *The Boston Family Institute* and developed an *Integrative Model of Family Therapy*. The **Duhls** and **Kantor** combined techniques from several models and created expressive, experiential, and nonverbal techniques, including *Family Sculpting*.

Ross Speck and Carolyn Attneave (1950s-1990s)

These two developed *Network Therapy* by assisting families in crisis by gathering their entire social network upward toward 50 people. Teams of therapists were used, and their emphasis was on breaking destructive patterns of relationship and mobilizing support. This is now an approach to therapy used to treat chemical-dependency struggles.

Conclusion

When reflecting upon the history of family therapy, we can see three primary themes that influenced the development of our field:

- The influence of **Psychoanalysis**—that is, individuals trained in psychoanalysis growing unsatisfied with the limitations of the individualistic lens, and experimenting with applying such concepts to working with families.

- Therapists well versed in the theory and practice of **Group Therapy** recognizing that the same principles apply to the family group.

- The race to cure **Schizophrenia**—and as a result, the development of human communications theory by Gregory **Bateson** that resulted in the dynamic and fresh approach to therapy built exclusively for the family out of the *Mental Research Institute*.

These three themes organize the narrative that is the history of the field of Marital & Family Therapy. When reviewing the role of each prominent figure in our field's development, placing them into one of these three categories will contribute toward retention and recall.

I hope you enjoyed taking a stroll down MFT Memory Lane, revisiting some familiar names and hopefully introducing yourself to many that you had not known as significant contributors to our ever-evolving profession. As you can see, our field grew from a group of brilliantly prolific, highly innovative and richly collaborative individuals. Our pioneers moved us beyond the individualistic, linear models of thinking and into the dynamic world of circularity and systems. As the early and late pioneers set the foundation for many approaches to therapy still practiced today, since then our field has continued to grow in many significant ways. There is no doubting that Marriage & Family Therapy has proven itself as a highly valued profession in meeting the mental health needs of our fellow citizens, becoming a landmark within the multi-disciplinary profession of human services and academia. I look forward to having you as a colleague and welcoming another contributor into such a vibrant and energizing professional community. But first, back to getting you ready to *Pass the National Licensing Exam!*

The next part of this Independent Study Guide will take you back through the theory and practice of Marriage and Family Therapy, including:

- Assessment in Marriage and Family Therapy
- Universal Concepts of a Systemic Therapist
- The Major Theories of Marriage & Family Therapy

Part III

The Theory & Practice of Marriage & Family Therapy

The Universal Family Therapist

As discussed earlier in this manual, the exam will ask questions through the lens of a *Marital and Family Therapist, Family Therapist*, or *Marriage and Family Therapist*. This identifies what the particular question is measuring. For instance, asking what a *Family Therapist* would do next is significantly different than asking what a *Symbolic-Experiential Therapist* would do next. When the question is tied to a specific theory (i.e. Symbolic-Experiential Family Therapy), that is your cue to channel your Inner-**Whitaker** and fall into the framework of that particular approach. This will guide your decision making process of which answer is *most correct*. In the instance that the question calls for a *Family Therapist*, it will be important to have a clear idea of what exactly that means in ways similar to when it is tied to a specific theory. As so, this manual delineates the makings of a *Universal Family Therapist*. Come test day, when you see the vignette pop up asking what a *Family Therapist* would do, keep these following concepts in mind while shifting into this theoretical orientation.

Moving from Symptom to System

As Marriage and Family Therapists, we pride ourselves in taking a radical shift when conceptualizing symptomology by looking beyond the individual and toward the system. Even when working with individuals, we are always conceptualizing their struggles within a systemic context. This tone is set with the very first phone call as we encourage the presence of as many family members available…

The Whole is Greater than the Sum of its Parts

This statement defines the concept of systems theory relative to human relationships. No one individual can be understood without understanding the system(s) in which he or she is a part of—and the dynamics between the various relationships within that system—and no system can be understood without understanding each individual within. Meaning, when individual *parts* become interrelated within a *system*, the interactions between creates something larger than the physical accumulation of the *parts*. There are dynamics occurring at the metaphysical level that make the whole larger than what is physically seen. In application to systems theory, no one individual can be assessed as functioning *independently* from the system in which they belong. In the case of emotional cutoff, it may appear that the individual is no longer impacted or affected by the system through proximity or surface-level emotion. However, the emotional cutoff is a mismanagement of the anxiety one is still carrying as a result of a past (systemic) relationship.

When parents or family members call to request therapy, it is important to encourage as many members of the family to join as possible. If the parent or spouse is resistant, it is appropriate to explain the nature of systemic therapies while requesting that all siblings and Dad join the session as well. This is the first step toward a primary aim of systemic therapies, which is *expanding the symptom* beyond the individual and toward the system. Again, if a parent is suggesting that only one child in the family is struggling, we understand that one individuals' symptom is likely a systemic problem. Several complex dynamics may be contributing to the symptom that ultimately involve every member in the system.

Genograms

Genograms are the go to assessment tool for systemically trained therapists. A genogram, when done in great detail, can provide all of the information necessary to fully understand a client system. Even when working with individuals, genograms are highly effective assessment tools and have curative factors resulting from the process of creating and reviewing them.

Building Relationships

As Marriage and Family Therapists, relationships are at the core of our practice. There are few predictors of effective outcomes that outweigh the quality of the therapeutic relationship. Also, as systemic therapists, we aim to maintain *neutrality* across all members of the family. As some approaches will intentionally align with the parental subsystem (**Haley's** Strategic and **Minuchin's** Structural), ultimately as family therapists we want to ensure that neutrality remains present and that all members of the family feel equally supported and valued by the work we do. This very act in and of itself is healing for the family as it models empathy, compassion, and the capacity to hold multiple views at the same time while finding worth in each of them.

> **Fun Fact!* Did you know that of the four major mental health professions (LP, LPCC, LICSW, LMFT) that Marriage and Family Therapists are the *least likely* to get sued by their clients? Many attribute this to our emphasis and training on *intentionally* building and maintaining relationships with *every* member of the family.

From Linear Causality to *Circular Causality*

The field of Marriage and Family Therapy is heavily based upon the concept of shifting from linear causality (psychodynamic, CBT) to *circular causality*. **Bateson** brilliantly illuminated upon the limitations of linear causality to understand human behavior, noting its failure to account for *communication* and *relationships*. His famous example of this uses the metaphor of a man kicking a boulder. This phenomenon can be measured and predictable. For example, based on how hard the man kicks the rock, at what angle, and with what form, we can predict the likely outcome on the spectrum of no injury to severe injury. A man could kick several boulders of similar physical attributes repeatedly, and the results will likely be similar. However, if a man were to kick a dog, the response would be incredibly unpredictable as it would be subjective to the dog as a living, breathing, and spontaneous biological mechanism. With this, a man kicking several dogs in similar ways would all have varied results.

Triangles

Triangles are everywhere, in every system, from our family to our work life to our recreational softball team. In any relationship, individuals will often bring in some third party as a means to help them manage anxiety—whether that be a parent, best friend, or bottle of 21-year-old single malt scotch.

Process/Content

Focusing on the **process** of communication (*how* people talk) rather than on its **content** (*what* they talk about) may be the single most productive shift a family therapist can make and serves as a key factor in our profession. This moves the dialogue from the surface (content) down to the emotional experience (process). Many theorists will agree that authentic healing takes place at this deeper level.

Family Structure

Minuchin's Structural Family Therapy continues to be one of the most widely practiced approaches to family therapy today. This is likely due to its approachable language and obvious pragmatic application to family life. Whether it be disengagement, enmeshment, disorganization, subsystems, or boundaries, all of these concepts are fluent throughout every family system. They are often easily distinguishable and clinically useful across the spectrum of family therapies.

The Meaning (Function) of Symptoms

In more traditional linear models, if a child was acting out, the behaviors in which the child externalized (e.g. bedwetting) would be the symptom that was treated—likely through individual therapy or the medical model. Family Therapists, on the other hand, are *always* interpreting *symptoms* as a metaphor for the larger (or, deeper) systemic problem within the family. Ultimately, the *symptoms* of an individual likely serve a homeostatic function, and the family would be at risk if it were to change or get better. The bedwetting may be a result of drinking too much water before bed, or, it can serve as a distraction allowing the family to focus away from Mom going into the basement every night to drink by herself.

The Family Life Cycle

Our profession deeply values and acknowledges the role of the family life cycle—not only in terms of the individual but the system as a whole. Families must reorganize to accommodate the growth and change of their members. New phases in the life cycle experienced by any of the family's members may likely have an impact on the system as a whole. The family life cycle is as follows:

- Leaving Home: single young adults
- The Joining of Families through Marriage: the new couple
- Families with Young Children
- Families with Adolescents
- Launching Children and Moving On
- Families in Later Life

Resistance

Tying into the family life cycle, families are naturally *resistant* to change. This is at the core of **Bateson's** systemic model that applied the concept of homeostasis to human systems. As each approach may offer a different lens to which resistance is approached and managed, the field at large can agree that resistance is an inherent part of family therapy.

Gender

As Family Therapists we must maintain awareness regarding gender in families. This is a product of the post-modern movement—and, the feminist approach to therapy that grew from it—that acknowledged the ways in which oppression can impact a family system both externally and internally.

Culture

As Family Therapists, we must also maintain awareness regarding the role of culture—particularly when cultural values may directly conflict with one another between the therapist and client(s). Ultimately, we must be sensitive to the cultural beliefs of our clients and manage therapy in ways that will not undermine, contradict, or offend our clients' cultural background.

Review

Essentially, you want to approach the questions on the exam as a systemic therapist that practices from the book—NOT, how *you* would address the concerns documented in the vignettes. The principles and concepts outlined above create an identity for the concept of a *Universal Family Therapist* and will assist you when shifting into the right mindset as you take the practice exams and actual exam.

Keep in Mind

As you can expect many vignettes to take the perspective of a *Family Therapist* (or *Marital & Family Therapist*), the exam will still tie vignettes to specific theories. For instance, as most will ask what a *Family Therapist* will do next, others may ask what would a *Symbolic-Experiential Therapist* would do next. Pay attention to these *qualifiers* particular to each question. When the question is tied to a specific theory, shift into that mindset as you read through each potential answer. Let us revisit the same question asked above except through the lens of a *Symbolic-Experiential Therapist* as opposed to the initial lens of a *Family Therapist...*

Sample Question

The mother of a 12-year-old boy calls to request that her son be seen for therapy. She reports him being withdrawn at home and acting out inappropriately at school (school has reported disrespectful language toward teachers and peers and refusal to work on occasion). Mom and the school staff agree that this is only the 12-year-old son's problem, as his younger sibling (age eight) is flourishing across all environments. A Marital and Family Therapist would do all of the following except:

a. Validate mom's concerns and struggles that her son is acting out inappropriately.
b. Aim to determine how the son's inappropriate behavior is occurring independently from his brother and parents.
c. Work with the son individually to explore why he is engaging in inappropriate behaviors.
d. Invite the entire family in to expand the symptom to the system.

Now, with the subtle shift from a *Family Therapist* to a *Symbolic-Experiential Therapist*, answer **C** that was considered incorrect in the previous question is now the correct answer. As it would be more appropriate for a *Family Therapist* to provide individual therapy, a *Symbolic-Experiential Therapist* would require that the whole family come in if they wish to work with he or she.

So, a firm understanding of the basic philosophical underpinnings, key terms, and primary interventions of each theory covered in the exam will be expected by the time your exam date arrives. As many other study manuals provide an exhaustive review of each theory— redundant to your graduate school experience—this approach condenses each theory down to its bare bones of what is needed for the exam. As so, once the condensed version of the theory is reviewed, you will have the opportunity to *apply* that theory to a vignette.

*Note: The glossary provided at the conclusion of this manual contains a list of all key terms as well as completed examples of each theory in application to the vignette.

Assessment in Universal Family Therapy

In relation to the theme of *Universal Family Therapy*, let us consider a general assessment approach taken from this perspective. As we will see, many of the theories we will review range from long-term treatment (mostly the *Transgenerational Models*) lasting up to several years to brief therapy (*MRI Models and some of the Post-Modern approaches*) being either time limited to 10 sessions or making strives to terminate around the 20 session mark. Most family therapy will fall somewhere in the middle and follow this general process:

The Early Phase: In the early phase you will be assessing the family to determine hypotheses regarding the presenting problems and any interactional dynamics that appear to be maintaining the problem. Once the assessment phase is nearing completion, you will begin moving into the resolution stage.

The Middle Phase: In the middle phase of treatment, time is focused on helping families to better identify and communicate their internal experiences of themselves and one another. When family members can become more aware of the thoughts and feelings that influence behavior, they begin to deal with one another in more constructive ways.

The Later Phase: Termination is often a collaborative process of the therapist and family coming to identify that the presenting problem has been resolved, and that the family has experienced out-of-session growth in how they experience one another. Once these changes have been maintained over an undetermined amount of time, therapy discontinues.

Assessment in Family Therapy

Assessment in family therapy may be formal or informal, quantitative or qualitative, or an assortment of the above. Regardless, family therapists will generally assess for the following dynamics:

- The presenting problem as identified by the family
- Recognizing the stage of the Family Life Cycle the family is in
- Considering the current family structure
- Attending to modes of communication style and patterns
- Drug or Alcohol Abuse
- Domestic Violence and/or Physical Abuse
- Extramarital Affairs
- Gender and Sexuality
- Multicultural Factors

The above factors apply directly to the working concept of a *Universal Family Therapist.* Beyond this general approach to assessment, the field does offer the following formal assessment tools and devices to measure various domains of family functioning. An exhaustive knowledge of each assessment is not necessary for the exam, but a capacity to identify each measure may come up. Because the likelihood of these assessments being mentioned on the exam is rare, consider how much time you would like to spend gathering more information on them.

FORMAL ASSESSMENT TOOLS AND DEVICES

The Global Assessment of Relational Functioning (GARF)

Systematic Assessment of Family Environment (SAFE)

Dyadic Adjustment Scale (DAS)

Self-Report Family Inventory (SFI)

Marital Satisfaction Inventory (MSI-R)

The McMaster Approach

Family Assessment Device (FAD)

Family Assessment Measure Version-III (FAM-III)

Family Environment (FES)

Parenting Alliance Measure (PAM)

Parenting Relationship Questionnaire (PRQ)

Parenting Satisfaction Scale (PSS)

Parenting Stress Index (PSI)

Partner Relationship Inventory

*DSM-V Notice

The National Exam has fully transitioned to using the DSM-V as the primary reference regarding diagnosis. The Exam *will* cover your capacity to differentiate between various mental disorders based on information presented in a client vignette. If you are familiar with the DSM-IV, consider the significant changes that took place with the launch of the DSM-V. If you are not familiar with either, review the general categories of psychopathology and the process of differential diagnosis.

You have now reviewed the working concepts of a *Universal Family Therapist* as well as a general overview of the assessment process in Marital & Family Therapy. Let us move on to reviewing each primary theory as organized by the particular domains on the National Licensing Exam...

Notice the category organizing each theory (see Figure 3.1). Having a general understanding of which underlying theories inform each primary category will provide structure and clarity—resulting in more accessible recall come test day.

Transgenerational Models

These approaches applied concepts from psychoanalysis to the family. The originators of each model were psychoanalytically trained prior to becoming interested in family dynamics. Essential themes of these models include how generations influence one another over time, and its impact on individual personality development and relational functioning. These models are long term, insight based, and growth is achieved through the process of *working through.*

Classical Schools

These models were the first approaches to therapy developed exclusively for the family as opposed to adapting individual psychology to the family system (i.e. *Transgenerational Models*). *MRI Systemic, Strategic,* and the *Milan Approach* were based in **Bateson's** *Human Communication Processes Model,* which as we reviewed earlier, integrated *cybernetics, general systems theory, theory of logical types,* and **Erickson's** use of *paradoxical interventions.* These approaches were brief and problem focused.

The *Experiential Models* (**Whitaker** and **Satir**) were more so influenced by *humanistic-psychology* and focused on the health of the individual as preceding the health of the family system.

Constructivist Models

These approaches were a new wave in family therapy, grounded in *Post-Modernism.* Here, therapy became more collaborative and strengths based. Clients were viewed as the experts on their own lives and the therapist's role became less about expertise and more about curiosity regarding the lived experience of the client.

The Theory and Practice of Marriage & Family Therapy

Transgenerational Models
Psychoanalytic Theory Applied to the Family System

Bowenian Family Therapy
Murray **Bowen**
Phillip **Guerin**
Thomas **Fogarty**

Betty **Carter** &
Monica **McGoldrick**
(Feminist Bowenian Therapists).

Contextual Family Therapy
Ivan Boszormenyi-Nagy

Object-Relations Theory
James Framo
Norman **Paul**
Jill & David **Scharff**

Classical Schools
Cybernetics and General Systems Theory

MRI Model (Palo Alto Group)
*Gregory **Bateson**
Jay **Haley**
*John **Weakland**
*William **Fry**

*Don **Jackson**
Virginia **Satir**
*Paul **Watzlawick**
Arthur **Bodin**

Strategic Family Therapy
Jay **Haley**
Cloe **Madanes** (*Strategic-Humanism*)
*Heavily influenced by Milton **Erikson**

Milan Systemic
Mara Selvini-**Palazzoli**
Luigi **Boscolo**

Gianfranco **Cecchin**
Guiliana **Prata**
Janet **Beavin**

Structural Family Therapy
Salvador Minuchin

Experiential Family Therapy
Carl **Whitaker**
Virginia **Satir**

**Napier, Roberto,
Bumberry, Keith,
Kempler, and Duhl**

Constructivist Models
Post-Modernism

Solution-Focused Therapy
Steven **DeShazer** & Insoo Kim **Berg**

Narrative Family Therapy
Michael **White** & David **Epston**

Collaborative Family Therapy
Harlene **Anderson** and Harry **Goolishan**

CBT-Family Therapy
John **Gottman**
Richard **Stuart**
James **Alexander**

Albert **Ellis**
Aaron **Beck**

Psycho-Education
Carol **Anderson**

Emotionally Focused Therapy
Susan **Johnson** and Leslie **Greenberg**

Internal Family Systems
Richard **Schwartz**

Figure 3.1

Theory Outline

As discussed earlier in this manual, notice that each theory is reviewed in direct relation to the domains measured on the exam. Take a moment to familiarize yourself with the outline as it will help to better differentiate between each theory while becoming acquainted with how the exam will measure your capacity to recall particular concepts and conceptualize various vignettes.

THE PRACTICE OF SYSTEMIC THERAPY (Domain 1)

Primary Contributor

Class of Family Therapy

Historical Overview

Essential Themes of Therapy

Key Terms

ASSESSING, HYPOTHESIZING, & DIAGNOSING (Domain 2)

Assessment

Diagnosing

DESIGNING & CONDUCTING TREATMENT (Domain 3)

Who is Involved

Treatment Duration

Goals of Therapy

Primary Interventions and/or Techniques

EVALUATING ONGOING PROCESS & TERMINATING TREATMENT (Domain 4)

Early Phase

Middle Phase

Later Phase

Termination

In Application to the Vignette

Multigenerational Family Therapy
(Bowen's Family Systems Approach)

THE PRACTICE OF SYSTEMIC THERAPY (Domain 1)

Primary Contributor: Murray **Bowen**

Secondary Contributors: Phillip **Guerin**

Thomas **Fogarty**

Monica **McGoldrick**

Betty **Carter**

Class of Family Therapy

Multigenerational Family Therapy (Bowen Family Systems Approach) is categorized under the *Transgenerational Models* of Family Therapy, as it applies principles of psychoanalytic theory to the family system while acknowledging the significance of past generations in relation to the individual and nuclear family in treatment (see **Figure 3.1**).

Historical Overview

Murray **Bowen** was a psychoanalytically trained psychiatrist and later pioneer of the Family Therapy movement after joining the *Race to Cure Schizophrenia*. As **Bowen** was studying individuals with schizophrenia, he recognized what he found to be a particularly emotionally-sensitive relationship between the schizophrenic patient and his or her mother. As this led him to experiment with engaging the mother and father in treatment, it eventually grew into his recognition of the entire family as an emotional system that was remarkably influenced by past generations and extended family members (Bowen, 1966). This concept grew into what remains as the most comprehensive theory in family therapy. Bowen went on record stating his primary interest was always more tied to developing a theory to fully understand how families function rather than clinical intervention.

In *2nd Generation Bowenian Therapy*, notably **Guerin** and **Fogarty**, focus was shifted away from the family of origin and toward joining with the symptomatic child—only drawing in extended family as directly related to the problem (Guerin, 1976). This was an attempt at *detriangulating emotional processes* within the nuclear family. **Bowen**, on the other hand, would jump right into the family of origin, as change within the family of origin will automatically influence change at the individual and nuclear level.

Monica **McGoldrick** and Betty **Carter** also identify with Bowen's model while bringing an emphasis to gender—**McGoldrick** and **Carter** are often referred to as *Feminist-Bowenian Therapists*.

Essential Themes of Therapy

The essential theme of **Bowen's** theory—and application to family therapy—is based on his identification of the inevitable and dialectical conflict between *individuality* and *togetherness*. According to **Bowen,** we all experience two biologically-based psychological capacities (Bowen, 1974):

(1) A *cognitive capacity* to realize our creative, individual potential to objectively accomplish tasks necessary for survival and enhancement. This capacity is rooted in *individuality*, is *non-reactive* and represents the actualization of our creative potential—which is exclusively rational and observable in the physical, material world. An example would be human's capacity over time to industrialize our world and advance in technologically sophisticated ways to not only prolong life, but improve the quality in which we experience it.

(2) An *affective capacity* that is more *reactive* and driven toward expanding our ability to *communicate* with and *connect to others*. This capacity is grounded in *togetherness*, is *subjectively experienced*, and is more prone to *emotional reactivity* yet still offers survival value.

Bowen's theory suggests that the primary challenge of mental health lies within our capacity to achieve and maintain a balance between these two forces (individuality and togetherness). **Bowen** found this to be an ongoing, dialectical process that is experienced at the individual level, family level, community level, societal level, and global level for our species as a whole. **Bowen** referred to the process in which individuals, microsystems (families), and macrosystems (societies) go about achieving such balance as *Self-Differentiation* (Bowen, 1974). *Self-Differentiation* is experienced throughout the lifespan and influenced within the family system as well as by past generations and extended family members.

Key Terms

Individuality & Togetherness:

Differentiation of Self:

Triangles:

Nuclear Family Emotional System:

Undifferentiated Family Ego Mass:

Family Projection Process:

Multigenerational Transmission Process:

Sibling Position:

Emotional Cutoff:

Societal Emotional Process:

ASSESSING, HYPOTHESIZING, & DIAGNOSING (Domain 2)

Assessment

As delineated in the assessment phase of treatment below, the process entails a rich history taking that trails back several generations. This may either be done as part of the *genogram* as an *assessment* or prior to the genogram as an *intervention*.

Diagnosis

This approach was non-pathologizing and maintained a systemic focus on the presenting problem.

DESIGNING & CONDUCTING TREATMENT (Domain 3)

Who is Involved

Multigenerational Family Therapists may work with individual family members, a partner dyad, an entire family, or various combinations of the above.

Treatment Duration

Treatment in this approach is often long term lasting up to several years.

Goals of Therapy

Multigenerational Family Therapy, much like the other *Transgenerational Models of Family Therapy*, is oriented toward *working through* the *underlying processes and conflicts* that fuel symptoms as opposed to focusing on symptom reduction (as we will see is the focus in several other approaches to family therapy). According to **Bowen,** the two processes that fuel symptoms experienced by individuals and families stem from *low levels of self-differentiation* and *chronic anxiety*.

As so, the primary goals for therapy are to:

(1) Decrease anxiety
(2) Increase levels of differentiation in as many family members as possible

Primary Interventions and/or Techniques

Detriangulate:

Nonanxious Presence:

Genogram (Guerin) / Family Diagrams (Bowen):

Process Questions:

Going Home Again:

Displacement Stories:

Coaching:

The "I" Position:

Relationship Experiments:

Person-to-Person Relationships:

EVALUATING ONGOING PROCESS & TERMINATING TREATMENT (Domain 4)

Therapy Structure

Many will claim that Multigenerational Family Therapy does not lend itself to a structure, given its long-term orientation and theoretical complexity. When analyzing the ongoing process of working from this approach, a pattern emerges that suggests three primary phases of this treatment:

(1) The Assessment Phase

Unlike the later approaches to family therapy, **Bowen's** approach includes a rich emphasis of history taking when coming to understand the family system and its individual members. During the assessment, the therapist will assess for patterns of *togetherness and individuality* by exploring individual's *family of origin*, the presence of *triangles*, and the various *levels of differentiation*.

(2) The Genogram Phase

After a thorough assessment of the family system and individuals within, the therapist and client(s) co-construct a *Family Diagram* (originally referred as by **Bowen**), or, more commonly known *Genogram* (*Family Diagrams* were later renamed as *Genograms* by Phillip **Guerin**).

(3) The Differentiation Phase

Here, the focus shifts toward reducing anxiety and increasing levels of differentiation of as many family members as possible. This process is informed by the thorough and in depth history taking of the family system and the individuals within that was completed in the prior two phases.

Applying Multigenerational Family Therapy to the Becker Family
(Bowen Family Systems Approach)

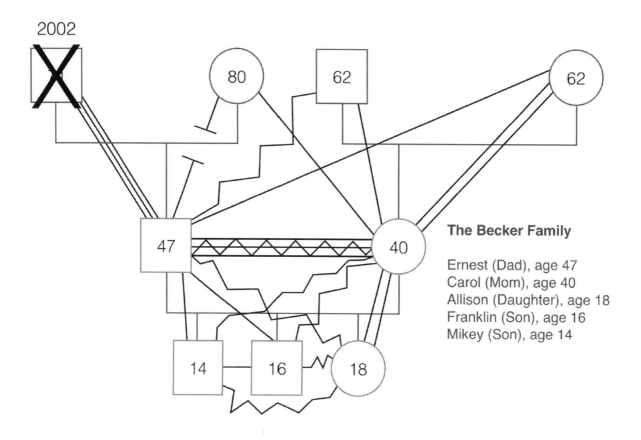

The Becker Family

Ernest (Dad), age 47
Carol (Mom), age 40
Allison (Daughter), age 18
Franklin (Son), age 16
Mikey (Son), age 14

The Beckers are a Caucasian, middle-class family pursuing therapy due to general family disconnection. Mom initiated the phone call stating that things are "out of control" and that "changes need to happen, and fast!" Mom further elaborated that she and her husband are very disconnected and have been for the past 11 years. She said he will work all day and come home to "decompress" in his workshop attached to the garage and spend most weekends with their two sons at various sporting activities and "guys-only outings." Mom reported that she and her husband have been sleeping in different bedrooms for the past three years. Mom said she will spend most days at her Mom's home—which is close in town—and as much time as she can with her daughter before she goes off to college in five months. Mom said she is very disconnected from her sons and her husband is very disconnected from his daughter. She reported the family being "split into two" and appeared quite desperate for change to occur. Mom requested that she, her husband, and her daughter come in as her two sons are refusing to attend family therapy.

**Applying Multigenerational Family Therapy to the Becker Family
(Bowen Family Systems Approach)**

Early-Phase Goals

1.

2.

Middle-Phase Goals:

1.

2.

Later-Phase Goals:

1.

2.

Overall Conceptualization of the Becker Family as Informed by Multigenerational Family Therapy

Contextual Family Therapy

THE PRACTICE OF SYSTEMIC THERAPY (Domain 1)

Primary Contributor: Ivan Boszormenyi-**Nagy**

Class of Family Therapy

Contextual Family Therapy is categorized under the *Transgenerational Models* of Family Therapy, as it applies principles of *psychoanalytic theory* to the *family system* while acknowledging the significance of *past generations* in relation to the individual and nuclear family in treatment (see **Figure 3.1**).

Historical Overview

Nagy was a Hungarian-American psychiatrist trained in *psychoanalysis* whose father was a judge. You will see the distinct influence this had on **Nagy's** development of *Contextual Family Therapy,* serving as a helpful reminder on the exam when questions come up related to this approach. *Contextual Family Therapy* integrates individual, interpersonal, systemic, and multigenerational dimensions of psychology to both the individual and the family system. Directly influenced by **Nagy's** childhood experiences of growing up with a father who was a judge, his model focuses on concepts of *Fairness* and *Relational Ethics*.

Essential Themes of Therapy

Nagy found that high functioning families shared two primary characteristics—*reliability* and *trustworthiness* (Boszormenyi-Nagy & Krasner, 1986). Understanding these two concepts through the lens of *Relational Ethics,* **Nagy** promoted that families must strive to maintain an equitable balance of *fairness* that transmits across generations. Based on this concept, **Nagy** found that individuals are born into a *legacy* based upon the prior experiences and actions of their parents and elder siblings, as well as a sense of *entitlement* related to what they feel they are inherently due from others and the world (objectively due) and what they are due in return based upon behavior toward others (subjectively due) (Boszormenyi-Nagy & Krasner, 1986). Subjective entitlements are stored and maintained in a *ledger* by each individual, tracking both *debts* and *entitlements* from within the family system.

The term *Contextual* refers to all individuals that are personally affected by the therapeutic interventions as well as **Nagy's** emphasis on the important role that the social and political *context* of the family plays in effective therapeutic outcomes.

This theory is in alignment with the other *transgenerational models* of family therapy that view underlying conflicts as fueling surface level symptoms, requiring a long-term process of gaining *insight* before *working through* the source of the issue.

There are four primary dimensions of individual and relational psychology that interact with one another (Boszormenyi-Nagy & Krasner, 1986):

1. **Facts:**

2. **Psychology:**

3. **Transactions:**

4. **Relational Ethics:**

Key Terms

Loyalty:

Legacy:

Entitlement:

Ledger:

Contextual:

Equitable Asymmetry:

Merit:

Filial Loyalty:

Split Filial Loyalty:

Revolving Slate of Injustice:

Debts or Filial Responsibility:

Destructive Entitlement:

Parentification:

Exoneration:

Deparentification Process:

ASSESSING, HYPOTHESIZING, & DIAGNOSING (Domain 2)

Assessment

Contextual family Therapy does not provide a structured assessment process, but like other *Transgenerational Models*, it will emphasize the importance of attaining a rich history of the family system throughout the prior generations—*Contextual Family Therapists* may likely use a *genogram* as an assessment tool. Primary themes of the assessment process will include (Boszormenyi-Nagy & Krasner, 1986):

- Maintaining an early focus on family resources. If the family does not have adequate resources in place (such as food, shelter, income) than this must be addressed prior to therapy being effective. This is a step toward building trust with the family and nurturing the therapeutic relationship.

- Monitoring the presence of and interactions between the four dimensions of individual and relational psychology.

- Tracking themes of *trust, loyalty, reliability,* and *fairness*

Diagnosis

This approach was non-pathologizing and maintained a systemic focus on the presenting problem.

DESIGNING & CONDUCTING TREATMENT (Domain 3)

Who is Involved

In *Contextual Family Therapy,* the therapist determines and directs who will come to therapy based on his or her determination of which individuals contain the richest resources for promoting change within the family. They will likely emphasize the significance of both parents being involved in treatment.

Treatment Duration

Like the other *Transgenerational Schools*, treatment is long term.

Goals of Therapy

Similar to **Bowen's** Model of Family Therapy, goals in *Contextual Family Therapy* are "umbrella" goals that will fit with each family that comes into treatment. Of them, include:

- Individuals taking responsibility for their behaviors toward others (requires *working through entitlements*).
- Reclaiming disowned parts of themselves (requires working through perceived *legacies*).
- Differentiating between *irrational guilt* (*legacies,* experienced objectively) and *justifiable guilt* (guilt based upon behaviors toward others, experienced subjectively).
- Achieving *exoneration* of self and others, thereby resulting in a family system balanced by *fairness* and consideration for others (Boszormenyi-Nagy & Krasner, 1986).

Primary Techniques and/or Interventions

The primary intervention identified in *Contextual Family Therapy* is one that models the very essence of *fairness* and *consideration* emphasized throughout the approach.

Multidirectional Partiality:

EVALUATING ONGOING PROCESS & TERMINATING TREATMENT (Domain 4)

Therapy Structure (Boszormenyi-Nagy & Krasner, 1986)

I. Early Phase of Therapy
- Early phases of *Contextual Family Therapy* focus on gathering a rich family history. This is done by gathering basic information, constructing a *genogram,* and having *each family member* explain his or her side of the story. This helps the therapist to understand the overall family system in terms of background facts, contextual factors, and to start recognizing the deeper motivational factors (the many terms associated with this approach, including: *hidden loyalties, ledger imbalances, destructive entitlements, parentification processes,* etc.).

II. Middle Phase of Therapy
- Address any issues requiring urgent attention as attained through the assessment phase (this is related to issues of social and financial welfare, violence, vulnerable individuals, etc.).
- Building off of the earlier phase of hearing each individual's side of the story, the therapist will deepen the conversation with each individual, taking their side as the dialogue evolves. The premise of this technique is to create a *balance* within the family system after the therapist is able to execute this with each member, and should not be confused with a technique of *joining.*
- Eventually have this dialogue shift toward mutual insight and shared accountability, paving way for *exoneration.*

III. Late Phase of Therapy
- As the work in the Middle Phase of Therapy is elaborated and expanded upon, it will eventually make way to family members learning to be more considerate of others in the family and taking responsibility for intentionally acting *ethically* toward others. Once these patterns are reinforced over time, the family will begin to experience desirable levels of *trustworthiness* and *fairness,* the overall goals of *Contextual Family Therapy.*

Applying Contextual Family Therapy to the Becker Family

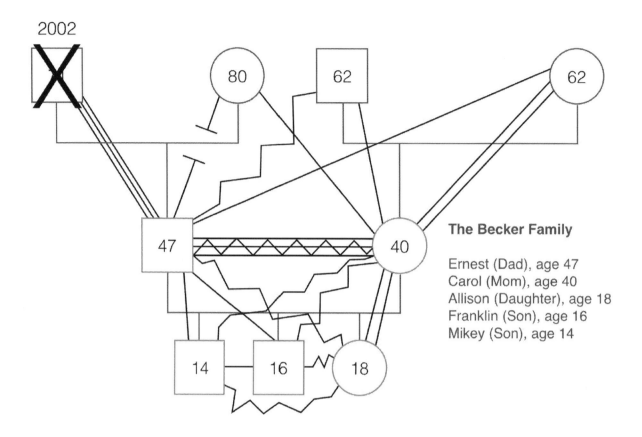

The Becker Family

Ernest (Dad), age 47
Carol (Mom), age 40
Allison (Daughter), age 18
Franklin (Son), age 16
Mikey (Son), age 14

The Beckers are a Caucasian, middle-class family pursuing therapy due to general family disconnection. Mom initiated the phone call stating that things are "out of control" and that "changes need to happen, and fast!" Mom further elaborated that she and her husband are very disconnected and have been for the past 11 years. She said he will work all day and come home to "decompress" in his workshop attached to the garage and spend most weekends with their two sons at various sporting activities and "guys-only outings." Mom reported that she and her husband have been sleeping in different bedrooms for the past three years. Mom said she will spend most days at her Mom's home—which is close in town—and as much time as she can with her daughter before she goes off to college in five months. Mom said she is very disconnected from her sons and her husband is very disconnected from his daughter. She reported the family being "split into two" and appeared quite desperate for change to occur. Mom requested that she, her husband, and her daughter come in as her two sons are refusing to attend family therapy.

Applying Contextual Family Therapy to the Becker Family

Early-Phase Goals

1.

2.

Middle-Phase Goals:

1.

2.

Later-Phase Goals:

1.

2.

Overall conceptualization of the Becker Family as informed by Contextual Family Therapy

Object-Relations Theory

THE PRACTICE OF SYSTEMIC THERAPY (Domain 1)

Primary Contributors: James **Framo**

Secondary Contributors: Norman **Paul**

Jill & David **Scharff**

Class of Family Therapy

Object-Relations Theory is categorized under the *Transgenerational Models* of Family Therapy, as it applies principles of *psychoanalytic theory* to the *family system,* while also acknowledging the significance of *past generations* in relation to the individual and nuclear family in treatment (see **Figure 3.1**).

Historical Overview

Object-Relations Theory, although grounded in traditional psychodynamic theory, took a shift from understanding individual motivation for seeking relationships as a result of instinctual drives (sex and aggression), and instead expanded it to a relational context—suggesting that individuals form relationships based on a fundamental need to seek relationships. Although the term *Object-Relations* stems back to the Freudian era, it developed as an independent theory throughout the 1940s and 1950s before being applied to the *Transgenerational Models* of Family Therapy by James **Framo** in the 1960s through the early 2000s.

Essential Themes of Therapy

This theory suggests that we can come to understand how adults relate to their environment and others by exploring how their experiences were shaped throughout infancy and early childhood (Framo, 1992). Meaning, if a child experienced consistent and reliable love, support, and nurturance throughout childhood, then they will likely predict similar behavior from others in their adult lives that remind them of their primary caregivers. However, if a child experiences extreme neglect or ongoing abuse throughout infancy and early childhood, in turn, they will likely predict similar patterns of behaviors from others in their adult lives whether they have abusive tendencies or not. This may result in the adult avoiding relationships altogether—despite the fact that there are potential partners that are highly unlikely to engage in abusive behaviors—or continue to find themselves drawn toward individuals that are abusive and remain in such relationships.

This theory posits that *objects* are typically internalized images of an individual's mother, father, or other primary caregiver throughout infancy and early childhood (Framo, 1992). These *objects,* internalizing exponentially throughout infancy, have the potential to influence individuals throughout the remainder of their adult and elderly lives. Although experiences later in life can reshape these patterns, it requires a process of *insight* and *working through,* similar to the other *Transgenerational Models* of Family Therapy. *Working through* such *internalized objects* is no small task, as **Framo** (1992) argues the extent to which individuals crave acceptance and approval from their parents is so strong that they will sacrifice the healthy development of their own ego identity to maintain the relationship.

For example, if a young daughter's father has developed a distain for women due to his mother talking harshly and nastily to him throughout his childhood, but is unable to *work through* his resentment independently due to a lack of *insight*, he may unconsciously *project* this resentment on to his daughter (a safer outlet). Because the child is powerless to change her external environment, she will instead internalize and repress aspects of the parents and incorporate them into her own personality. Over time, this will subtly encourage his daughter's development of relating to men in harsh manners, similar to her paternal grandmother. Now, the only way for the father to express his resentment is dependent upon the daughter continuing to identify with her father's *internalized object* of how women act toward men. To continue to meet her father's needs—which results in a sense of acceptance and approval—will require the daughter to unconsciously sacrifice a healthy ego development.

Key Terms

Projection:

Projective Identification:

Insight:

Working Through:

Interpretation:

Transference:

Countertransference:

Object:

Introject:

ASSESSING, HYPOTHESIZING, & DIAGNOSING (Domain 2)

Assessment

Object-Relations Theory does not provide a structured assessment process, but like other *Transgenerational Models,* will emphasize the importance of attaining a rich history of the family system throughout the prior generations—*Object-Relations Therapists* may likely use a *genogram* as an assessment tool. Primary themes of the assessment process will include (Framo, 1992):

- Exploring early childhood experiences and the clients' interpretation of them.
- Exploring the individual's past and present relationship to their primary caregivers.
- Exploring their current relationship style and areas in which they may be struggling to establish healthy, long-term relationships.

Diagnosing

This approach was nonpathologizing.

DESIGNING & CONDUCTING TREATMENT (Domain 3)

Who is Involved

Much like *Contextual Family Therapy,* the therapist will determine who is involved based upon each individual's direct relationship to the problem. *Object-Relations Therapists* will likely emphasize the significance of family of origin work given its profound impact on adult functioning.

Treatment Duration

Similar to the other *Transgenerational Models* of Family Therapy, this treatment approach is long term.

Goals of Therapy

Similar to the other *Transgenerational Models* of Family Therapy, the primary goals of this approach are to develop *insight* and begin *working through* unresolved conflict while developing new ways of behaving governed by a healthy, central ego (Framo, 1992). Again, this theory will look beyond symptom relief and focus on underlying conflicts and processes that unconsciously fuel the maladaptive behaviors that cause symptoms. This theory will specify that goals are open-ended and will often change as the individual and family experiences growth and change. Ideally, individuals will develop healthy egos and begin relating to others maturely; that is, being open to experience as opposed to unconsciously predicting behavior. This will allow individuals to interact with their partners in ways free of *projecting* unresolved conflict and relate to others in the world in relatively undistorted ways (Framo, 1992).

Primary Interventions and/or Techniques

This theory does not define a list of specific interventions, and instead, therapists engage in the therapeutic process with openness and a capacity to adjust the approach to the unique needs of the individual or family system. As so, the approach encourages a consistent use of *listening, responding to unconscious material, interpreting, working with transference and countertransference, empathy,* and *therapeutic neutrality,* but does not lay out a specific structure or process.

EVALUATING ONGOING PROCESS & TERMINATING TREATMENT (Domain 4)

Therapy Structure (Framo, 1992)

I.   Early Phase of Therapy
   - Early phases of *Object-Relations Theory* focus on assessing for early childhood experiences, exploring the individual family members' past and present relationship to their primary caregivers and exploring their current relationship style and areas in which they may be struggling to establish healthy, long-term relationships.

II. Middle Phase of Therapy
   - The middle-phase of therapy will entail fostering *insight* through exploring past relationships, making room to uncover and understand the meaning of their current behaviors in relation to experiences throughout early childhood, and then begin *working through* unresolved and internalized conflicts.

III. Late Phase of Therapy
   - As the work in the Middle Phase of Therapy is elaborated and expanded upon, individuals can begin to experiment with developing new behaviors and ways in which they interact with themselves and others in the world. This will foster later life experiences that will reshape *internalized objects* from the past, freeing the individuals to relate to other in mature, non-distorted ways.

James Framo's Approach

James **Framo** (1992) offered some relatively unique adjustments to the more traditional *Object-Relations Theory* approach detailed thus far. **Framo** strongly encouraged the importance of working with the adult client and his or her family of origin. For example, if a male and female couple came in for couple therapy reporting that the husband is struggling to connect in deep, intimate ways with his wife, and the assessment phase draws out a history of the husband growing up with an emotionally distant mother, **Framo** would suggest that the husband come back to see him with his mother and father. He believed that working through the core relationship that resulted in the *internalized object* fueling his emotional distance with his wife will resolve the conflict within the marriage. Although many clients will be resistant to this recommendation, **Framo** identified a concept he terms **The Dirty Middle,** which refers to the middle of therapy when *insight* is achieved but *working through* is at an impasse, typically resulting from a pronounced divide between each partner's philosophy of marriage or dispute over a seemingly irreconcilable disagreement. **Framo** would use *The Dirty Middle* as *leverage* for getting each individual to bring in their family of origin.

Applying Object-Relations Theory to the Becker Family

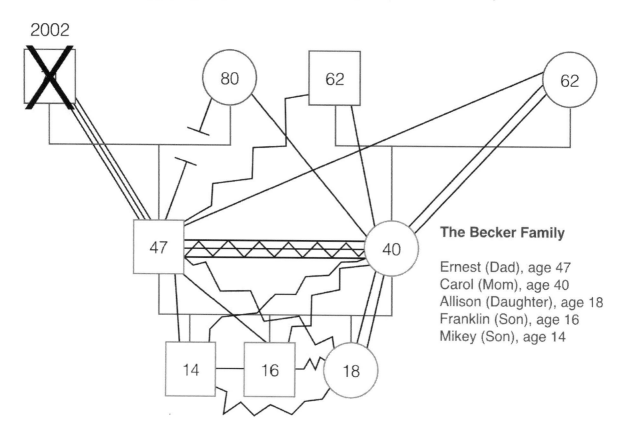

The Becker Family

Ernest (Dad), age 47
Carol (Mom), age 40
Allison (Daughter), age 18
Franklin (Son), age 16
Mikey (Son), age 14

The Beckers are a Caucasian, middle-class family pursuing therapy due to general family disconnection. Mom initiated the phone call stating that things are "out of control" and that "changes need to happen, and fast!" Mom further elaborated that she and her husband are very disconnected and have been for the past 11 years. She said he will work all day and come home to "decompress" in his workshop attached to the garage and spend most weekends with their two sons at various sporting activities and "guys-only outings." Mom reported that she and her husband have been sleeping in different bedrooms for the past three years. Mom said she will spend most days at her Mom's home—which is close in town—and as much time as she can with her daughter before she goes off to college in five months. Mom said she is very disconnected from her sons and her husband is very disconnected from his daughter. She reported the family being "split into two" and appeared quite desperate for change to occur. Mom requested that she, her husband, and her daughter come in as her two sons are refusing to attend family therapy.

Applying Object-Relations Theory to the Becker Family

Early-Phase Goals

1.

2.

Middle-Phase Goals:

1.

2.

Later-Phase Goals:

1.

2.

Overall Conceptualization of the Becker Family as Informed by Object-Relations Theory

Similarities & Differences of the Transgenerational Models

Similarities

- Informed by Psychoanalytic Theory as applied to the family system.
- Long-Term Treatment.
- Emphasize *insight* & *working through* as opposed to symptom relief.
- Endorse that unresolved conflictual patterns are transmitted across generations.
- Find that experiences from our early childhood within our family of origin influence how we relate to others as adults.
- Use Genograms as assessment tool.
- Emphasize the importance of history-taking.
- Identify *transference* & *countertransference* as therapeutic tools.
- Will work with families in various client-dynamics as relevant to the presenting problem.

Differences

Key Characteristics: *Bowen Family Therapy*

- Emphasizes the role of *anxiety* and promotes the encouragement of *self-differentiation* of each family member as ultimate goal of therapy.
- Therapist remains *neutral* and acts as *coach*.

Key Characteristics: *Contextual family Therapy*

- Emphasizes the roles of reliability, *trustworthiness*, and *fairness*.
- Ultimate goal is to experience *exoneration*, have individuals become accountable for their actions, and achieve balanced levels of *fairness* and *consideration toward others* in the family system.
- *Multidirectional Partiality* over neutrality.

Key Characteristics: *Object-Relations Theory*

- Individuals create *objects* throughout early childhood, mostly based on their mother, father, and/or primary caregiver, which influence their adult lives.
- Stated that the need for acceptance from parents is so strong that children sacrifice their own healthy ego development.
- Emphasized working primarily with the individual and his/her family of origin (Framo).
- Ultimate goal is to develop a healthy central-ego, allowing individuals to relate to others in mature, undistorted ways.

Figure 3.2

Notes on the Transgenerational Models

MRI Systemic Approach

THE PRACTICE OF SYSTEMIC THERAPY (Domain 1)

Primary Contributors:
Gregory **Bateson** (non-clinical)
Don **Jackson** (founder of MRI)
Virginia **Satir**
Jay **Haley**
John **Weakland**
Paul **Watzlawick**

Secondary Contributors: Richard **Fisch** (reorganized MRI as Brief Therapy Center)

Class of Family Therapy

The MRI Systemic School is categorized under the *Classical Schools* of Family Therapy (see **Figure 3.1**). These were the first models developed from the ground up exclusively for families, promoting the practice of Marriage & Family Therapy as a distinct field of study.

Historical Overview

MRI Systemic was the initial approach to Marriage and Family Therapy that grew out of the still famous *Mental Research Institute* in *Palo Alto*. The MRI Systemic Approach is grounded in Gregory **Bateson's** integrated *Human Communication Processes Model*, primarily influenced by *General Systems Theory* and *Cybernetics*. This approach also borrows the rich contributions of Milton **Erickson's** use of *paradoxical interventions*. As opposed to the *Transgenerational Models* previously discussed, which adapted *psychoanalytic theory* to the family system, these approaches are grounded in traditional *General Systems Theory* and offer *pragmatic, action-oriented interventions* aimed at providing *symptom relief* in a relatively brief amount of time (often, 10 sessions or less) (Weakland, Fisch, Watzlawick, & Bodin, 1974).

Essential Themes of Therapy

This approach finds that families get *stuck* in problematic, *interactional cycles of repetitive behaviors* which prevent the family system from appropriately adjusting to environmental changes (Weakland et al., 1974). Failure to appropriately adjust to environmental changes often stem from failed attempts at solving the problem in the first place. *Family Systems* get stuck in repetitive behavioral cycles when the response to a failed solution is to do *more-of-the-same* (Watzlawick, Beavin, & Jackson, 1967). For instance, if a child is acting out because he is not allowed to attend sleepovers now that he is in the seventh-grade, instead of the parents adjusting to the child's developmental milestone by granting more freedom they punish the child for requesting to attend a sleepover. When the child acts out even more, the parents increase the punishment.

The basis of this model is to provide symptom relief as related to the presenting complaint rather than interpret meaning or exploring familial events (quite the contrast with the *Transgenerational Models* previously reviewed) (Watzlawick et al., 1967). This is done in a pragmatic, action-oriented and methodical manner. The therapists will first assess for the cycle of problematic interactions and then intervene to break the cycle by using straightforward or paradoxical directives. As so, the responsibility for change falls upon the therapist's capacity to effectively execute this methodology. Therapy is terminated once the presenting issue is resolved.

Key Terms

First-Order Change:

Second-Order Change:

Problem as Attempted Solution:

More of the Same:

Report and Command Functions:

Metacommunication:

Complementary Relationship:

Symmetrical Relationship:

ASSESSING, HYPOTHESIZING, & DIAGNOSING (Domain 2)

Assessment

Assessment is delineated in the therapy structure portion below. Essentially, assessment included a clear, yet brief description of the problem. Once the problem was fully understood, the therapist(s) would identify the behavioral interactional patterns that maintain it, and intervene with the use of a paradoxical intervention.

Diagnosing

This approach is nonpathologizing and systemic in nature.

DESIGNING & CONDUCTING TREATMENT (Domain 3)

Who is Involved

Far fewer family members are involved in this approach, again contrasting the *Transgenerational Models*. Often, only one or two family members will attend therapy. *MRI Systemic* would often use a *Team Approach* to therapy; meaning, several therapists gathering to consult on the case, hypothesize, and at times interchangeably work with the family (Weakland, 1974).

Treatment Duration

Treatment in this approach is brief, limited to 10 sessions whether symptom relief is achieved or not.

Goals of Therapy

Resolve current problem and provide symptom relief and create *second-order change.*

Primary Interventions and/or Techniques

Paradoxical Intervention:

Positioning:

Prescribing the Symptom:

Restraining the Progress of Change:

Out-of-Session Directive:

EVALUATING ONGOING PROCESS & TERMINATING TREATMENT (Domain 4)

Therapy Structure

This treatment approach offers a structured method applied to *every* family in six steps (Weakland et al., 1974):

1. Introduction to the treatment setup

2. Inquiry and definition of a single problem

3. Estimation of the solution (the positive feedback) maintaining the problem (the unwanted behavior)

   a. solution is to deny that a problem exists (thus, clients need to *act*)

   b. solution is to solve a problem which does not exist (thus, clients need to *stop acting*)

   c. solution is an effort to solve a problem within a framework that makes solution impossible (thus, client needs to *act differently*)

4. Setting goals for treatment (e.g. for *second-order change,* identify the rules that support the dysfunctional solution and which, therefore, need to be changed)

5. Selecting and making behavioral or strategic interventions

   a. *Reframe* the problem to induce compliance

   b. Use of *paradoxical interventions*, such as:

      • *Outpositioning* (exaggerate to absurd levels)

      • *Prescribing the presenting symptom* (in hopes of compliance, defiance, or exposure of family relationships that maintain the problem)

      • *Restraining the progress of change* (slow down, don't change too fast, or don't change at all)

6. Termination

Applying MRI Systemic Family Therapy to the Becker Family

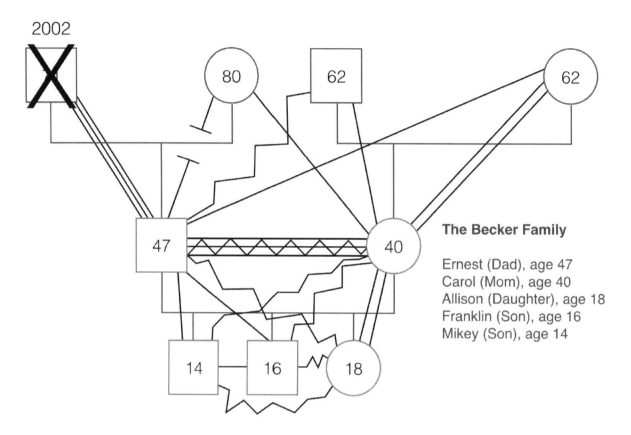

The Becker Family

Ernest (Dad), age 47
Carol (Mom), age 40
Allison (Daughter), age 18
Franklin (Son), age 16
Mikey (Son), age 14

The Beckers are a Caucasian, middle-class family pursuing therapy due to general family disconnection. Mom initiated the phone call stating that things are "out of control" and that "changes need to happen, and fast!" Mom further elaborated that she and her husband are very disconnected and have been for the past 11 years. She said he will work all day and come home to "decompress" in his workshop attached to the garage and spend most weekends with their two sons at various sporting activities and "guys-only outings." Mom reported that she and her husband have been sleeping in different bedrooms for the past three years. Mom said she will spend most days at her Mom's home—which is close in town—and as much time as she can with her daughter before she goes off to college in five months. Mom said she is very disconnected from her sons and her husband is very disconnected from his daughter. She reported the family being "split into two" and appeared quite desperate for change to occur. Mom requested that she, her husband, and her daughter come in as her two sons are refusing to attend family therapy.

Applying MRI Systemic Family Therapy to the Becker Family

Early-Phase Goals

1.

2.

Middle-Phase Goals:

1.

2.

Later-Phase Goals:

1.

2.

Overall Conceptualization of The Becker Family as Informed by MRI Systemic Family Therapy

Strategic Family Therapy

THE PRACTICE OF SYSTEMIC THERAPY (Domain 1)

Primary Contributors: Jay **Haley**
                               Cloe **Madanes**

Class of Family Therapy

Strategic Family Therapy is categorized under the *Classical Schools* of Family Therapy (see **Figure 3.1**). These were the first models developed from the ground up exclusively for families, promoting the practice of Marriage & Family Therapy as a distinct field of study.

Historical Overview

Jay **Haley** eventually broke off from the *MRI Group* to study with Salvador **Minuchin** for 10 years at the *Child Guidance Clinic.* Shortly after he formed the *Family Therapy Institute* in Washington D.C. where he eventually developed his own brand of therapy. Along with his then wife, Cloe **Madanes,** the two introduced *Strategic Family Therapy,* a development which merged **Bateson's** *Systemic* concepts with Salvador **Minuchin's** emphasis of the *Family Structure.*

Essential Themes of Therapy

Strategic Family Therapy continued to emphasize many of the principles offered from the *MRI Systemic Approach*—primarily, brief, pragmatic, solution-focused interventions—while adding a critical component. **Haley,** quite obviously influenced by **Minuchin,** also drew attention to the significance of the family structure—particularly, the *Parental Hierarchy. Strategic Family Therapy* poses that symptoms stem from a faulty organization within the family and serve a function in maintaining its structure and homeostasis (i.e. resistance to change) (Haley, 1963). *Strategic Family Therapy* emphasizes that the hierarchical arrangement of the family members is essential in resolving problems. A notable contribution of this theory—mirroring **Minuchin's** *Structural Family Therapy*—was **Haley's** intentional alignment with the parental generation when dealing with child-focused problems. **Haley** found that bringing parents together to work on their child's problem can both realign problematic hierarchies and serve to strengthen the couple's relationship.

Haley (1963) also emphasized the significance of the *Family Life Cycle,* as the process in and of itself inevitably results in *positive feedback loops* that disrupt *homeostasis.* Failing to adjust accordingly to the family life cycle results in the development or maintenance of symptoms and ongoing problems.

Key Terms

Directives:

Ordeal Therapy:

Aligning with Parental Generation:

Unbalancing:

Presenting Problem as Metaphor:

ASSESSING, HYPOTHESIZING, & DIAGNOSING (Domain 2)

Assessment

The structure of therapy is less precise than *MRI Systemic* other than the first session; that is outlined in great detail. **Haley** emphasized the importance of therapy starting well if it is to end well.

The Four Stages of the First Session (Haley, 1963):

1. *Social Stage*: Therapist aims at making clients comfortable (joining)
2. *Problem Stage*: The therapist will ask each person's perspective on the problem, usually starting with the Father. The therapist will ensure that no one is interrupted, and will attentively listen but will not interpret.
3. *Interaction Stage*: Therapist continues to attentively observe but not interpret, while noting observations of information on sequences, hierarchies, triangles, and alliances.
4. *Goal Setting Stage*:
   - Learn what solutions have been tried but failed (*MRI Systemic*).
   - Focus shifts to the here-and-now and on creating successes—via directives aimed at small changes.
   - Shifts in structure and hierarchy remain as appropriate structural goals.

DESIGNING & CONDUCTING TREATMENT (Domain 3)

Who is Involved

Fewer family members, often only one or two—only more if they are directly related to the identified problem. *Strategic Family Therapy* will emphasize the importance of having both parents involved in treatment.

Treatment Duration

Strategic Family Therapy is not as brief as *MRI Systemic* but more brief than *Milan Systemic*, landing right in the middle of the three *Systemic Approaches* to Family Therapy as far as treatment duration.

Goals of Therapy

Much like the *MRI Systemic Approach*, **Haley** and **Madanes** aimed to alter the behavioral interactions of the family members in hopes of achieving symptom relief but differ in their equally important effort to also change the structure of the family and parental hierarchy.

Primary Interventions and/or Techniques

Paradoxical Interventions:

Reframing:

Metaphoric Task:

Pretend to Have Symptom:

Incongruous Hierarchies:

Therapy Structure

After the initial, structured first session, subsequent sessions will use specific interventions aimed at achieving goals set in the first session while avoiding to focus on marital issues. Instead, a preferred intervention as engaging the couple through their parental roles (i.e. creating a situation in which they collaborate on helping a child) (Haley, 1973). **Madanes** (1990) also focused on appropriate ways for children to help their parents.

Strategic-Humanism

Primary Contibutor: Cloe **Madanes**

Historical Overview

Madanes eventually branched off herself to create a unique brand of *Strategic Family Therapy* which she referred to as *Strategic-Humanism*. This approach maintains principles from *Strategic Family Therapy* while introducing concepts borrowed from *Humanism*, mainly increasing individual family members' ability to soothe and love as opposed to attempting to gain control over one another (Madanes, 1990). **Madanes** considers this as more of a *growth-oriented* model that views *love & happiness* as appropriate goals of therapy.

Essential Themes of Therapy

Strategic-Humanism endorses that each individual is continually presented with a range of choices as to what to make of him or herself and the present circumstances. **Madanes,** in this new approach, views *all* problems as stemming from the conflict between *Love & Violence* (Madanes, 1993).

Madanes (1990) hypothesized four ways in which individuals go about resolving this conflict:

1. To dominate and control (behavioral problems)
2. Desire to be loved (anxious & depressive problems)
3. Love and protect (related to problems of abuse and neglect)
4. Repent and forgive (problems related to sexual and/or physical abuse)

Strategic-Humanism entails *triangulation, dramatizations, pretending* (ask the child to pretend to have the symptom and the parents to pretend to help the child), and *make-believe play* (when a child protects his parents through symptomatic behavior, she is covertly helping them; here, this becomes intentional and used as a *directive*) (Madanes, 1993).

Applying Strategic Family Therapy to the Becker Family

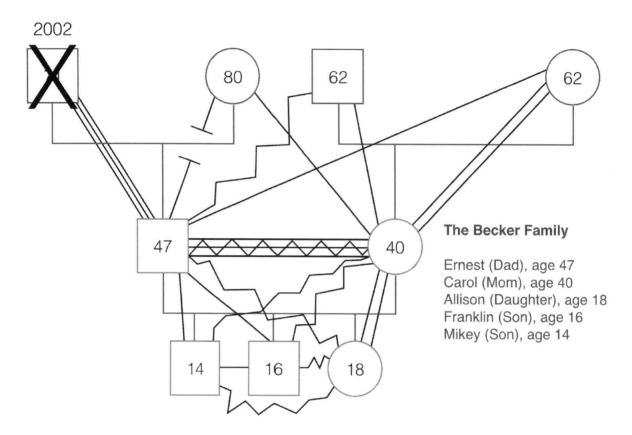

The Becker Family

Ernest (Dad), age 47
Carol (Mom), age 40
Allison (Daughter), age 18
Franklin (Son), age 16
Mikey (Son), age 14

The Beckers are a Caucasian, middle-class family pursuing therapy due to general family disconnection. Mom initiated the phone call stating that things are "out of control" and that "changes need to happen, and fast!" Mom further elaborated that she and her husband are very disconnected and have been for the past 11 years. She said he will work all day and come home to "decompress" in his workshop attached to the garage and spend most weekends with their two sons at various sporting activities and "guys-only outings." Mom reported that she and her husband have been sleeping in different bedrooms for the past three years. Mom said she will spend most days at her Mom's home—which is close in town—and as much time as she can with her daughter before she goes off to college in five months. Mom said she is very disconnected from her sons and her husband is very disconnected from his daughter. She reported the family being "split into two" and appeared quite desperate for change to occur. Mom requested that she, her husband, and her daughter come in as her two sons are refusing to attend family therapy.

Applying Strategic Family Therapy to the Becker Family

Early-Phase Goals

1.

2.

Middle-Phase Goals:

1.

2.

Later-Phase Goals:

1.

2.

Overall Conceptualization of The Becker Family as Informed by Strategic Family Therapy

Milan Systemic Approach

THE PRACTICE OF SYSTEMIC THERAPY (Domain 1)

Primary Contributors:
Mara Selvini **Palazzoli**
Guiliana **Prata**
Luigi **Boscolo**
Gianfranco **Cecchin**

Class of Family Therapy

Milan Family Therapy is categorized under the Classical Schools of Family Therapy (see **Figure 3.1**). This model was an extension of the MRI Group, heavily influenced by **Bateson's** Systemic Concepts as well as Strategic's paradoxical interventions, as introduced in Milan, Italy. It too was one of the initial approaches to therapy developed exclusively for families, contributing to the development of Marriage & Family Therapy as a distinct field of clinical practice and academic study.

Historical Overview

The Milan Group Center for the Study of the Family was founded by Mara Selivini **Palazzoli** in 1971, and along with her associates, published *Paradox and Counterparadox* in 1978. The approach started off as a close replica of the MRI Group, mirroring **Bateson's** *systemic-orientation* and relying upon *Strategic's* regular use of *paradoxical interventions*. In the 1980s, **Boscolo** and **Cecchin** split from **Palazzoli** and **Prata**. **Boscolo** and **Cecchin,** often referred to as the *Later Milan Group,* became less adaptive to *paradoxical interventions* and instead made efforts toward becoming a purer *systemic model* (Cecchin, 1987). As an account of their new professional identity, they published *Milan Systemic Family Therapy* in 1987.

> ***Note:** On the exam, it will be important to be able to differentiate between *Early Milan* and *Later Milan,* as this section of the manual will outline for you.

Essential Themes of Therapy (Early Milan Group)

The Early Milan Group was predominantly influenced by the *MRI-Group* and *Strategic Family Therapy* approaches. They endorsed the concept that family interactions are governed by a set of rules that may be adapted through the use of *paradoxical intervention* (Selvini Palazzoli, Boscolo, Cecchin, & Prata, 1980). Each family was seen by a therapist dyad (one male, one female) while being observed—live—by other members of the therapy team. Each session had five delineated parts, and sessions were held one month apart (Selvini Palazzoli et al., 1980). It was hypothesized that having sessions one month apart would allow for families to appropriately react to the intervention. Treatment was limited to 10 sessions over the course of one year—as so, it was often referred to as the *long-term brief therapy.* The *Early Milan Group* approach was characterized by two basic interventions—*positive connotation* and *ritual*—meant to introduce new ways of thinking into the family system (Selvini Palazzoli et al., 1980). The intervention was not dependent upon the family actually following through with the prescription; instead, the family would benefit from merely considering new ways to think about the *problem.*

Key Terms

Epistemology:

Epistemological Error:

Games:

Analogical Message:

Digital Message:

Metacommunication:

Punctuation (different than Structural):

Time:

ASSESSING, HYPOTHESIZING, & DIAGNOSING (Domain 2)

Assessment

Based on the primary principle of *hypothesizing* through the *Team Approach,* assessment was ongoing based upon new information and the family's adjustment to it as it arised. Initial *assessment* came in the form of a phone call, where one therapist would discuss with the family basic demographics and a general overview of the family including their expectations and presenting problem. This information would provide the content of the first *pre-session,* where the *Therapy Team* would begin to develop hypotheses that would be explored, validated, and readjusted as necessary during the *session phase* of each meeting. This process (minus the phone call) would continue throughout the duration of treatment (Selvini Palazzoli et al., 1980).

Diagnosing

This approach was nonpathologizing and viewed problems families experience systemically.

DESIGNING & CONDUCTING TREATMENT (Domain 3)

Families were seen by a male-female dyad and observed by other members of the therapy team. Sessions were held with at least one month apart allowing for the intervention to take effect.

Who is Involved

As many family members that are directly related to the problem would be involved. Typically, number of clients was relatively fewer with the exception of additional members as appropriate to the hypothesis. The *Early Milan School* was ahistoric and problem focused.

Treatment Duration

The *Early Milan Approach* was referred to as the *Long Term Brief Therapy,* as treatment was limited to 10 sessions but were held at least one month apart.

Goals of Therapy

The goals of the *Early Milan School* were to open families to accommodating and adjusting to new information and beliefs (new meaning) to maintain healthy systemic functioning (Selvini Palazzoli et al., 1980).

Primary Interventions and/or Techniques

Positive Connotation:

Rituals:

Paradoxical Prescription:

Neutrality & Irreverence:

Counterparadox:

A Learning Process:

Hypothesizing:

Team Approach:

EVALUATING ONGOING PROCESS & TERMINATING TREATMENT (Domain 4)

Therapy Structure
Each therapy session had five parts (Selvini Palazzoli et al., 1980):
1. *The Pre-Session*: The team would meet without the family to build an initial hypothesis.
2. *Session*: The team would meet with the family to check hypothesis (validate or modify).
3. *Intersession*: The team would meet privately to discuss and form an intervention.
4. *Intervention*: The therapist would return to deliver the intervention to the family. The intervention would take the form of either a *positive connotation* or prescription of a *ritual*—either of which were always given in the form of a statement leaning *against change* (use of *paradox* to address family's natural resistance to *change*).
5. *Post-Session Discussion*: The team would debrief on the discourse of the session and make preliminary plans and hypotheses for the following session.

THE LATER MILAN GROUP

The *Later Milan* group split—**Palazzoli** and **Prata** in one group, and **Boscolo** and **Cecchin** in the other.

Palazzoli and Prata

These two became focused on interrupting the destructive family games which disturbed families through the use of *the invariant prescription* (Selvini Palazzoli, Cirillo, Selvini, & Sorrentino, 1989).

Key Terms

The Dirty Game:

Primary Interventions (Techniques)

The Invariant Prescription:

Boscolo and Cecchin

These two moved away from any use of *paradoxical intervention* aimed at changing behavior and instead focused exclusively on introducing new information into the family system—an effort, in their words, to move toward more of a pure systemic approach to family therapy (Boscolo, Cecchin, Hoffman, & Penn, 1987). The goal became having families create a new *epistemology* to allow for new ways of operating. Their primary interventions were less directive and more process based, identified through the concepts of *hypothesizing, circularity,* and *neutrality. Circular Questioning* was the only defined intervention.

Primary Interventions (Techniques)

Circular Questioning:

Applying Milan Family Therapy to the Becker Family

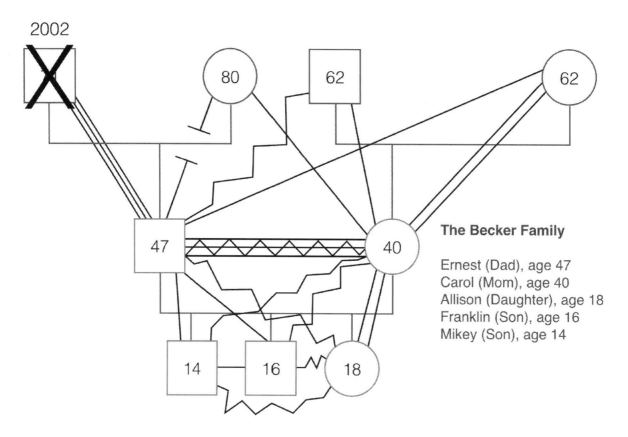

The Becker Family

Ernest (Dad), age 47
Carol (Mom), age 40
Allison (Daughter), age 18
Franklin (Son), age 16
Mikey (Son), age 14

The Beckers are a Caucasian, middle-class family pursuing therapy due to general family disconnection. Mom initiated the phone call stating that things are "out of control" and that "changes need to happen, and fast!" Mom further elaborated that she and her husband are very disconnected and have been for the past 11 years. She said he will work all day and come home to "decompress" in his workshop attached to the garage and spend most weekends with their two sons at various sporting activities and "guys-only outings." Mom reported that she and her husband have been sleeping in different bedrooms for the past three years. Mom said she will spend most days at her Mom's home—which is close in town—and as much time as she can with her daughter before she goes off to college in five months. Mom said she is very disconnected from her sons and her husband is very disconnected from his daughter. She reported the family being "split into two" and appeared quite desperate for change to occur. Mom requested that she, her husband, and her daughter come in as her two sons are refusing to attend family therapy.

Applying Milan Family Therapy to the Becker Family
(be sure to differentiate between *Early Milan* and *Later Milan* based on interventions used and treatment goals)

Early-Phase Goals

1.

2.

Middle-Phase Goals:

1.

2.

Later-Phase Goals:

1.

2.

Overall Conceptualization of the Becker Family as Informed by Milan Family Therapy
(be sure to differentiate between *Early Milan* and *Later Milan* based on interventions used and treatment goals)

Comparing & Contrasting MRI Systemic, Strategic, & The Milan Approach

Common Factors of All Three Approaches

- Bateson's Human Communications Processes Model
- Grounded in Cybernetics and General Systems Theory
  - Homeostasis, Positive/Negative Feedback
  - Circular Causality, 1st/2nd Order Change
- Families get stuck in behavioral interactional cycles
- Families are naturally resistant to change
- Use of paradoxical interventions
- Problem Focused, pragmatic, action oriented

- Reframe problem to induce compliance
- Few family members present, only those directly related to the identified problem.
- Therapy Terminates once symptom is relieved
- Structured, brief in nature and ahistoric
- Therapist is responsible for change
- Favored out of session directives
- Often used a "team approach" (*less true of *Strategic*)

Particulars of MRI Systemic

- Structured 6-Step Process used with EVERY family
- Sessions limited to 10 sessions spaced one-week apart (or fewer sessions based on symptom relief)
  - Terminates after 10th session whether problem is resolved or not
- Concept of *more of the same behavior*
- Favored Paradoxical Interventions:
  - Positioning
  - Prescribing the Symptom
  - Restraining the Progress of Change
- Problem is resolved when clients:
  - learn *to act*
  - learn *to stop acting*
  - learn to *act differently*

Particulars of Strategic

- Structured 1st session (4 Stages)
- Emphasized *joining* with clients
- Emphasized the significance of the family structure (following his studies with Minuchin)
- Aimed to strengthen parental hierarchy (would intentionally join with parental subsystem)
- Would use in-session directives
- Emphasizes the significance of the *family life cycle*
- Therapy is brief, but not limited to 10 sessions
- Favored Paradoxical Interventions:
  - Ordeal Therapy
  - Repetitive Rituals
  - Pretending to have the Symptom

Particulars of The Milan Approach

- Each session had 5 delineated tasks
- Sessions were held at least 1-month apart, while limited to 10 sessions (the long-term brief therapy)
- Always used a team approach and 1-way mirror (role of hypothesizing)
- Emphasized epistemology as informing the rules that keep families stuck
- Relied on two primary interventions:
  - Positive Connotation
  - Ritual

Later Milan Group

- Palazzoli & Prata
  - *Dirty Game & Invariant Prescription*
- Boscolo & Cecchin
  - *Circular Questioning* (dropped paradox)

Notes on MRI Systemic, Strategic, & The Milan Approach

Structural Family Therapy

THE PRACTICE OF SYSTEMIC THERAPY (Domain 1)

Primary Contributor: Salvador **Minuchin**

Class of Family Therapy

Structural Family Therapy is categorized under the *Classical Schools* of Family Therapy (see **Figure 3.1**). It was one of the initial approaches to therapy developed exclusively for families, advancing Marriage & Family Therapy as a distinct field of clinical practice and academic study.

Historical Overview

Salvador **Minuchin** was a child psychiatrist born and raised in Argentina. He was trained early on by Nathan **Ackerman** (The *Father of Family Therapy*, who undoubtedly sparked **Minuchin's** interest in working with families). He was eventually appointed as director of the *Philadelphia Child Guidance Clinic*, and while Jay **Haley** studied under him, it was there where he developed the approach known as *Structural Family Therapy*.

> ***Fun Fact:*** In a poll sent out to Marriage & Family Therapists across the United States, the vast majority of practitioners identify with being influenced by *Structural Family Therapy* in their clinical practice more than any other approach to Family Therapy. This is likely due to its pragmatic, easily understood and applied concepts to understanding and working with families.

Essential Themes of Therapy

Minuchin viewed and understood families as a system structured through set patterns and rules that govern family interactions (1974). **Minuchin** found within the larger family system lies multiple sets of *subsystems* that are interdependent with and to the *whole*. **Minuchin** advised that therapists should, "Look at the family as more than an aggregate of differentiated subsystems and instead as an organism in itself" (Minuchin & Fishman, 1981). Family structure may be understood as an organized pattern in which families interact within—comprised of *roles, communication styles,* and *interactional styles* that are determined by *covert* and *overt* rules. These *rules* become evident to the therapist as the family is observed over time in the here-and-now of the therapeutic encounter, and serve as a primary source of promoting change within the family system. In *Structural Family Therapy* change is concerned with shifting the structure of the family in a way that is more *open* and *flexible* (i.e. responsive to the external environment) and less *rigid* and *closed* (i.e. non-responsive to the external environment) (Minuchin, 1974). As each family will create a working structure congruent to the idiosyncrasies of their *whole*, a *universal* and *necessary* structural component to all families—as stated by **Minuchin** and later endorsed by **Haley** in *Strategic Family Therapy*—is developing an *effective hierarchical structure* (i.e. a high functioning executive subsystem, such as two parents).

Key Terms

Subsystems:

Boundaries:

Rigid Boundary:

Diffuse Boundary:

Clear Boundary:

Disengaged Systems:

Enmeshed Systems:

Complementarity:

Hierarchy:

Intervening:

Conflict Management:

Coalitions:

ASSESSING, HYPOTHESIZING, & DIAGNOSING (Domain 2)

Assessment

Assessment takes place over time and requires that all members of the nuclear family be present in session, as the therapist relies upon what is observed in the here-and-now of in-session behavior. The therapist will track the following themes and concepts as observed in session (Minuchin & Fishman, 1981):

- Boundaries
- Complementarity
- Hierarchy
- Conflict Management

Diagnosing

This approach was nonpathologizing and viewed the family as the client. As so, diagnoses were not prescribed.

DESIGNING & CONDUCTING TREATMENT (Domain 3)

Who is Involved

Structural Family Therapy will work with the *entire Nuclear Family*, as each member plays a significant role in maintaining dysfunctional structural patterns. This approach is more ahistoric and concerned with the here-and-now of the family structure and interactions, likely leaving out extended family members and ignoring the role of previous generations.

Treatment Duration

Structural Family Therapy is more of a short-term therapy, but not necessarily a *brief therapy*. This approach will not limit any number of sessions, but does aim to terminate therapy once a higher functioning structure is attained, typically within 10-20 sessions.

Goals of Therapy

The ultimate goal in this approach is to alter, reorganize, and restructure the family system in a way that promotes problem solving capacities and encourages growth in each individual while mutually supporting the family *whole*—done so in a manner that benefits the entire system. What results is a healthy, high-functioning, and well-defined system characterized by two primary elements (Minuchin & Fishman, 1981):

- A functioning spousal subsystem (generational hierarchy)
- Clear boundaries between all individuals and subsystems

As opposed to the briefer therapies coming out of the MRI Group, goals are not achieved by any single intervention and instead occur over time after a series of interventions.

Primary Interventions and/or Techniques

Joining & Accommodating:

Mimesis:

Intensity:

Planning:

Structural Family Mapping

Know how to interpret your Structural Family Maps. Below is a table created to demonstrate the basic characteristics, but much like a genogram, various symbols and hierarchical arrangements add to the complexity of this assessment/intervention. Take the next couple of pages to draw in your Structural Family Map logos sought through various resources.

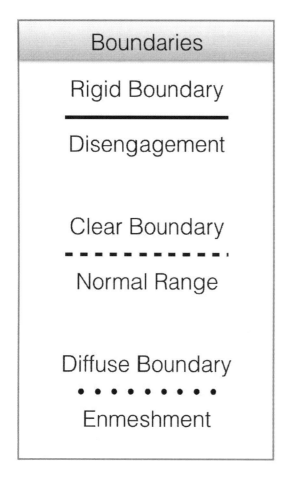

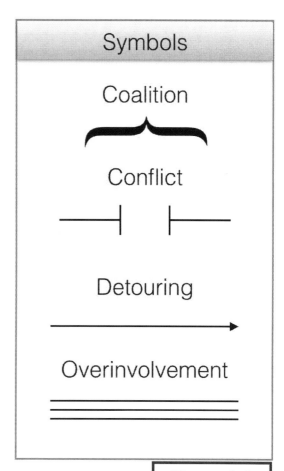

Figure 3.3

Structural Family Maps

Enactments:

Spontaneous Behavioral Sequences:

Challenging Family Assumptions:

Challenging the Symptom:

Reframing:

Affective Intensity:

Shaping Competence:

Boundary Making:

Unbalancing:

Punctuation (different than Milan):

EVALUATING ONGOING PROCESS & TERMINATING TREATMENT (Domain 4)

The *Focus of Treatment* is always determined by the therapist working with the family based upon the problem presented by the family, but more so concerned with the systemic processes that are underlying the problematic situation (e.g. *diffuse boundaries, coalitions*, etc.) (Minuchin & Fishman, 1981). This approach does adhere to a *structured* (no pun intended by me, but perhaps intended by **Minuchin** himself) process outlining three phases of therapy along with a list of *key elements* to *assess* for and effective *therapeutic interventions* aimed at promoting *structural change* and *growth*.

Therapy Structure

The structure of *Structural Family Therapy* can be understood through the division of three linear phases (Minuchin & Fishman, 1981):

1. The *Joining and Accommodating* Phase
2. The *Mapping the Family Structure* Phase
3. The *Intervening* Phase

Applying Structural Family Therapy to the Becker Family

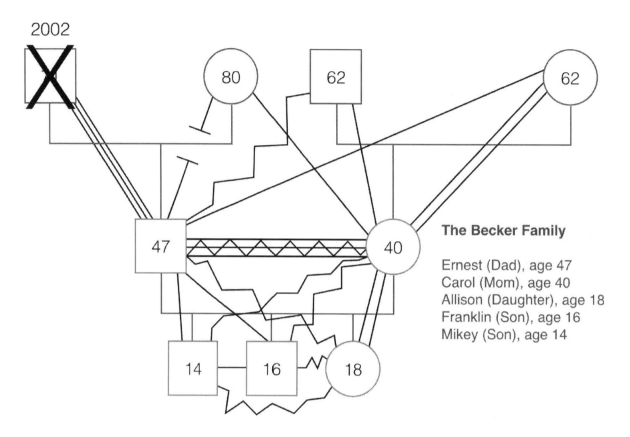

The Becker Family

Ernest (Dad), age 47
Carol (Mom), age 40
Allison (Daughter), age 18
Franklin (Son), age 16
Mikey (Son), age 14

The Beckers are a Caucasian, middle-class family pursuing therapy due to general family disconnection. Mom initiated the phone call stating that things are "out of control" and that "changes need to happen, and fast!" Mom further elaborated that she and her husband are very disconnected and have been for the past 11 years. She said he will work all day and come home to "decompress" in his workshop attached to the garage and spend most weekends with their two sons at various sporting activities and "guys-only outings." Mom reported that she and her husband have been sleeping in different bedrooms for the past three years. Mom said she will spend most days at her Mom's home—which is close in town—and as much time as she can with her daughter before she goes off to college in five months. Mom said she is very disconnected from her sons and her husband is very disconnected from his daughter. She reported the family being "split into two" and appeared quite desperate for change to occur. Mom requested that she, her husband, and her daughter come in as her two sons are refusing to attend family therapy.

Applying Structural Family Therapy to the Becker Family

Early-Phase Goals

1.

2.

Middle-Phase Goals:

1.

2.

Later-Phase Goals:

1.

2.

Overall Conceptualization of the Becker Family as Informed by Structural Family Therapy

Similarities & Differences of Structural Family Therapy and the 3 Systemic Schools

Similarities

- Individual behavior changes as family *context* changes
- Families are *rule-governed systems*
- *Therapy is present-oriented* with therapist in highly directive role
- *Process* more important than content
- *Therapy is problem-oriented; therapist is pragmatic (i.e. what works)*
- *The presenting problem functions in family to support present interactions*
- Change context by changing repetitive *behavior sequences of interaction*
- Assessment & Treatment: Observing, Hypothesizing, Probing & Testing, Intervening, & Examining Results
- Use of Therapeutic *Contracts & Behavioral Tasks*
- Interpretation used to *reframe rather than insight-* oriented
- "Joining" as crucial process
- Use of Therapeutic Paradox
- *Brief Therapy* (10 to 20 sessions)

Differences

Key Characteristic of Structural Family Therapy

- *Changing boundaries between subsystems* is primary means of creating change.
- Therapist uses in-session directives (& confrontations), particularly enactments.
- *Entire Family* is present.
- Much consideration given to the Individual and Family Life Cycle; particularly in *strengthening and supporting the executive subsystem (traditional hierarchy)*

Key Characteristics of 3 Systemic Schools

- *Use of "Positive-Feedback"* to change the reason the presenting problem (the maladaptive behavior) is maintained by the interactions.
- Therapist uses out-of-session directives or prescriptions (rather than actively directs or confronts) to change current out-of-session behavioral sequences.
- One or two family members (e.g. MRI).
- Little consideration given to the Individual and Family Life Cycle; particularly in *strengthening and supporting the executive subsystem (traditional hierarchy)*

Forisha, 2014

Figure 3.4

Notes on Structural vs. the Three Systemic Schools

Symbolic-Experiential Family Therapy

THE PRACTICE OF SYSTEMIC THERAPY (Domain 1)

Primary Contributor: Carl **Whitaker**

Secondary Contributors: August **Napier**
David **Keith**
Walter **Kempler**
Thomas **Malone**
Laura **Roberto**

Class of Family Therapy

Symbolic-Experiential Family Therapy is categorized under the *Classical Schools* of Family Therapy (see **Figure 3.1**). It was one of the initial approaches to therapy developed exclusively for families, contributing to the development of Marriage & Family Therapy as a distinct field of clinical practice and academic study.

Historical Overview

Symbolic-Experiential Family Therapy was one of the two movements that grew out of *humanistic-psychology* and *gestalt therapies*. The approach shifted focus from symptom relief and behavioral change to the healing attributes inherent within the *growth process* experienced by each individual in the family (the other of which being Virginia **Satir's** *Human Validation Process Model* discussed next). *Experiential Therapies* may be distinguished from *Humanistic Psychology* at both the applied and theoretical level. While still emphasizing the concept of *being* and *becoming*, *Experiential Therapies* are more so concerned with the concepts of *co-being* and *co-becoming* (i.e. growth experienced by the individual through interaction and dialogue between his or her self and the interpersonal context of his or her life) (Forisha, 2013).

Carl **Whitaker** was the driving force and primary contributor to the development of *Symbolic-Experiential Family Therapy*. He too was a psychoanalytically-trained psychiatrist who grew both frustrated and bored with the limitations of the medical model and traditional psychoanalysis. As so, **Whitaker** daringly began to experiment with what was then an unorthodox practice within his profession—actually *listening* to his patients. When **Whitaker** would engage in such a *devious* act, astonishingly, he found that the patient was actually capable of independent growth and healing. Despite the obvious positive effects experienced by his patients, Emory University was unimpressed and demanded **Whitaker** to make the department more *psychoanalytic*. In response, **Whitaker**—along with his *entire* faculty—resigned from the University and began the *Atlantic Psychiatry Clinic* where the *Symbolic-Experiential* approach to Family Therapy prospered.

*Note: What a testament of the degree to which **Whitaker's** students and colleagues believed in him and his vision, resigning from their faculty positions—some of which were tenured—to be a part of his movement. Pretty cool!

Another prominent figure in this approach was Walter **Kempler,** a *Gestalt Therapist* trained directly under *Fritz Perls,* who introduced many themes of *Gestalt Therapy* (e.g. *unfinished business*) to working with families and took a shift from the more *purely systemic* schools by tending to the *individual's growth* over the family system as a whole.

Essential Themes of Therapy

Experiential Family Therapies identified that *emotional suppression* was often at the source of individual and family dysfunction (Whitaker & Bumberry, 1988). It asserted that individuals thrive in environments of support and safety, allowing for open expression and nurturing authentic growth. This therapy took an abrupt shift from the other *Classical Schools* previously discussed by abandoning structured therapy sessions. Instead, it emphasized clinicians remaining attuned to his or her *self as a therapist* and relying upon that for spontaneous, experiential intervention and therapeutic discourse.

Instead of depending on theory, **Whitaker** endorsed that therapists need to rely on themselves, becoming more of *who they are* rather than regurgitating the textbook (Whitaker, 1989). In session, **Whitaker** would always strive to be *authentic* when working with families. By remaining aware of his own anxieties and emotional reactions to what he was experiencing in the here and now of the therapeutic encounter, he remained open to spontaneous and creative interventions, thereby *evoking the emotional experience of the family* and its individual members. **Whitaker** found this very act of authenticity helped family members become more aware of their own emotional experiencing. This empowered them to become more authentic and "real" themselves—an essential theme of *Symbolic-Experiential Therapies* (Napier & Whitaker, 1988).

Other essential themes include: The primacy of experience, affect, person of the therapist, spontaneity and creativity, freedom and existential encounters, present-centeredness, and global vs. specific goals (Whitaker & Bumberry, 1988).

The Stance and Role of Therapist

This approach takes a shift in the stance and role of the therapist when working with families, serving as an essential element differentiating it from others discussed throughout this manual. Let us review:

- The use of a **Co-therapist**: By developing a *co-therapy relationship* that is more important to the therapists than their relationship to the family, *they can rely on their interpersonal intimacy to sustain them rather than expecting the client family to meet their needs* (Napier & Whitaker, 1988).
- Role as therapist to the family mirrors that of a *grandparent role*. Therapists accept parenting functions only temporarily and remain free to return them to the real parents at any moment. A therapist, like a grandparent, is involved and loving with the "children" and grandchildren—but is not essential to the function of the family.

This better prepared families to be responsible for themselves outside of session (Napier & Whitaker, 1988).

- The therapist declines taking on the role of *expert,* and instead, the responsibility to change lies upon the family (radical shift from the MRI Schools). The therapist does not have better solutions for the family than the family already has themselves (Napier & Whitaker, 1988).

- Therapists recognize their inability to rely on transference of feelings from important prior relationships to provide the power and content for therapy. In contrast to individual therapy, the relationships between and among the family members are more critical and salient than the relationship between any one family member and the therapist (Napier & Whitaker, 1988).

Key Terms

Person of the Therapist:

Existential Encounter:

Therapy of the Absurd:

Individuation:

Family Interaction:

ASSESSING, HYPOTHESIZING, & DIAGNOSING (Domain 2)

Assessment

Whitaker stated that therapy begins with the initial phone call, setting the tone for the *first interview* process that may extend into as many sessions as necessary based upon family defensiveness. The first phone call allows the therapist an opportunity to demand the whole family be present if they wish to be seen, the first step toward winning *the battle for structure* (Whitaker & Keith, 1981). From there, this approach takes a competency-based approach to assessment and leans away from diagnoses and problems. During the assessment phase, the therapist will remain mindful of *the family life cycle* as well as the *transgenerational belief system* (Whitaker & Keith, 1981). The *Symbolic-Experiential Therapist* will assess all the way out to the extended family and community and back to the internal worlds of each individual family member. This is the therapists attempt at gaining a thorough understanding of the system as a whole as well as the idiosyncrasies of each individual member, including particular attention to: *subsystems, emotional age vs. chronological age* of each member, *triadic patterns* and *dyadic collusions, teaming,* and *individual dynamics* (Whitaker & Bumberry, 1988).

Diagnosing

This approach is non-pathologizing. When clients would inquire about a possible diagnosis, **Whitaker** would typically respond with a *therapeutic double bind.* That is, a relational diagnosis that is unlikely to change.

DESIGNING & CONDUCTING TREATMENT (Domain 3)

Who is Involved

Symbolic-Experiential Therapists took a radical stance that *all members of the family*, including at least two generations, must be in attendance for the early therapy sessions. Therapists practicing from this approach would often refuse to see only parts of a family, affirming that the entire family must participate for any hope to achieve meaningful and lasting change.

Treatment Duration

This approach traditionally has families meet for weekly sessions, until later phases of treatment where it may be appropriate for families to start coming monthly. Given its emphasis on *growth*, therapy may go on as long as needed and will typically span anywhere between six months to two years.

Goals of Therapy

Therapy is conducted in a manner that increases each family members' sense of *belongingness* to the family while simultaneously encouraging the freedom to *individuate* (i.e. become more of themselves) (Whitaker, 1989). Goals aim to increase creative expression and develop an environment where individuals feel safe to be emotionally expressive with and toward one another. Individuals are encouraged to grow in ways congruent to their authentic selves.

Whitaker and **Keith** (1981) identify 10 general goals in *Symbolic-Experiential Family Therapy:*

1. Increase the level of stress
2. Development of family nationalism (shared anxiety)
3. Expand relationships with extended family
4. Expand the relationships to culture and community
5. Develop a sense of family boundaries
6. Separate the generations
7. Family learns to play
8. Develop a we-they. Therapist-family split (models constant cycle of separating and joining)
9. Explode the myth of individuality—the family should believe in itself as a unit, with a strong sense of its absurdity
10. Each member should be more of himself

Whitaker defined *curative factors* as elements that must be present prior to any actual healing or growth taking place. First, **Whitaker** stated that families must begin to see and appreciate that they are a unit—all in the battle toward health together. Lastly, and most notably, **Whitaker** believed that the single most important element to effective therapy is the therapist's own personality and psychological health (Whitaker, 1989).

Primary Interventions and/or Techniques

Before reviewing the techniques associated with this approach, let us remember that **Whitaker's** mantra advocated against reliance upon theory, technique, or intuition, as he found them to hinder clinical work. He elaborated that although none of these can be avoided when working with families, they are never to be offered to families as anything other than just what they are and *always* with a sense of *absurdity* (Whitaker & Bumberry, 1988). What he described as more important to the *art* of family therapy rather than explicit techniques were *metatechniques* (i.e. technique of techniques), such as timing, application of emphasis, how & when to apply pressure, when to back off, or when to be cautious. **Whitaker** viewed the therapist not as a clinician, but as an *Artist & Healer* in the manner of a Zen Master (Napier & Whitaker, 1988).

> *****Note:** Until you are licensed, you are not able to advertise yourself as a Marriage & Family Therapist, Family Therapist, Couple Therapist, etc., as they are protected titles by law, BUT, no one is stopping you from putting *Artist & Healer* on your business cards.

Battle for Structure:

Battle for Initiative:

Expanding Distress:

Activating Constructive Anxiety:

Redefining Symptoms:

Fantasy Alternative:

Affective Confrontation:

Co-Therapist:

Degrees of Craziness:

Teaming Roles:

Therapeutic Double Bind:

Bilateral Pseudo-Therapy:

Bilateral Transference:

Flight Toward Health:

Other Common Strategies or Useful Techniques offered by Whitaker (1976):
- Convey basic empathy for the family.
- Develop a liaison with the husband/father as a means of engagement (this reflected Whitaker's view of contemporary male inadequacy).
- Treat the children like children and not like peers. Play with the children.
- Maintain the importance of the person and growth of the therapist. Whitaker stated that as individuals (and, as therapists), we must grow until we die.
- Redefine symptoms as efforts for growth.
- Probe the unconscious and tickle the defenses (Ackerman's term) of each family member.
  - *Invade* family's dynamic operation
  - Use *personal confrontations*
  - *Increase pathology* and implicate the whole family scene, converting it into *absurdity*
  - *Model Fantasy* alternatives to real life stress

EVALUATING ONGOING PROCESS & TERMINATING TREATMENT (Domain 4)

Structure of Therapy

This approach to therapy does not offer a structure, and as **Whitaker** would argue, does not even lend itself to being considered a theory—such a consideration would defeat the very premise of the approach. The *focus of therapy*, as **Whitaker** would define, entailed maintaining efforts geared toward the *growth* of all individuals involved in the family which often focused around the successful completion of developmental tasks.

Although **Whitaker** advised against relying upon structure, it was still important to remain aware of where families were in their subjective growth process. This helped to identify when families were ready for termination. Therapy can be understood through three vaguely defined phases (Roberto, 1991):

Early Phase

> Here, the therapist must win the Battle for Structure while the family must win the Battle for Initiative.

Middle Phase

> Achieve reorganization around the interpersonally expanded symptom.

Later Phase

> The family begins to operate as a mobile milieu therapy unit within the family-co-therapist suprasystem.
>
> > ***Note**: During any phase of treatment, any move on the *whole family's* part to terminate contact is supported and encouraged. If a family all of the sudden stops showing up for sessions or making contact with the therapist, it is assumed that they experienced *a flight toward health* and no longer require therapy—desirable results were achieved.

Whitaker endorsed the importance of keeping the family *interested* in therapy, allowing for deeper meaning and understanding. A good way to monitor whether or not therapy was maintaining interest was to measure the degree to which the therapist felt that he or she was personally benefiting or growing from the experience. This was another radical position taken by **Whitaker** that therapists should be intentional about benefiting from their work with clients.

Carl Whitaker's Tips for Helping Therapists Stay Emotionally Alive (this will likely not be covered on the exam, but I felt inclined to include anyway)

- Relegate every significant other to second place.
- Learn how to love. Flirt with any infant available. Unconditional positive regard probably isn't present after the baby is three years old...
- Develop a reverence for your own impulses, and be suspicious of your behavior sequences.
- Enjoy your mate more than your kids, and be childish with your mate.
- Fracture role structures at will and repeatedly.
- Learn to retreat and advance from every position you take.
- Guard your impotence as one of your most valuable weapons.
- Build long-term relationships so you can be free to hate safely.
- Face the fact that you must grow until you die. Develop a sense of the absurdity of life—yours and those around you—and thus learn to transcend the world of experience. If we can abandon our missionary zeal we have less chance of being eaten by cannibals.
- Develop your primary process for living.
- Evolve a joint craziness with some one you are safe with.
- Structure a professional cuddle group so you won't abuse your mate with the garbage left over from the day's work.
- As Plato said, "Practice dying."

(Whitaker, 1976)

> *Note: It is reported that **Whitaker** retired from practice with over a two year wait-list of clients lined up to see him, all the while charging $300 per session in the 1970s...

Applying Symbolic-Experiential Family Therapy to the Becker Family

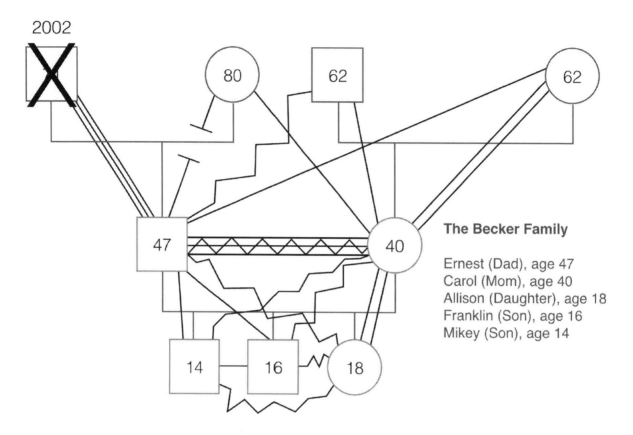

The Becker Family

Ernest (Dad), age 47
Carol (Mom), age 40
Allison (Daughter), age 18
Franklin (Son), age 16
Mikey (Son), age 14

The Beckers are a Caucasian, middle-class family pursuing therapy due to general family disconnection. Mom initiated the phone call stating that things are "out of control" and that "changes need to happen, and fast!" Mom further elaborated that she and her husband are very disconnected and have been for the past 11 years. She said he will work all day and come home to "decompress" in his workshop attached to the garage and spend most weekends with their two sons at various sporting activities and "guys-only outings." Mom reported that she and her husband have been sleeping in different bedrooms for the past three years. Mom said she will spend most days at her Mom's home—which is close in town—and as much time as she can with her daughter before she goes off to college in five months. Mom said she is very disconnected from her sons and her husband is very disconnected from his daughter. She reported the family being "split into two" and appeared quite desperate for change to occur. Mom requested that she, her husband, and her daughter come in as her two sons are refusing to attend family therapy.

Applying Symbolic-Experiential Family Therapy to the Becker Family

Early-Phase Goals

1.

2.

Middle-Phase Goals:

1.

2.

Later-Phase Goals:

1.

2.

Overall Conceptualization of the Becker Family as Informed by Symbolic-Experiential Family Therapy

Satir's Human Validation Process Model
(Satir's Communications Approach)

THE PRACTICE OF SYSTEMIC THERAPY (Domain 1)

Primary Contributor: Virginia **Satir**

Class of Family Therapy

Satir's Human Validation Process Model is categorized under the *Classical Schools* of Family Therapy within the domain of *Experiential Family Therapies* (see **Figure 3.1**). It was one of the initial approaches to therapy developed exclusively for families and advanced the development of Marriage & Family Therapy as a distinct field of clinical practice and academic study.

Historical Overview

Satir's Human Validation Process Model was one of the two *Experiential Therapy* movements that grew out of *humanistic psychology* and *gestalt therapies.* The movement shifted focus from symptom relief and behavioral change to the healing attributes inherent within the *growth process* experienced by each individual family member (the other of which being **Whitaker's** *Symbolic-Experiential Therapy* previously discussed). *Experiential Therapies* may be distinguished from *Humanistic Psychology* at both the applied and theoretical level. While still emphasizing the concept of *being* and *becoming, Experiential Therapies* are more so concerned with the concepts of *co-being* and *co-becoming* (i.e. growth experienced by the individual through interaction and dialogue between his or her self and the interpersonal context of his or her life) (Forisha, 2013).

Virginia **Satir,** often referred to as the *Mother of Family Therapy,* was reverently known for her *warmth, compassion,* and *genuineness.* Beginning her career as a social worker—wanting to help families—she soon became involved in the humanistic psychology movement before joining the *MRI Group* in Palo Alto to study human communication processes under Gregory **Bateson.** After serving as the Clinical Director at the *MRI Brief Therapy Center,* **Satir** went on to establish her own approach to therapy based upon the very characteristics in which she became known for—aforementioned above.

Ultimately, **Satir** believed in the *goodness of people* and the importance of interconnectedness among humanity. Eventually, her ideas went beyond family treatment to incorporate issues regarding spiritual growth and world peace.

> *****Note**: In 1986 at the AAMFT Annual Meeting, **Satir** was honored on her 70th birthday. She received a standing ovation that lasted for *over 45-minutes*—the vast majority of the audience was in tears.
> (Forisha, 2013, personal recollection)

Essential Themes of Therapy

With a notable influence from humanistic psychology, **Satir** believed that individuals are naturally growth oriented, intrinsically striving toward fulfilled potential, wholeness, and authenticity (Satir, Banmen, Gerber, & Gomori, 1991). Her therapy endorsed the natural goodness within us all, and that deep down we all desire to be sensitive and genuine with one another. **Satir's** therapy proposed that various life events can block these natural tendencies, and that conveying genuine care and acceptance toward another was the source of helping them overcome their fears. This not only opened them to new experiences, but to others. **Satir** (1987) had a mystical ability to empathize, courageously and compassionately joining her clients as they explored the depths of their scariest places.

Satir (1987) believed that all therapy and growth involved *warmth*, *genuineness*, and *congruent communication*.

Satir et al. (1991) viewed *self-esteem* (self-worth) as a primary source of fulfillment and happiness, considering it to be the most significant factor in family relationships. She would—metaphorically—refer to *self-esteem* as the *pot*. Family dysfunction was more likely if individuals within the family had an *empty pot*. Congruently, healthy family functioning flowed when individuals experienced having a *full pot*. Communication was the gauge in which individuals measure one another's *pot level*.

In any given interaction, **Satir** acknowledged three primary and present elements: *The Self*, *The Other*, and *The Context* (Satir et al., 1991). Leveling is the process leading to balanced decisions that honor all three identified parts of the relationship. This context sets the stage for dysfunctional communication styles that plague family health.

Satir (1987) is also known for her effective *use of touch* with clients while in session.

Satir Communications Therapists operate off of four primary assumptions (Satir et al., 1991):

1. People naturally tend toward positive growth.
2. All people possess the resources for positive growth.
3. Every person and every thing or situation impact and are impacted by everyone and everything else.
4. Therapy is a process involving interaction between therapist and client; and, in this relationship, each person is responsible for him or her self.
    (Satir et al., 1991)

Key Terms

Primary Survival Triad:

Body, Mind, and Feelings:

Communication:

Self-Worth:

Dysfunctional Communication Styles (or, Survival Stances):

Placaters:

Blamers:

Computers:

Distractors:

Levelers (congruence):

Model Integration Analysis:

Role-Function Discrepancy:

ASSESSING, HYPOTHESIZING, & DIAGNOSING (Domain 2)

Assessment

Satir's Communications Approach outlined an assessment process geared toward three themes (Satir et al., 1991):

1. The family system's symptomatic behavior.
2. Communication patterns and stances.
3. The influence and exploration of family of origin issues.

Diagnosing

This approach was *nonpathologizing* and strengths based, drawing attention to the clients' potential and inherent goodness. Diagnostics were *systemic* in nature and *expanded to the system,* not any one individual.

DESIGNING & CONDUCTING TREATMENT (Domain 3)

This approach blends **Whitaker's** spontaneity and creativity with MRI's structure to therapy (i.e. relying on therapist's use of self while adhering to a process).

Who is Involved

Satir did not take nearly as radical of a stance as the *Symbolic-Experiential Therapists,* and would likely meet with whomever desired to attend a session.

Treatment Duration

Length of treatment was never predetermined or time limited. Therapy would go on for as long as needed depending on the particulars of each client encounter.

Goals of Therapy

The ultimate goal in therapy was *growth,* and along with *Experiential Therapy's* philosophy, *growth in the individual will result in symptom reduction across the family system.* As *growth* was found to be hindered by incongruent and dysfunctional communication, *Satir's Communications Approach* identifies three goals for improving communication in the family system (Satir et al., 1991):

1. Increase Congruent Communication
2. Improved Self-Esteem, including a recognition and appreciation for the individuality of each member of the family.
3. Growth—as self-esteem is recognized and nurtured, individuals are able to actualize their growth potential.

Primary Interventions and/or Techniques

Instead of outlining simplified *techniques*, **Satir** developed what she referred to as *Vehicles for Change*, such as:

Role of Therapist:

Modeling Communication:

Metaphors:

Self-Mandala:

Parts Party:

Temperature Reading:

Family Reconstruction:

Family Sculpting:

EVALUATING ONGOING PROCESS & TERMINATING TREATMENT (Domain 4)

Therapy Structure (Satir et al., 1991)

Early Phase

- *Stage One*: Status Quo (homeostasis)
- *Stage Two*: Introduction of a Foreign Element (the therapist)

Middle Phase

- *Stage Three*: Chaos (homeostasis disrupted)
- *Stage Four*: New Possibilities/New Options and Integration (uncovers possibility for change and more adaptive ways of communicating)

Later Phase

- *Stage Five*: Practice/Implementation (experience change and explore feelings openly)
- *Stage Six*: Attainment/The New Status Quo
  (Satir et al., 1991)

Termination

Applying Satir's Human Validation Process Model to the Becker Family
(Satir's Communications Approach)

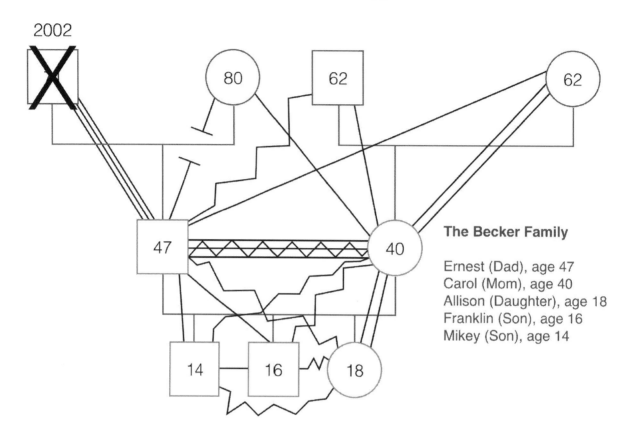

The Becker Family

Ernest (Dad), age 47
Carol (Mom), age 40
Allison (Daughter), age 18
Franklin (Son), age 16
Mikey (Son), age 14

The Beckers are a Caucasian, middle-class family pursuing therapy due to general family disconnection. Mom initiated the phone call stating that things are "out of control" and that "changes need to happen, and fast!" Mom further elaborated that she and her husband are very disconnected and have been for the past 11 years. She said he will work all day and come home to "decompress" in his workshop attached to the garage and spend most weekends with their two sons at various sporting activities and "guys-only outings." Mom reported that she and her husband have been sleeping in different bedrooms for the past three years. Mom said she will spend most days at her Mom's home—which is close in town—and as much time as she can with her daughter before she goes off to college in five months. Mom said she is very disconnected from her sons and her husband is very disconnected from his daughter. She reported the family being "split into two" and appeared quite desperate for change to occur. Mom requested that she, her husband, and her daughter come in as her two sons are refusing to attend family therapy.

Applying Satir's Human Validation Process Model to the Becker Family
(Satir's Communications Approach)

Early-Phase Goals

1.

2.

Middle-Phase Goals:

1.

2.

Later-Phase Goals:

1.

2.

Overall Conceptualization of the Becker Family as Informed by Satir's Human Validation Process Model

(Satir's Communications Approach)

Emotionally Focused Couples Therapy

THE PRACTICE OF SYSTEMIC THERAPY (Domain 1)

Primary Contributors: Susan **Johnson**
                              Leslie **Greenberg**

Class of Family Therapy

Emotionally Focused Couples Therapy (EFT) is primarily classified as an experiential approach but does not qualify as a *Classical School of Family Therapy* given its inception taking place in the 1980s. Given its emphasis on the lived experience, integrative nature, and late introduction to the field, it fits well within the other Post-Modern approaches.

(See Figure 3.1)

Historical Background

Emotionally Focused Couples Therapy was developed in the 1980s by Susan **Johnson** and Leslie **Greenberg.** Essentially, it is an experiential approach to therapy that is grounded in attachment theory. Integrative by nature, it also incorporates principles and concepts from Psychodynamic, Systemic, and Behavioral Therapies.

Given the rich literature and research emphasizing the life-long impact that attachment styles have on adult relational functioning, **Johnson** and **Greenberg** were able to develop a short term, structured approach to couples therapy focusing on reprocessing emotional responses that organize attachment behaviors. Beyond it being one of the first approaches to therapy developed exclusively for adult couples, its structure lends itself to research quite well—which has demonstrated that 70-75% of couples view their relationships as no longer distressed after 10-12 sessions of EFT, and these results appear to be less susceptible to relapse than in other approaches (Greenberg & Johnson, 1988).

Essential Themes of Therapy

As a result of insecure attachment styles developed throughout infancy and early childhood (i.e. mistrust and unreliability toward others), adults learn to hide their *primary emotions* (i.e. actual emotions, such as fear or desire for connection) and instead express *secondary reactive emotions* which are generally defensive in nature and deconstructive to effective couple dialogue (Greenberg & Johnson, 1988). The reactive *secondary emotions* evolve into *negative interaction patterns*—such as, pursuer/blamer and withdrawer/defender—which serve to intensify the fear that partners are not trustworthy; thus, maintaining the *negative interactional pattern* and further suppressing the expression of *primary emotions*.

EFT aims to reprocess emotional responses that organize attachment behaviors, freeing individuals to engage in adult relationships in more desirable ways through creating and experiencing secure attachments (Johnson, 2004). The goal here is to create a safe atmosphere where individuals can access their *primary emotions*, establish *emotional bonds*, and disrupt the *negative interactional sequences.* By accessing primary emotions, individuals are better able to understand their partner's experience and respond to them with empathy and compassion as opposed to reactivity and defensiveness. This process alters the negative interactional pattern by developing secure bonds and constructive ways of managing conflict. Accessing primary emotions and expressing them to one's partner will prime new responses—this process is at the core of cultivating change in EFT (Johnson & Greenberg, 1988).

For example, prior to working with an EFT Therapist, when Carol felt threatened that Ernest was going to abandon her, she would anxiously respond by becoming more and more focused on "what's wrong" (pursuer) which influenced Ernest to move further away from the relationship (withdrawer). The further Ernest would move away, the more desperately Carol would attempt to save the relationship through aggression and anger (blamer). After working through the *de-escalation process* and accessing their *primary emotions* in session, Carol is able to now understand Ernest's *withdrawal* (response to secondary emotion of annoyance) as his *fear* of being emotionally hurt (primary emotion), and Ernest is able to understand Carol's insistent pursuance (response to secondary emotion of frustration) as her *fear* of abandonment (primary emotion). This will open the couple to relating to one another more authentically and work toward establishing a more stable, *secure bond.*

The success of this process is dependent upon the therapist's capacity to join with the couple and establish trusting relationships (utilizes the Rogerian principles of *unconditional positive regard, empathy,* and *non-judgment*). In EFT, the therapist will often work with one partner at a time in the presence of the other. As the couple enters therapy with varying degrees of mistrust toward one another, the therapist must first establish safety, enabling each individual to access primary emotions as his or her partner bears witness (Johnson, 2004). As each individual emotionally processes with the therapist, the therapeutic relationship will contribute to the observing partner not feeling sided against.

Key Terms

Primary Emotions

Secondary Emotions:

Attachment:

Softening:

Interactional Patterns:

Primary Needs:

Bonding:

ASSESSING, HYPOTHESIZING, & DIAGNOSING (Domain 2)

Assessment

Assessment in EFT occurs through Stage I of this structured approach to couple therapy, which will be outlined in detail in the *Evaluating Ongoing Process & Terminating Treatment* Domain. Assessment will operate off of two primary principles (Johnson, 2004):

1. **Looking Within**: Exploring how each partner constructs his or her emotional experience of relatedness.

2. **Looking Between**: Exploring how partners engage each other and identifying each individual's role in the creation and maintenance of negative interactional patterns.

Diagnosing

This approach is *nonpathologizing*. Diagnostics were *systemic* in nature and *expanded to the couple system*, not any one individual. Partners are not seen as sick, developmentally delayed, or unskilled; instead, they are simply stuck in deconstructive yet habitual ways of managing emotions and relating to others.

DESIGNING & CONDUCTING TREATMENT (Domain 3)

This approach is structured into three stages, each containing outlined steps as the couple works through the process.

Who is Involved

Both partners must be present for this therapy to be effective in relation to the couple system. EFT can work with individuals, but if the presenting complaint is directly related to a current relationship it will be strongly encouraged that the partner attends therapy conjointly. EFT Therapists will often work exclusively with an individual as they emotionally process downward toward primary emotions; however, it will require that the partner is present and observing this process in order for it to directly alter the negative interactional pattern.

Treatment Duration

EFT Therapists are traditionally able to effectively work through the three phases within 12-20 sessions.

Goals of Therapy

EFT promotes that effective couples therapy addresses the security of the bond, creates mutual accessibility to emotional experiences, and cultivates empathic, constructive responsiveness from each partner toward the other.

- De-escalate the problematic interactional cycle that maintains attachment insecurity and relationship distress by creating a therapeutic alliance and accessing unacknowledged primary emotions.
- Promote identification with disowned attachment needs and fears and promote acceptance of the others partner's experience; thus, creating new responses and altering negative interaction cycles.
- Create emotional engagement through the expression of specific needs and wants of each partner.
- Facilitate the emergence of new solutions to old problematic relationship issues through the consolidation of new positive and cycles of attachment behavior.
(Johnson & Greenberg, 1988; Johnson, 2004)

Primary Interventions and/or Techniques

Much like **Satir's** approach, EFT does not necessarily define any detailed interventions as much as it promotes themes to be carried throughout the discourse of therapy. The primary theme throughout EFT is the use of *Empathic Reflection.* Johnson (2004) stated that the EFT therapist will move recursively between three primary tasks:

1. Monitoring and actively tending to and nurturing a positive therapeutic alliance.
2. Expanding and restructuring primary emotional experiences.
3. Structuring enactments meant to either clarify present patterns of interaction or step by step, shape new, more positive patterns in interactional couple dynamics.

EFT Therapists are also intentional about:
- **Validating** each client and creating a strong alliance/therapeutic safety.
- **Focusing the Session:** Engaging clients to remain attuned to the creation of new, more responsive interactional patterns and expressing primary emotions (not getting caught up in managing day-to-day conflict).
- **Slowing down the Processing:** Making sure clients cultivate a capacity to sit with their primary emotions and pain, as well as their partner's.
- **Organizing:** Creating coherence between partners by reflecting/summarizing the growth and change as it takes place throughout the discourse of treatment.

EVALUATING ONGOING PROCESS & TERMINATING TREATMENT (Domain 4)

Therapy Structure

As discussed, EFT is a structured approach carried out in three phases:

- Phase I: Cycle De-Escalation and Stabilization
    1. Establish therapeutic alliance and clarify core issue as attachment-based.
    2. Identify the negative interactional cycle that maintains attachment insecurity.
    3. Access underlying emotions driving the interactional positions.
    4. Reframe the problem as a cycle based on attachment needs/fears.
- Phase II: Restructuring Interactional Positions/Patterns
    5. Promote identification with disowned attachment needs.
    6. Promote acceptance of and responsiveness to each partner's new construction of experience.
    7. Create emotional engagement by facilitating the expression of specific needs and wants.
- Phase III: Consolidation and Integration
    8. Facilitate the emergence of new solutions to old problematic relationship issues.
    9. Consolidating new positions and cycles of attachment behavior.
    (Johnson, 2004)
- Termination once Phase III tasks are independently maintained by the couple.

Applying Emotionally Focused Couple Therapy to Ernest and Carol Becker

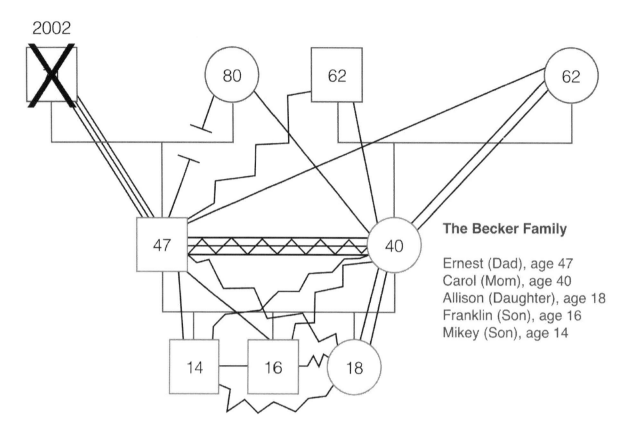

The Becker Family

Ernest (Dad), age 47
Carol (Mom), age 40
Allison (Daughter), age 18
Franklin (Son), age 16
Mikey (Son), age 14

The Beckers are a Caucasian, middle-class family pursuing therapy due to general family disconnection. Mom initiated the phone call stating that things are "out of control" and that "changes need to happen, and fast!" Mom further elaborated that she and her husband are very disconnected and have been for the past 11 years. She said he will work all day and come home to "decompress" in his workshop attached to the garage and spend most weekends with their two sons at various sporting activities and "guys-only outings." Mom reported that she and her husband have been sleeping in different bedrooms for the past three years. Mom said she will spend most days at her Mom's home—which is close in town—and as much time as she can with her daughter before she goes off to college in five months. Mom said she is very disconnected from her sons and her husband is very disconnected from his daughter. She reported the family being "split into two" and appeared quite desperate for change to occur. Mom requested that she, her husband, and her daughter come in as her two sons are refusing to attend family therapy.

Applying Emotionally Focused Couple Therapy to Ernest and Carol Becker

Early-Phase Goals

1.

2.

Middle-Phase Goals:

1.

2.

Later-Phase Goals:

1.

2.

Overall Conceptualization of Ernest and Carol Becker Informed by Emotionally Focused Couple Therapy

Social Constructivism
The Post-Modern Wave in Marital & Family Therapy

This manual has thus far walked you through the *Transgenerational* and *Classical Schools* identified within the field of Marital & Family Therapy. Next came the *Post-Modern* wave, shifting the nature in which we understood couples and families from a systemic perspective.

Before getting into the theories, it is important to mention that *Post-Modernism* was not only a shift in how we view individual, couples, and families within culturally-informed societies but a shift in *epistemology* of how we understand and attribute meaning to our shared existence. As so, let us walk through a brief review of the three competing epistemologies to better understand the nature of the *Post-Modern* movement...

EPISTEMOLOGY (or, how do we know what we know?)

Epistemology essentially asks the question, "How do we know what we know?" Or, more specifically, what is *truth*, and how do we come to understand, promote, and share in truth both individually and collectively?

There are currently three competing frameworks within the realm of *epistemology*:

- *Pre-Modernism*
- *Modernism*
- *Post-Modernism*

Pre-Modernism

Pre-Modernism interprets *Truth* with an uppercase "T." From this orientation, it is assumed that there is an ultimate *Truth* that brings meaning to our shared existence, and that although this truth is not visually or behaviorally observed in the physical world, it is a deeply felt, intuitive experience. *Pre-Modernism* may be best understood through the concept of religion. For example, we exist because God chose us as His children, to spread His word, and to live in His light. Here, the church may be viewed as the primary institution governing knowledge.

Upside: This orientation lends itself to deeply felt meaning, can be highly relational, and helpful toward others.

Downside: Also lends itself to being too authoritarian and close minded when considering other means of derived meaning.

Modernism

Modernism interprets *truth* with a lowercase "t." From this orientation, *truth* is hypothetical and derived through empiricism (i.e. science). We can only know *truth* based on *theory*, and we can only know *theory* based on probabilities and *not* certainties. This orientation made its rise through academia and knowledge-based institutions. Here, the University is the primary institution governing knowledge.

Upside: Rational, Objective (can be observed and measured in the physical world), and Self-Correcting (understanding can change based on the introduction of new information).

Downside: This orientation is also prone to being authoritarian and impersonal by privileging the normative.

Post-Modernism

Post-Modernism proposed relief to the ongoing dissonance between the heavily competing *pre-modern* and *modern* epistemologies, stating that *neither* of which—in and of themselves—can truly account for the lived experience of each individual. It argued that there is no absolute truth, that reality is continually constructed and deconstructed by each individual. As so, *Post-Modernism* viewed *truth* as a series of lowercase "t's" (*truth* as hypothetical) while also acknowledging the role of the *individual* (**personal**) and *politics* (the society in which the individual exists). So, here we see that *post-modernism* understands *truth* through the equation of "t + p + p."

Upside: Favors both *intuition* and *rationality,* and is socially useful by including the element of dialogue. It was also experienced as liberating the conflict between *pre-modernism* and *modernity.*

Downside: As rational as it was, it was also prone to *irrationality* as it lacked a sufficient basis and lends itself to ideological extremism (i.e. when *truth* is interpreted as *equaling* the *personal* and the *political* through a narrow, mircosystemic lens as opposed to the concept rightfully being applied to the human family as a whole, making room for the infinite experiences of the *personal* and *political*) (Forisha & Volini, 2014).

Having a clear understanding of just what *post-modernism* is all about should help in identifying the particulars of the *post-modern* theories in relation to the *transgenerational* and *classical* schools. This graph should help keep things in perspective…

The Three Competing Epistemologies

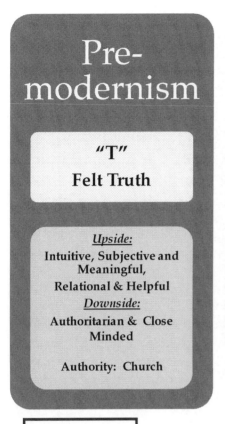
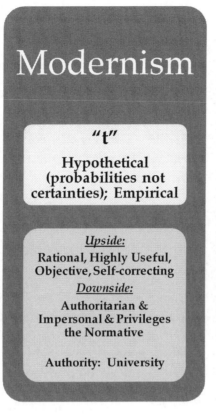
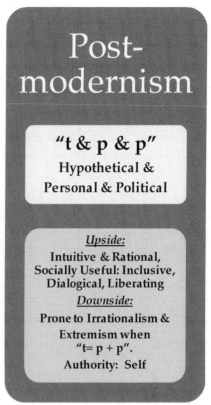

Pre-modernism

"T"
Felt Truth

Upside:
Intuitive, Subjective and Meaningful, Relational & Helpful
Downside:
Authoritarian & Close Minded

Authority: Church

Modernism

"t"
Hypothetical (probabilities not certainties); Empirical

Upside:
Rational, Highly Useful, Objective, Self-correcting
Downside:
Authoritarian & Impersonal & Privileges the Normative

Authority: University

Post-modernism

"t & p & p"
Hypothetical & Personal & Political

Upside:
Intuitive & Rational, Socially Useful: Inclusive, Dialogical, Liberating
Downside:
Prone to Irrationalism & Extremism when "t= p + p".
Authority: Self

Figure 3.5

Forisha & Volini, 2014

POST-MODERNISM

Post-Modernism was a philosophical movement—taking off in the late 20th century—that served as a departure from *modernism.* Having a widespread impact on how we experience and come to understand culture and society, the concept has been applied to a variety of movements within the domains of art, music, literature, and philosophy among many others. Essentially, it was meant to liberate and free individuals from the constraints of *pre-modernistic* and *modernistic* orientations toward living through the encouragement of subjective expression and the prescription of idiosyncratic meaning. *(T)truth* was no longer dictated by religious or academic institutions, and instead, was understood subjectively through the lived experience of the individual. As *Post-Modernism* was the movement that made way for the shift in *epistemology,* the exam will focus more on the concept of *Social Constructivism,* a term that falls under the umbrella of *Post-Modern* philosophy.

SOCIAL CONSTRUCTIVISM

Social constructivism—both sociological and philosophical in nature—aims to answer the question of how subjective meaning (*post-modernism*) becomes a social fact. Essentially, the concept is based upon the process in which individuals learn about themselves, others, and the world at large through what is observed and experienced—and thus, interpreted by the individual—within the group they grow up in (i.e. family, community, culture, etc.). Growing up is a process of interpreting experiences from our environment, creating *constructs* based on those interpretations and organizing them as a map for our actions and predicting/interpreting new experiences. So, we come to understand that no one experience can be understood directly—instead, everything is filtered through the mind of the observer and experienced subjectively. No one individual could ever fully understand the lived experience of another.

Application to Family Systems

When considering what we have reviewed from the *Transgenerational* and *Classical Schools* of Marital & Family Therapy, we can begin to identify how *Post-Modernism* fills in two significant gaps— (1) how the behaviors of each family member are influenced by their subjective beliefs and (2) and how those beliefs are shaped culturally in ways that are not experienced universally across the nuclear system. This was a break away from *objectivity*, as family therapy shifted away from a reliance on scientific methods to understand systemic patterns of interaction and toward emphasizing the importance of the individual's *experience* and *interpretation* of his or her problems. *Meaning*, and not *behavior*, became the determining factor in helping families achieve symptom relief and higher levels of satisfaction.

So, considering that the manner in which individuals relate to the world is heavily influenced by their social context, therapies aimed toward *deconstructing* these interpretations and meanings—thus, making room for new ways of understanding ourselves and others within the social world we share. We will come to see how these themes played out in the development of the *Post-Modern* theories we are about to review—primarily, *Solution-Focused Therapy, Narrative Therapy*, and *Collaborative Therapy.*

Solution-Focused Family Therapy

THE PRACTICE OF SYSTEMIC THERAPY (Domain 1)

Primary Contributors: Steven de **Shazer**

Insoo Kim **Berg**

Class of Family Therapy

Solution-Focused Therapy falls under *Post-Modern* domain of Marital & Family Therapy. Given its focus on the subjective, lived reality of each individual and guiding therapy in a way that promotes new ways of interpreting experience—both individually and collectively— concepts of *Social Constructivism* flow throughout this approach to therapy.

Historical Overview

Solution-Focused Therapy was developed out of the Brief Family Therapy Center (BFTC) in Milwaukee, Wisconsin during the late 1970s. The BFTC group—started by **Shazer** and **Berg**—was initially influenced by **Shazer's** experiences at *MRI* (i.e. therapy as being brief, relying on few interventions, and not being concerned with history or underlying pathology). As the approach shared these basic similarities with the *MRI Model*, there was a sharp contrast between *MRI* being *problem focused* and the BFTC group being *solution focused* (i.e. focusing attention *away* from the problem brought in by the family, and instead, illuminating upon what the family was doing when the problem is not present). Further, instead of the therapist being responsible for effective therapy outcomes (*MRI Model*), *Solution-Focused Therapists* believed that clients already had the strength and knowledge to solve their own problems, making the therapist's job to help them identify those internal resources through the art of asking questions that reframe their interpretation of the problem.

Essential Themes of Therapy

Solution-Focused Therapists argued that the therapist needs to know very little information about the actual problem in order to help the family resolve it, and that often, the solution is not necessarily related to the problem in the first place (De Jong & Berg, 2000). Instead of focusing on the problem, the therapist maintains a primary interest on what the family is already doing that works for them—thus drawing attention to existing solutions and future possibilities. Essentially, *Solution-Focused Therapy* aimed to help families identify what is working and to then be intentional about doing more of it. In turn, *problems* are indirectly resolved and families begin to experience more of what they are wanting and less of what they are not wanting.

Key Terms

Solution and Future Focus:

Strengths and Resources:

Beginner's Mind:

Change is Constant:

Language and Meaning:

Hope:

Solution-Focused Therapists assess for the various levels of *commitment to change* presented by clients at the onset of therapy. Clients will typically fall within one of the three defined categories:

Visitor:

Complainant:

Customer:

ASSESSING, HYPOTHESIZING, & DIAGNOSING (Domain 2)

Assessment

The assessment process includes a very brief exploration of the client problem—again, very little is needed to be known about the *problem* since the family already contains the *solution* (De Jong & Berg, 2000). Once there is a basic understanding, therapy shifts to the intervention phase. Even as the therapist explores the *problem*, he or she always remains intentional about pointing out strengths or resources as opportunities present themselves.

Diagnosing

Solution-Focused Therapies share in a nonpathologizing, strengths-based approach to therapy by shifting the focus away from any form of individual diagnosis.

DESIGNING & CONDUCTING TREATMENT (Domain 4)

Who is Involved

Solution-Focused Therapists will likely work with whomever shows up for therapy. If they find that other family members may play an important role in reaching goals, it may be encouraged for them to attend following sessions but not enforced.

Treatment Duration

Solution-Focused Therapy is BRIEF. Therapy will conclude as soon as the desired solution is achieved.

Goals of Therapy

Goal setting in this approach is a *collaborative* endeavor between client(s) and the therapist. Clients will initially define the goals—which typically identify their preferred solutions to the identified problem—and the therapist will then assist in assuring they are specific, attainable, and fall within the scope of therapy (Miller, Duncan, & Hubble, 1996).

Goals will generally include a two-part process of (1) identifying specific preferred behaviors and interactions and (2) increasing the number of times these specific preferred behaviors and interactions occur (Miller et al., 1996). It is important in this approach that goals are measurable and easily identifiable. For instance, clients will be encouraged to explore how they will know when the problem is solved (*hint hint, *miracle question*, hint hint).

Primary Interventions and/or Techniques

Formula First Session Task:

Miracle Question:

Exception Questions:

Scaling Questions:

Compliments:

EVALUATING ONGOING PROCESS & TERMINATING TREATMENT (Domain 4)

Therapy Structure (de Shazer, 1985; De Jong & Berg, 2000; Miller et al., 1996)

- *Early Phase* (First Session): Throughout the first session, the therapist joins with the family through non-judgmental interest to create a sense of comfort and safety. The therapist will also address client complaints while giving compliments for present and/or past strengths and resources. Throughout, three processes are highlighted:

    1. Define the problem using the family's language while assessing for the possibility of unexplored solutions.

    2. Exceptions are identified, highlighted, and further explored.

    3. As exceptions are highlighted, goals begin to establish.

        - *Formula First Session Task* and *Miracle Question* are executed at this phase.

- *Middle Phase* (Goal Setting Stage): Here (as early as the second session), the client(s) and therapist collaboratively identify how the problem will be solved and how they will know when the problem has been resolved.

    - *Scaling Questions, Exception Questions*, and *Compliments* are used throughout the rest of therapy.

- *Later Phase* (Third Session and On): The therapist continues to inquire about positive patterns, and as they occur, the therapist encourages the client(s) to be intentional about doing more of what is working. If no positive patterns are emerging, the therapist will explore the client's situation in greater detail through a process of deconstruction.

    - *Scaling Questions, Exception Questions*, and *Compliments* are used throughout the rest of therapy.

- *Termination:* Treatment ends when *problem* has been resolved.

Applying Solution-Focused Therapy to the Becker Family

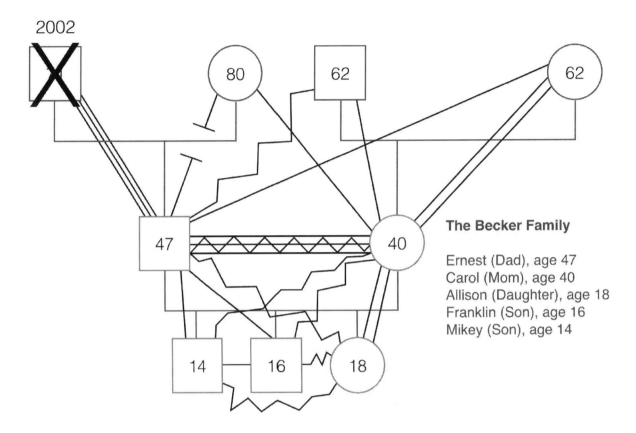

The Becker Family

Ernest (Dad), age 47
Carol (Mom), age 40
Allison (Daughter), age 18
Franklin (Son), age 16
Mikey (Son), age 14

The Beckers are a Caucasian, middle-class family pursuing therapy due to general family disconnection. Mom initiated the phone call stating that things are "out of control" and that "changes need to happen, and fast!" Mom further elaborated that she and her husband are very disconnected and have been for the past 11 years. She said he will work all day and come home to "decompress" in his workshop attached to the garage and spend most weekends with their two sons at various sporting activities and "guys-only outings." Mom reported that she and her husband have been sleeping in different bedrooms for the past three years. Mom said she will spend most days at her Mom's home—which is close in town—and as much time as she can with her daughter before she goes off to college in five months. Mom said she is very disconnected from her sons and her husband is very disconnected from his daughter. She reported the family being "split into two" and appeared quite desperate for change to occur. Mom requested that she, her husband, and her daughter come in as her two sons are refusing to attend family therapy.

SOLUTION-FOCUSED THERAPY |175

Applying Solution-Focused Therapy to the Becker Family

Early-Phase Goals

1.

2.

Middle-Phase Goals:

1.

2.

Later-Phase Goals:

1.

2.

Overall Conceptualization of the Becker Family informed by Solution-Focused Therapy

Narrative Family Therapy

THE PRACTICE OF SYSTEMIC THERAPY (Domain 1)

Primary Contributors: Michael **White**
David **Epston**

Class of Family Therapy

Narrative Family Therapy falls under *Post-Modern* domain of Marital & Family Therapy. Given its focus on the subjective, lived reality of each individual and guiding therapy in a way that promotes new ways of interpreting experience—both individually and collectively—concepts of *Social Constructivism* flow throughout this approach to therapy.

Historical Overview

Narrative Family Therapy is most commonly associated with Michael **White,** an Australian therapist who constructed a framework to therapy based upon the dual influence of Michel **Foucault** (a European philosopher at the forefront of the *Post-Modern* movement) and David **Epston** (a clinician from New Zealand that focused on the individual narratives that people construct in therapy). Grounding the approach in the *Post-Modern* view of no absolute reality—instead, reality as a social construct—**White** viewed therapy as an environment where people can reflect on the narratives they have constructed about themselves, identifying their life experiences that influence them and creating new narratives congruent to ways in which they want to begin living. The development of this approach established its roots through the 1970s and 1980s before being introduced to the mental health field at large in 1990 through the publication of **White** and **Epston's** *Narrative Means to Therapeutic Ends.* Since then, *Narrative Therapy* has blossomed into a prominent approach to individual, couple, and family therapy across the world.

Essential Themes of Therapy

Narrative therapy is a collaborative approach that places clients as the experts of their own lives. Therapy becomes a process of freeing people from the oppression of their own problems through coming to view them as metaphors of the stories they have created about themselves (White & Epston, 1990). **White's** approach states that over time, people develop self-narratives comprised of life events that eventually emerge into a theme. Individuals are then prone to identifying with all information congruent with their narrative and neglecting information that may contradict it. For example, an individual whose narrative suggests that he is a failure—developed as an account of life experiences—will overly focus on events in which he fails and likely ignore or discredit events where he found success.

As so, these narratives come to exert a powerful influence over individuals' lives both introspectively and relationally, and problems become an externalized metaphor of their narrative. Therapy aims to help clients in deconstructing the narrative they bring in to therapy before constructing a new narrative more reflective of their desired ways of experiencing themselves and others (White & Epston, 1990). This approach will also emphasize the role that the social and political world have on the development of undesirable narratives.

Key Terms

Narrative Metaphor:

Constitutionalist Self:

Problem-Saturated Stories:

Preferred Narrative:

Subjugated Story:

ASSESSING, HYPOTHESIZING, & DIAGNOSING (Domain 2)

Assessment

Narrative Therapy does not propose a structured assessment process, but identifies the exploration of three domains during the early (assessment) phases of therapy (White & Epston, 1990):

1. *Knowing the Person Apart from the Problem*: During the joining and assessment phase, the therapist will intentionally inquire about learning of the individual in ways not related to the problem. This sets the stage for externalizing the problem, identifies strengths and resources, and expands the client's sense of self beyond the problem and toward competence.
2. *Identifying Unique Outcomes*: The therapist will intentionally draw attention to times in the client's life when the problem is not a problem. These can occur historically, presently, or be future oriented by engaging imagination and anticipation.
3. *Mapping Effects*: Essentially, the therapist will explore ways in which the problem has affected the client as well as how the client has affected the life of the problem.

Diagnosing

Through the awareness of the larger social and political influences that challenge themselves and their clients, *Narrative Therapists* do not objectively label problems with pathological or systemic diagnoses.

DESIGNING & CONDUCTING TREATMENT (Domain 3)

Who is Involved

Narrative Therapists do not state a particular stance on who is required to attend therapy, and will likely work with whomever is present and willing to come. It may be assumed that resolution of the problem can be achieved on an individual basis and does not require the system as a whole to participate.

Treatment Duration

Narrative Therapy does not identify with being either a brief, long-term, or somewhere-in-the-middle approach to therapy. Therapy will continue until each individual develops a desirable narrative and will likely vary with each client.

Goals of Therapy

Ultimately, the goal of *Narrative Therapy* is to alter the problem-saturated story to better reflect the preferred narrative, as defined by the client (White & Epston, 1990).

Primary Interventions and/or Techniques

Deconstruction Questions:

Externalizing the Problem:

Externalizing Questions:

Unique Outcomes (Sparkling Events):

Relative Influencing Questioning:

Mapping the Influence of the Problem:

Mapping the Influence of the Person:

Landscape of Action Questions:

Landscape of Meaning Questions:

Preference Questions:

Therapeutic Letters:

Therapeutic Certificates:

Collaborative Case Notes:

Clients as Consultants:

EVALUATING ONGOING PROCESS & TERMINATING TREATMENT (Domain 4)

Falling in line with the *Post-Modern* orientation of subjectivity, *Narrative Therapy* does not necessarily provide a structured, phase-based discourse of treatment and instead suggests that each client contact will vary. The therapist must adjust to the unique circumstances and idiosyncrasies of each client encounter. Keep in mind, **White** and **Epston** (1990) will suggest the necessity of starting with a unique outcome, specifying that "it is only necessary that one unique outcome be identified in order to facilitate performance of new meaning.

Termination occurs when the new narrative is solidified and its extension into the future is explored.

Applying Narrative Family Therapy to the Becker Family

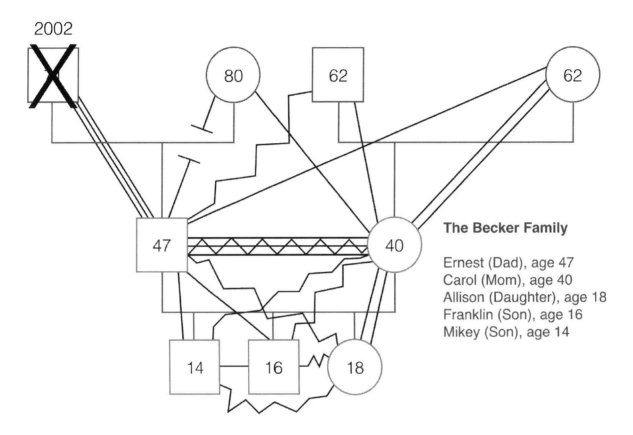

The Becker Family

Ernest (Dad), age 47
Carol (Mom), age 40
Allison (Daughter), age 18
Franklin (Son), age 16
Mikey (Son), age 14

The Beckers are a Caucasian, middle-class family pursuing therapy due to general family disconnection. Mom initiated the phone call stating that things are "out of control" and that "changes need to happen, and fast!" Mom further elaborated that she and her husband are very disconnected and have been for the past 11 years. She said he will work all day and come home to "decompress" in his workshop attached to the garage and spend most weekends with their two sons at various sporting activities and "guys-only outings." Mom reported that she and her husband have been sleeping in different bedrooms for the past three years. Mom said she will spend most days at her Mom's home—which is close in town—and as much time as she can with her daughter before she goes off to college in five months. Mom said she is very disconnected from her sons and her husband is very disconnected from his daughter. She reported the family being "split into two" and appeared quite desperate for change to occur. Mom requested that she, her husband, and her daughter come in as her two sons are refusing to attend family therapy.

Applying Narrative Family Therapy to the Becker Family

Early-Phase Goals

1.

2.

Middle-Phase Goals:

1.

2.

Later-Phase Goals:

1.

2.

Overall Conceptualization of the Becker Family informed by Narrative Family Therapy

Other Theories Covered on the Exam

This manual has walked you through the dominant theories that will be covered on the exam—that is, those deemed by the regulatory board as exerting the most influence on the study and practice of Marital & Family Therapy at large. We will now *briefly* review some lesser-known approaches—many of which are gaining momentum in their notoriety—that may also be covered on the written exam. As the exam will not expect a broad knowledge base of these approaches, nor a demonstration of their direct application, it will be important to know the general overview and key terms associated with each.

Collaborative Languages Approach

Primary Contributors: Harry **Goolishan**

Harlene **Anderson**

Karl **Tomm**

Tom **Anderson**

Theory Overview

Collaborative Family Therapy, primarily developed by **Goolishan** and **Anderson**, is most concerned with the role that *language* and *conversations* play in the development and maintenance of relational discord and general dissatisfaction. Much in line with the *Post-Modern* and *Social-Constructivism* orientation of reality being socially constructed, this approach believed that the very process of social construction occurs directly through dialogue, language, and communication as it forms a living narrative. As each individual's very sense of meaning (i.e. their living narrative) occurs through a process of dialogue and communication, so too does the individual's development of problems and solutions. The goal of therapy thus becomes changing the manner in which people talk about themselves, their problems, and the world at large—making room for new meanings and adapting the lived narrative both individually and collectively.

Therapeutic Process

The landmark of the therapeutic process in this model is the therapist taking a **not-knowing approach** (i.e. not taking an expert position and downplaying the use of technique). Through this orientation, the therapist creates a dialogue of open curiosity, where therapist and client can co-create a rich interchange aimed toward constructing new meanings and exploring possibilities.

Example

When a client reports feelings of depression, instead of assuming that they know what *depression* is (perhaps as specified by the DSM), the therapist would inquire about the *client's experience of depression*. They would ask, "Depression, hmm...What does that mean to you, to be *depressed?*" Or, "Depression, hmm...I am not quite sure I know what you mean by that, please, say more about your experience of feeling depressed..." The therapist here would understand that there is no one way to be depressed and that the very essence of depression is a subjective experience. This not only helps clients feel less pathologized, but encourages them to explore the meanings they have attributed to depression and the manner in which that may contribute to the ongoing experience.

As so, therapists in this approach will *not* prescribe a diagnosis, hypothesize outside of the in-session co-created dialogue, or utilize any predetermined interventions or techniques.

Key Terms and Themes

Not-Knowing Approach: This identifies the stance of the therapist not taking on the role of expert, diagnostician, or interventionist. Instead, they remain open and curious to the lived experience of each individual, as only the individual can serve as expert to their own lives.

Problem-Determining System: This concept states that problems arise and maintain themselves based upon the nature in which individuals continue to communicate about them. It is the language that is used regarding the problem within the system that maintains the problem. By changing the way individuals talk about the problem, new meanings are prescribed and possibilities are explored—thereby, disillusioning the problem.

Language: Language is at the foundation of this approach, and therapists will intentionally adapt to the style and form of language used by clients as a means of joining and entering their internal world.

Inventive Questioning: This was a concept introduced by Karl **Tomm,** used to help families in finding new ways of communicating, behaving, and creating meaning.

Reflecting Team: Tom **Anderson** developed what he found to be a more *collaborative* approach to using a reflecting team as opposed to the more traditional, expert-based models (thing Milan Systemic). In this approach, Anderson would have a team of other *collaborative therapists*—that is, those taking a *not-knowing approach*—observe a family behind a one-way mirror. Instead of the observation team consulting on the case in private, the family would be invited to *observe the observation team* as they discussed the family's case. Then, the family would be invited to reflect on their experience of observing the observation team.

Feminist Family Therapy

Primary Contributors: Peggy **Papp**

Olga **Silverstein**

Marianne **Walters**

Betty **Carter**

Deborah **Luepnitiz**

Rachel **Hare-Mustin**

Historical Overview

Feminist Family Therapy grew directly from the Feminist Movement, which aimed to define, establish, and defend equal political, economic, and social rights for women in what was then a blatantly patriarchal society. It was the intention that such a movement would create equal opportunities for women in the domains of education, employment, and overall social status.

This influenced the practice of Family Therapy in several significant ways. The wave started in 1978 after the first published article on the topic—*A Feminist Approach to Family Therapy* by Rachel **Hare-Mustin**—caused some rather large waves in the professional community. Many of the primary concepts in which the field of Family Therapy was based upon were now being identified as sexist and counterintuitive to the very goal it was trying to accomplish—as we will now see, the argument for this was compelling.

Consider the History of the Development of the Field of Family Therapy as discussed in Part II of this Manual. As the various theories, concepts, and ideas developed one by one, expanding significantly upon the manner in which we understand and treat the family system, there was no mention of or accounting for *gender differences.* The theories indirectly assumed that males and females will benefit equally from the identified interventions. When looking back on many of these concepts through a *post-modern* lens, many of the concepts that were largely accepted by our profession may now give us some reason to second-guess their appropriateness...

Primary Criticisms offered by Feminist Family Therapy

Neutrality: Neutrality aims to ensure that each family member feels validated, accepted, and equally invested in by the therapist. At first, this concept seems hard to deny as anything but appropriate. *Feminist Family Therapy* suggests that issues arising in families and relationships that are accounted for by the societal oppression endured by women must be acknowledged and emphasized. In doing so, alignment with the oppressed group may better serve the family moving forward than maintaining neutrality and siding with both the oppressed individual as well as the individual in the family whose behaviors perpetuate the cycle of oppression that is harming the female client. In cases where the conflict within the system is fueled by a dynamic of inequality, a therapist remaining neutral in the midst of that only perpetuates the oppressive cycle. As so, in Feminist Family Therapy, the therapist may intentionally align with the individual struggling under oppressive cycles to draw attention to the inequality inherent within the system.

Cybernetics: *Cybernetics* suggests that all problems in the system are maintained by the recursive nature of ALL OF ITS parts, indirectly suggesting that everyone is equally involved in the ongoing nature of problems. If we expand the family system to the microsystem of societal oppression at large, this concept may maintain the homeostasis and "status quo" of the current oppressive nature of Western society endured by women.

Circularity: Along with the concept of *Cybernetics*, *circularity* aims to expose the circular nature of all problems, expanding it to a systemic issue in which both parties share responsibility. *Feminist Therapists* viewed this as "blaming the victim" in instances of rape, incest, or domestic abuse endured by women.

Bowen's Differentiation: *Feminist Family Therapists* viewed the distancing between emotionality and rationality, and **Bowen's** emphasis on increasing rationality as not accounting for the gender differences suggesting that women experience the world more emotionally (subjectively) as men do more rationally (objectively). This would suggest that the woman is responsible to act against the organic nature of her neurological wiring and assimilate to the more natural relational style of men. It also fails to acknowledge the richness associated with the emotional experience and the positive impact it may have on the family system.

Overview of Approach to Therapy

Feminist Family Therapy is a political approach to therapy that aims to alter the patriarchal and hierarchical implications of many therapies and shift toward a more *egalitarian* relationship with clients.

Goals of Therapy

- Engage in dialogue that draws awareness to the ways in which societal, macrosystemic dynamics may be oppressive and consider how these dynamics may manifest the family microsystem.
- Based on the awareness of societal oppression, empower individuals to CHOOSE and construct their desired roles, challenging the societal messages that tell them what it means to be a male or female.
- Explore issues of power and control in the system.
- Help men to become more in touch with their emotional side and empower women to move beyond their prescribed societal limitations.

Internal Family Systems (IFS)

Primary Contributor: Richard **Schwartz**

Essential Elements

Internal Family Systems (IFS) was developed by Richard **Schwartz** based on years of interpretive analysis of his own work with clients. A theme **Schwartz** continued to encounter was the client's use of language when referring to their different "parts." For instance, when you're sitting with a client who is working through a difficult decision, common language used would be to say, "A part of me wants to leave my marriage, while another part of me still believes we can work through this affair." Schwartz grew increasingly intrigued by this phenomenon and eventually based his entire approach off of it. IFS is about internalizing the concept of the system and investigating the existence of and interactions between our various "parts."

Key Terms and Themes

The Self: *IFS* states that every person as a true *Self* that is stable, unchanging, and always positive. The *Self* is what allows us the capacity to heal, to foster insight, and to endorse compassion. The *Self* is the key part of each individual which governs the rest of our parts. It exists exclusively and purely within each individual. This concept parallels the soul, freewill, mindfulness as a means of connecting to the spirit of the Buddha, etc.; however, it does not suggest any religious connotation.

IFS states that our parts are organized into three categories:

Exiles: Exiles are our wounded parts. Whether it be traumatic experiences, neglect, profound sadness etc. They are the parts we bury deep down inside because they are too painful to acknowledge. By keeping them buried deep down inside, we protect them from being damaged again by the outside world.

Managers: Managers are what allow us to keep our *Exiled* parts buried deep down inside. The role of our Manager parts is to manage the day-to-day living. These are the ways in which we manage our stress and strive to maintain a sense of comfort, contentedness, and avoid conflict or situation that could potentially harm our Exiled parts or potentially create new ones.

Firefighters: When our internal system recognizes that our Managers are failing to protect our Exiled parts, Firefighters must step in to either prevent or manage crises. Firefighter parts may express themselves through abusing alcohol or drugs, self-harm, withdrawal and isolation, dissociation, or rage and violence.

Therapeutic Process

As the *Managers* and *Firefighters* help to protect the *Exiled* parts from coming to the surface—becoming vulnerable to re-injury or too painful for the individual to confront—a parallel process occurs that prevents these parts from healing. As long as the *Exiled* parts remain *Exiled*, they will remain a part of us and interfere with our quality of life. The purpose of *IFS* is to create a safe space where the *Self* can give permission for the *Manager* and *Firefighter* parts to step to the side, allowing the *Exiled* parts to come to the surface. The *IFS* Therapist guides the client through a process in which his or her various parts engage in dialogue with the *Exiled* parts. This process ultimately leads to the *Exiled* parts being healed. From there, the client can negotiate and reassign roles for his or her *Manager* and *Firefighter* parts that are more authentic and fulfilling.

For example, a 32-year-old male who was sexually abused when he was 6-years-old is experiencing difficulty maintaining intimate relationships and has acted out violently when he feels his partner is getting too close to him. This violence is an example of his *Firefighter* part protecting his *Exiled* part that is mistrustful of the world based on past experiences. He has now found himself in a pattern where he hasn't dated in three years and instead focuses on work and recreation (these would be his *Manager* parts helping to get him by on a day-to-day basis). This young man's *IFS* Therapist would find ways for his *Manager* and *Firefighter* parts to step aside, creating a safe space for his *Exiled* part (in this case, a terrified, helpless 6-year-old boy) to come to the surface. The *IFS* Therapist may instruct the client to close his eyes, and describe how he sees his 6-year-old self. This can be done in great detail. This process will continue into a dialogue where the 23-year-old self can talk to his 6-year-old self, and give his 6-year-old self a voice he wasn't able to find 17 years ago. As a result of this process, the 6-year-old self can heal. When our *Exiled* parts heal, we create space inside of ourselves for more positive experiences and are able to develop more constructive roles for our various parts.

Goal of Therapy

The ultimate goal in *IFS* is to have *the self* become the organizer and leader of the other various parts, creating lesser of a need for *Managers* and *Firefighters*.

Cognitive-Behavioral Family Therapy

Primary Contributors: Richard **Stuart**

Historical Overview

Cognitive Therapy, Behavioral Therapy, and *Cognitive-Behavioral Therapy* (CBT) are some of the most highly recognized approaches to therapy. CBT continues to offer the community a boastful review of quantitative analysis endorsing its effectiveness with various conditions. Unlike the approaches we have reviewed thus far, CBT follows a model of linear causality—that is, problems are caused by the behavior or event that preceded it. Let's do a brief review of the primary concepts offered from this approach…

Classical Conditioning: A concept introduced by Ivan Pavlov demonstrated a learning process that took place when a previously neutral stimulus was paired repeatedly with a potent, response-eliciting stimulus. When this pairing occurred enough times, the previously neutral stimulus would then elicit a response in the absence of being paired with a potent stimulus. The classic example: Every time the dog would be fed (presentation of food is a potent stimulus) the experiment would ring a bell (a neutral stimulus)—the dog would see/smell the food and begin to salivate. After this process occurred enough times, ringing the bell alone would result in the dog beginning to salivate despite there being no food present. John Watson applied this concept to human behavior. This concept develops a relationship between a *stimulus* and a *behavior*.

Operant Conditioning: A concept introduced by B.F. Skinner, demonstrated that a learning process in which behavior is highly responsive to—or, even controlled by—its consequences. Meaning, a child goes to eat a cookie out of a cookie jar every afternoon. If the only consequence of eating the cookie is the sheer pleasure of enjoying a delicious cookie, the consequence would serve as a *positive reinforcement* and likely encourage the behavior to be repeated. However, if the child gets scolded and grounded by his parents for eating a cook before dinner, despite enjoying the cookie, the more potent consequence would be the *punishment* of being scolded and grounded which would likely discourage the behavior being repeated. *Positive* or *Negative Reinforcement* encourage the behavior to be repeated. *Punishment* discourages the behavior being repeated.

Key Terms and Themes

Primary Reinforcer: These types of reinforcement are determined biologically such as survival, food, and sex.

Secondary Reinforcer: These are learned consequences that have been deemed as desirable by the individual, and as so, acquire reinforcing properties. These can be consequences such as monetary rewards, positive feedback, and/or earning privileges.

Premack Principle: This is when a high-probability behavior serves as the positive reinforcer for a low-probability behavior. An example of this would be an adolescent getting to go to a friend's house (high-probability behavior) after he cleans his room (low-probability behavior).

Target Behavior: The behavior in which the therapy aims to change.

Baseline: This establishes how often the target behavior is currently taking place—frequency and duration.

Functional Analysis of Behavior: This includes an assessment of the likely antecedents and consequences of the target behavior.

Therapeutic Process

This approach maintains a focus on current behaviors, is time limited, and aimed at symptom relief. Goals in this approach are highly concrete and easily measurable. The therapist will identify the *target behavior* along with a *baseline* of the frequency and duration of the *target behavior* before developing a *functional analysis of behavior* addressing the likely antecedents and consequence of the *target behavior*. The goal is to then increase the number of positive behaviors through the implementation of positive reinforcement and thereby decrease the frequency of problematic behaviors. Through this process, couples will learn concrete communication and problem-solving skills, and once put to regular use will serve as the determining factors of a healthy relationship.

Richard **Stuart** is most recognized for developing an approach to couples therapy aimed at developing new, more functional ways of behaving within the relationship that were found to be mutually satisfying by each partner.

Branches of Cognitive-Behavioral Family Therapy

Functional Family Therapy

Developed by Thomas **Sexton,** *Functional Family Therapy* is an *evidence-based* approach to Family

Therapy that addresses violent and criminal behavior in adolescents. The three-phase process process aims to (1) *engage the family* by decreasing blame and negativity and increasing alliances and a family, (2) *implement behavioral change* by building on competencies congruent with the family, and finally (3) *generalize* the behavioral competencies by building support and maintaining the changes over time (Sexton, 2010).

Rational-Emotive Family Therapy

REFT, developed by Albert **Ellis,** finds an individual's illogical beliefs and distortions serving as the foundation for emotional distress. In therapy, family members are taught to recognize the problem-causing pattern:

A-B-C, in which events in the family (A) are influenced by irrational beliefs (B) and result in a problem (C).

Cognitive Family Therapy

Originated by Aaron **Beck** in the 1970s, *Cognitive Family Therapy* suggests that individuals hold a set of conscious and unconscious *core beliefs,* or, a *schema,* about themselves and their families through which they interpret and evaluate one another's behavior. Therapy focuses on addressing these *schemas* and *core beliefs* directly through developing more functional ways of interpreting and evaluating one another's behavior.

Network Therapy

Network Family Therapy is a model developed by Ross **Speck,** Carolyn **Attneave,** and Uri **Ruevini** throughout the mid 1970s. They outlined a set of procedures designed to work specifically with families in crisis, not meant to be a substitute for traditional family therapy.

Network Family Therapy is a time-limited, goal-directed approach developed to help families in crisis assemble and utilize their own social network—including relatives, friends, neighbors, co-workers, etc.—which then become collectively involved in developing new options and solutions for dealing with future crises as they arise (Ruevini, 1979). This serves to disrupt dysfunctional patterns within the family and activate the healing processes inherent within a social network.

This approach will generally involve a team of at least two, but as many as six therapists, to meet with as many available members of the family's broader social network for three to four hours per session over the span of three to eight sessions (Ruevini, 1979). This approach has been known to assemble networks from 5-45 members, and may also be commonly used to address alcohol-use.

Psychoeducation and Enrichment

Psychoeducational Family Therapy, primarily developed and endorsed by C.M. **Anderson**, is the preferred approach to family therapy when an individual is suffering from a severe and persistent mental illness—including, but not limited to, bipolar disorder, schizophrenia, psychotic illnesses, and some personality disorders. The approach is meant to empower the family to work with the mental illness in resourceful and constructive ways. It helps the family learn about the nature of the illness and develop skills to best serve the support of the individual. It also endorses the importance of self-care for others in the family, encouraging them to intentionally find ways of taking care of themselves as they take care of their family member. In this approach, the emphasis is on education about the illness—for both the individual and the family members—resources, and coping skills.

Medical Family Therapy

Similar to *Psychoeducation, Medical Family Therapy* aims to provide education about the physical illness and what is to be expected moving forward upon initial diagnosis. It aims to promote a constructive and intentional adaptation to the illness and provides resources and skills for managing problematic patterns related to symptoms. It not only serves the individual but the family members as well who will also be impacted by the illness.

Family Preservation Program

This is a brief, intensive, crisis intervention implemented when children are at risk of being removed from the home. It sets services in place and teaches necessary skills to prevent foster care placement in situations where that is not within the best interests of the family.

Family Focused Therapy

This is an approach to therapy developed specifically for individuals with Bipolar Disorder, and has many elements of *Psychoeducation*.

Other Concepts & Terms to Know

The Circumplex Model

The Circumplex Model was designed as an assessment measure to bridge the gap between research, theory, and practice within the field of Marital & Family Therapy. It identifies 16 different types of couple and family relationships by focusing on three central dimensions of marital and family systems: *Cohesion, flexibility,* and *communication* (Olson, Russell, & Sprenkle, 1989).

This model developed self-report scales based off of *The Circumplex Model* referred to as *FACES* (Family Adaptability and Cohesion Evaluation Scale) which measures a family's level of *cohesion* and *flexibility.*

There are four levels of *cohesion*: disengaged, separated, connected, and enmeshed (Olson et al., 1989).

There are four levels of *flexibility:* chaotic, flexible, structured, and rigid (Olson et al., 1989).

Communication, the third dimension, facilitates movement between the other two dimensions (*cohesion* and *flexibility*) (Olson et al., 1989).

The assessment produces *The Couple and Family Map. The Couple and Family Map* depicts the *closeness* and *flexibility* areas derived from the *FACES* self-report measure. Families aim to achieve *balance* measured on a scale of *balanced,* to *mid-range,* to *unbalanced. Balanced* families are *structured* and *flexible* with healthy degrees of *separation* and *connection* (Olson et al., 1989).

The Couple and Family Map has since been adopted by the *PREPARE/ENRICH* assessment.

The Timberlawn Model

Originated by Robert **Beavers** during a 1976 study on healthy families volunteering to perform predetermined tasks led to the identification of two primary scales that measured family patterns: *Family Competence* and *Family Style* (Beavers & Hampson, 1990).

Competence: Measured on a range from adequate, to midrange, to severely dysfunctional.

Stylistic: Measured through the dimensions of *centripetal, centrifugal,* and *mixed.*

Centripetal: Family members look to get their needs met *within* the family system.

Centrifugal: Family members look to get their needs met *outside* of the family system.

***Note:** A trick I used to remember the differences between these two terms was to illuminate the word **pet** within centri**pet**al. The visual of a healthy family, out to a picnic, sitting around a yellow lab, on a beautiful spring day, immediately served as a reminder that this family likely gets its needs met *within the system.*

The next portion of this manual will explore other relevant factors pertaining to the practice of marriage and family therapy covered on the exam, including:

- Multicultural Practices in Marital & Family Therapy
- Sex Therapy
- Ethics
- HIPAA
- Managing Crisis Situations
- Violence & Abuse
- Drug & Substance Abuse
- Research Trends & Findings

Much like the other domains, the exam will measure both your general knowledge of these concepts as well as your capacity to effectively apply them to the here and now of a therapeutic encounter. A basic skill base in relation to the following concepts is best nurtured out in the field through client encounters, supervision, and clinical case consultation…

Part IV

Clinical Considerations & Concepts

Multicultural Practice in Marriage & Family Therapy

Marriage and Family Therapy has fully embraced the importance of considering contextual factors when working with clients, particularly in relation to their ethnic, racial, and cultural make-up. Ethnicity, for instance, is deeply tied to the families in which it is transmitted. Referring to a common ancestry through which individuals have evolved, it provides and shares the very values and customs that will have a profound impact on an individual's development (McGoldrick, Giordano, & Preto, 2005). Beyond its transgenerational influences, ethnicity is also impacted by:

Culture of Origin	Spirituality
Gender	Sexuality
Age	Socio-Political
Socio-Economic Status	Oppression/Discrimination
Religion	Inequality

The cultural context in which ethnicity exists will directly influence the manner in which individuals go about receiving help—whether it be through the church, community, medical doctors, psychotherapists, a shaman, or drugs and alcohol among many others—Marriage and Family Therapists must be attuned to the presence and significance of these phenomena.

The exam is going to measure your capacity to identify various themes within particular cultures and ethnicities in relation to receiving mental health services. For instance, if it states that your client is of Asian-American descent, what can we *objectively* assume about the relationship between Asian-Americans and mental health? Depending on your training in delivering culturally-sensitive therapies, this may or may not be congruent with your personal philosophy; however, as we discussed in Part I, this exam is *not* about what *you* would do as a family therapist so be sure to stay in a congruent mind-set.

There may only be a few questions on the exam pertaining to working with specific ethnic groups, so you may decide the extent to which you want to familiarize yourself with this objective approach to multicultural therapy. In the case that you want to go all-in, or at least skim through the primary themes, the recommended text in the field is *Ethnicity and Family Therapy* by Monica McGoldrick, Joe Giordano, and Nydia Garcia Preto. The text, in its third edition, provides an exhaustive review on delivering culturally-sensitive therapies with families and individuals from over 40 different ethnic groups.

Remember, when contextual factors impair a Family Therapist's ability to remain neutral and nonjudgmental, or put the clients' needs beyond the scope of the therapist's competencies, it is appropriate to provide a referral to another therapist that may better serve the particular individual or family.

Notes on Multiculturalism

Notes on Multiculturalism

Notes on Multiculturalism

Sex Therapy

The evolution of Sex Therapy as a distinct approach has proven itself as a useful addition to our profession. Essentially, Sex Therapy is a treatment approach geared toward addressing issues of sexual dysfunction stemming from psychological distress. Sex Therapy addresses a list of concerns that fall within the domain of an individual's or couple's sex life, including, but not limited to: premature ejaculation, low-libido, unwanted sexual fetishes, erectile dysfunction, lack of sexual confidence, working through a sexual assault, sexual addiction, pain experienced during intercourse, and difficulty reaching orgasm. The goal of Sex Therapy is to assist individuals and couples in experiencing a desirable and satisfying sex life.

When practicing *Sex Therapy*, and something that the exam may cover, it is important to differentiate between *Sexual Dysfunction* and *Sexual Disorders*.

Sexual Dysfunction: A <u>physiological</u> arousal or performance problem. *This requires a MEDICAL referral.*

Sexual Disorder: A <u>psychological</u> arousal or performance problem. *This can be treated by a SEX THERAPIST.*

There are several theorists that have contributed to the development of Sex Therapy as a distinct approach. Let's review some of the key contributors and their primary concepts and interventions.

General Key Terms

Spectatoring: When sexually active, one focuses all mental attention on his or her own sexual behavior (or, quality of performing that sexual behavior). This can either be a result of performance anxiety or result in experiencing performance anxiety.

Coital Alignment Technique (CAT): An intervention used to increase mutual stimulation through full body contact (male learns to position and maneuver on top of the woman).

Masters & Johnson

Masters and **Johnson** pioneered the development of sex therapy, integrating a medical and behavioral understanding of sexual (dys)function with behavioral interventions (Leiblum, 2007).

Four-Stage Model of the Sexual Response (Lieblum, 2007)
- Excitement Phase (initial arousal)
- Plateau Phase (at full arousal, but not yet orgasm)
- Orgasm
- Resolution Phase (after orgasm)

Key Terms of Masters & Johnson

Sensate Focus: This is an intervention that allows couples to ease into sex and overcome inhibition by becoming more familiar with one's body through a series of touch, identifying please responses and connecting mind and body.

Squeeze Technique: This intervention is used to work through pre-ejaculation. Prior to the male reaching orgasm, the partner squeezes the penis to disrupt the orgasmic process.

Helen Singer Kaplan

Kaplan developed **Psychosexual Therapy** which combined Master's and Johnson's Behavioral Therapy with Object-Relations Theory. Her emphasis was to introduce the concept of *sexual desire* into Sex Therapy (Lieblum, 2007).

Key Terms of Kaplan

Stop-Start Technique: To treat pre-ejaculation in men. Preferred source of stimulation would occur until until male reaches premonitory sensations, then stimulation stops. This process is repeated allowing the male to build a greater tolerance for pleasure as well as better control over his body. Also, it builds confidence by extending the duration of sexual interaction.

Triphasic Sexual Response: Kaplan included *sexual desire, excitement,* and *orgasm* to better explain sexual intercourse.

Bridge Maneuver: This intervention calls for the manual stimulation of the female in an effort to produce orgasm. This would gradually decrease as treatment progresses and partner can begin to fill that role.

David Schnarch

Schnarch combined Object-Relations Theory with Intergenerational Theories resulting in an approach that identified sexual life as a means of storytelling, sharing one's story with his or her partner through intercourse (Lieblum, 2007). His goals include differentiation of each partner and disregards the concept of dysfunction, attributing sexual struggles only to the degree to which partners have effectively differentiated.

Leslie & Joseph LoPiccolo

Focused on the development of techniques to treat physiological sexual dysfunction.

Key Terms of LoPiccolo

Directed Masturbation Training: To treat anorgasmic women, this technique helps a woman to touch herself, and then her partner, in various ways to trigger her orgasm.

Maintaining Ethical, Legal, & Professional Standards

Domain 6 will measure your capacity to maintain ethical, legal, and professional standards when conducting Marital & Family Therapy. When preparing for this section, keep in mind that this is the *National* Licensing Exam, and not your *State* Licensing Exam. As the governing licensing board in your respective state likely has a list of laws, rules, and statutes pertaining to the practice of Marriage and Family Therapy, know that these vary across the nation and will not be measured on the National Exam. Instead, the exam will call for a working knowledge of the AAMFT Code of Ethics, which may be found at **www.aamft.org**.

A notable addition to the AAMFT Code of Ethics, as of January first, 2015, was the addition of guidelines for providing technology-based therapy (i.e. online therapy, telephone therapy etc.). Familiarize yourself with the recommendations offered from AAMFT along with the rest of the primary principles of our profession's Code of Ethics.

Keep in mind: You can memorize the AAMFT Code of Ethics in its entirety, but this *knowledge base* will not necessarily prepare you to work through the complex case vignettes that the exam will present. The exam will measure your capacity to *apply* the AAMFT Code of Ethics to challenging case scenarios. When it comes to this domain, there is no better means of preparation than *Field Experience, Clinical Supervision,* and *Clinical Case Consultation.* Keep this in mind as you consider whether or not you want to take the National Exam fresh out of graduate school or invest in your professional development.

Some tips to keep in mind pertain to questions that would require knowledge of local state laws as applied to the case scenario. For instance, if the question involves an adolescent client wanting to consent for his or her own mental health services without parental knowledge, know that states vary on how to best navigate such a situation. As so, the *next best step* for a Marital & Family Therapist would be to refer to the local state laws and statutes regarding this legal matter. If your state allows 16-year-olds to consent for their own treatment, and that is provided as a potential correct answer, remember that the law does not generalize across the country, and in the nature of this exam, defer to referring to the local state laws in which the Marital & Family Therapist is licensed.

Refer to the AMFTRB website, **www.amftrb.org** for a breakdown of what is expected of you for **Domain 6.** Within will provide some detailed expectations of how to conduct ethical, legal, and professional standards. If you find yourself struggling with the test questions pertaining to ethics, talk things over with your clinical supervisor or refer to the book *User's Guide to the AAMFT Code of Ethics,* written and published by the American Association for Marriage and Family Therapy (2013). This text will walk you through real-life client scenarios while outlining what to consider when navigating through ethical dilemmas.

> *****Note:** Use the following pages to organize your notes as you prepare for **Domain 6.** As rich client scenarios come up in consultation or supervision, jot them down! Best Prep? **Practicum and post-graduate field experience.**

Notes on Ethics

Notes on Ethics

Notes on Ethics

Notes on Ethics

Notes on Ethics

Health Insurance Portability & Accountability Act (HIPAA)

The National Exam will measure your working knowledge of maintaining compliance with the Health Insurance Portability and Accountability Act (HIPAA). This is a federal mandate that transcends state bylaws applying to each applicant regardless of his or her state-governing board. HIPAA guidelines apply to any mental health provider that works in a clinic or practice setting where health insurance records are submitted and shared to third parties (i.e. health insurance companies). Even if you work exclusively from a fee-for-service basis, if another provider bills insurance electronically, all providers must adhere to HIPAA guidelines.

When maintaining a client's right to privacy and confidentiality, know how to navigate the following situations:

- Who has the right to access the client's file?
- When is it appropriate to share the mental healthcare treatment of a client with others?
- What may the therapists maintain private from the client that is in his or her file?
- Who has right to receive notice of therapy services being rendered to a particular client?
- When is a Release of Information required, and when is it not?
- Does a subpoena from an attorney require therapist disclosure and/or release of the client file?
- Does a court order from a judge require a therapist's disclosure and release of the client file?
- What rights do minors have regarding healthcare privacy?

HIPAA will become common practice as your near the completion of your required supervision hours for licensure, making this yet another knowledge domain that will come naturally on the exam if you allow yourself to first focus on professional development.

For instance, when reading through the questions above, did you know off hand that a therapist has the right to decline a client access to his or her therapy progress notes along with anything else in the file that the therapist deems as being potentially harmful to the client? If you did, your agency has done a nice job of preparing you to practice in a HIPAA-Compliant manner. If not, no problem. Review the HIPAA guidelines for Mental Health Professionals.

Defer to the U.S. Department of Health and Human Services (**www.hhs.gov**) for a thorough review of HIPAA, particularly the PDF document directly related to HIPAA in Mental Health.

Note: http://www.hhs.gov/ocr/privacy/hipaa/understanding/special/mhguidance.html
Note: Use the following pages to organize your notes as you prepare for the knowledge domains covering HIPAA. As rich client scenarios come up in consultation or supervision, jot them down! For instance, as your colleague runs down his client, Peggy Sanders, shouting that she forgot her antidepressant medication in his office, know that it's a HIPAA No-No! Best Prep? **Practicum and Post-Graduate Experience!**

Notes on HIPAA

Notes on HIPAA

Notes on HIPAA

Managing Crisis Situations

Crisis Intervention is a new Domain (5) on the National Licensing Exam. This Domain will measure an applicant's capacity to:

- Assess the severity of a crisis situation and determine what immediate interventions are needed, including:
  - The presence of suicidal harm
  - Risk of violence to client *from* others
  - Client's potential for self-destructive and/or injurious behaviors toward self and/or others

- Understand your role as a professional in legal matters, including:
  - Court-ordered cases
  - Testimony
  - Expert witness
  - Custody hearing

Some things to keep in mind as you prepare for this Domain. When a client presents themselves as suicidal, the *next best step* will *always* be to perform a formal suicide assessment. Suicide assessments are typically brief in nature and provide a concrete road map for appropriate next steps. Having them documented and filed will also help protect you against any potential liability. A crisis assessment should include the role of the client's trauma history, cultural and other contextual factors, and a list of referrals to any potentially helpful resources during the client's time of need. The intervention should be collaborative and leave the client with an identified plan of how to maintain prevention of harm to themselves or others into the future. It may then be appropriate to develop a new therapy goal that has the client develop skills to independently manage his or her own crisis situations that may arise in the future.

Remember, in crisis situations, clients still have rights to privacy and confidentiality. Making a *mandated report* or practicing your *duty to warn* in any situation outside of what is necessary and justified by law will make you liable for breaching confidentiality.

For instance, to make a mandated report regarding a client's suicidal ideation *requires* the presence of a *plan* and *intent*. Clients need to feel comfortable in expressing their feelings of suicidal ideation as it is often a symptom to be worked through in various treatment contexts. If there is mistrust that the therapist will inaccurately file a mandated report, it could prevent the client from being open and honest about experiences vital to the therapeutic healing process.

Also, be mindful that the *duty to warn* act—a law coming out of the landmark case of *Tarasoff vs. Regents* in **1974**—varies from state to state. In the interest of the National Licensing Exam, it would always be appropriate for a Marital & Family Therapist to consult with his or her local state bylaws when in a situation suggesting the potential to practice the *duty to warn*. In any situation, there must *always* be evidence of an *imminent* risk-of-harm to an identified individual or group of individuals. If the potential of death is not *imminent*—such as, the intentional spreading of HIV—than the practitioner is not protected to break confidentiality under this law.

> ***Note:** Use the following pages to organize your notes as you prepare for **Domain 5.** As rich client scenarios come up in consultation or supervision, jot them down! Best Prep? **Clinical practicum and post-graduate field experience.**

Notes on Managing Crisis Situations

Notes on Managing Crisis Situations

Notes on Managing Crisis Situations

Family Violence & Physical Abuse +
Chemical Abuse

A consensus has yet to be reached regarding intervention with partner violence in family therapy. The traditional model suggested splitting the two into individual therapies (the man in a group with other violent men and the woman in a support group for other victims of abuse). This was the result of the Feminist critiques on the current state of family therapy—as detailed in the previous section on Feminist Family Therapy—which reinforced a "blame-the-victim" mentality. As this shift provided support for the victim, it pathologizes the male to the fullest extent.

In the later 90s, Virginia **Goldner** (2004) and Gillian **Walker** integrated the concept of separate treatment programs *with* conjoint couple therapy. They maintained the Feminist perspective that violence is the responsibility of the man, continuing to have men taking responsibility for their violent behaviors a primary goal. Along with this, the two introduced the benefits of conjoint couple therapy as being part of the process once the violence has stopped. This dynamic addresses that although a woman is *not* equally responsible for her partner's violent behaviors, that the partners are both equally stuck in a process of interaction that must change (Goldner, 2004).

If the abuse is currently ongoing, conjoint couple therapy would serve as an inappropriate intervention and other resources must be sought until the abuse discontinues. At that point, conjoint couple therapy can be not only appropriate but highly beneficial in an effort to maintain the discontinuation of the abuse into the future (Goldner, 2004).

Abuse and Children

> At all costs, protect the child! Know when to make a mandated report and how to assess for the potential of abuse (acting timid, reactive flinching, defensiveness, acting out aggressively in inappropriate contexts—particularly if it is in response to a trigger).

Drug and Substance Abuse

Always be sure not to overlook the role of drug or substance abuse. If the vignette suggests that drug or alcohol abuse is currently an ongoing problem, it would be appropriate to refer the individual to receive drug and alcohol treatment. Family Therapy has been empirically endorsed as an effective treatment modality for individuals (adolescents *and* adults) experiencing chemical dependency/abuse, particularly *Family Focused Therapy*—as a supplemental and concurrent approach to the individual's chemical-dependency treatment.

Research Trends & Findings

Many of my colleagues identified the questions pertaining to research trends and findings as being the most challenging on the exam. Much of this has to do with the fluid and ever-evolving nature of our field, as we are fortunate to have a wealth of passionate and prolific researchers continually evolving our empirically-supported knowledge base of what is actually working in clinical practice (evidence-based practices) and identifying the trends our families are experiencing in society. It will be important to know of the many **evidence-based practices** of family therapy in relation to particular diagnoses and client contexts.

Multi-Dimensional Family Therapy

An evidence-based family therapy model found to be effective in treating *adolescent substance abuse* (Liddle, 2010).

Family-Based Interventions

Carr (2000) conducted an exhaustive literature of controlled trials measuring the effectiveness of family-based interventions. The review found family therapy to be an effective treatment for the following disorders of **childhood and adolescence:**

- Oppositional-Defiant Disorder
- Aggressive Behaviors
- AD-HD
- Conduct Disorder
- Delinquency
- Substance Abuse
- Anxiety
- Depression

Parent-Child Interaction Therapy (PCIT)

Chaffin, Funderburk, Bard, Valle, and Gurwitch (2011) found Parent-Child Interaction Therapy to reduce the recidivism of child abuse in families over time.

Adult Disorders

Depression

A similar meta-analysis conducted by Barbato and D'Avanzo (2008) found couples therapy to be *as effective* as individual therapy in the treatment of individual depression. Similarly, their research also endorsed that couples therapy is more effective in treating relational distress (a risk factor for adult depression) than individual therapy.

Substance Abuse

O'Farrell and Fals-Stewart (2003) performed a meta-analysis concluding that various approaches to Marital and Family Therapy benefit individuals struggling with chronic chemical use as well as their families. As Family Therapy is not intended to be used as the approach to treat and cure the addiction, it was endorsed as an effective concurrent, supplemental approach to an individual's chemical-dependency treatment.

Major Mental Illness (SPMI)

As discussed earlier in this manual, *Psychoeducational Approaches* to family therapy have been found to be effective in helping families cope with the stressors associated with serious and persistent mental illness. Remember, Family Therapy is not an appropriate intervention in attempting to *heal* or *cure* a major mental illness, but is highly appropriate in helping the individual and his or her family members to learn about the nature of the illness and effective ways of coping and managing.

Couple Conflict

Emotionally Focused Couples Therapy (EFT) has earned empirical support documenting its effectiveness with couples experiencing distress, and that changes made in therapy are stable over time (Johnson, 2004).

Divorcing and Step Families

There are several articles documenting the effectiveness of using family therapy as an intervention when families are going through transitions of divorce and creating step-families.

There you have some nuts and bolts of the foundational support earned by the field of marriage and family therapy. Spend some time exploring some other evidence-based practices earning credibility, as the AMFTRB continually updates questions on the exam with new research findings and trends. Because it would be out of reach to keep editions of this manual up to date with all new research findings, remain knowledgeable of the current research trends in the following areas of family functioning:

Divorce: The impact it has on children in the early phase, middle-phase, and later phase.

LGBT-Q: The number of families with parents or children identifying with the LGBT-Q community.

Family Life Cycle: Stay up to date on all relevant research pertaining to the family life cycle.

Adoption: Implications for effective treatments and current trends in adjustment.

Evidence-Based Practices: New practice orientations that are proving themselves either effective or ineffective as far as evidence-based outcomes.

Research Methods & Techniques

The national exam is starting to measure your ability to understand basic methods of research and analyzing statistics. This likely reflects AAMFT's push toward establishing evidence-based practices as well as filling the literature with relevant research findings. I won't go into too much detail here, but will provide a basic review of primary terms and concepts. If you are looking for more depth, I encourage you to access the free e-textbook by Anol Bhattacherjee at: http://scholarcommons.usf.edu/cgi/viewcontent.cgi?article=1002&context=oa_textbooks.

And while you are at it, be sure to shoot her an email (listed in the e-textbook) in thanks of this remarkably generous contribution to our field.

Introduction to Research

Ultimately, research (i.e., science) aims to create and establish the very knowledge that entails our studies. In the interest of Family Science (the comprehensive discipline to which family therapy falls within), research plays a specific role. For example, research allows our profession to establish *evidence-based practices,* meaning, proof that what we are doing actually works. That our therapy provides symptom relief to particularly common struggles that bring both individuals and relational groups to therapy. Why is this so important? Because this is what helps us to get paid. Need any more rationale than that? Insurance companies will continue to acknowledge our license as a valid healthcare service so long as we are producing findings that endorse our methods are not only effective, but effective in the short-term. That means insurance companies will end up paying us less as we relieve their consumers of mental health ailments in a relatively brief period of time.

Beyond *evidence-based practices,* research helps us to understand how individuals and families are evolving over time. Research provides us with an understanding of what factors contribute to relational conflict, and what interventions can be done to support families in experiencing more satisfaction. Research, in many ways, ties the link between theory and practice. Undoubtedly, it plays a significant part in maintaining our profession's identity and relevancy within the highly competitive market of therapy and counseling. As these brief paragraphs help to establish a basic understanding of the relationship between family therapy and research, let's review some basic concepts.

Scientific Research

The two pillars of scientific research include the *theoretical level* and the *empirical level*. As the *theoretical level* is largely conceptual and somewhat abstract in nature (i.e., how we *think* about and *make sense of* various phenomenon and the relational/interactional dynamics between (i.e., observation based), the *empirical level* then tests the theoretical hypotheses to determine how well they reflect observations of reality (i.e., method/measurement based; Bhattacherjee, 2012). If the empirical findings align with the initial theory, the theory is refined and strengthened accordingly as it is now supported by data. If the empirical findings contradict the theoretical hypothesis, then the theory needs to change in ways that better reflect the empirical findings. Over time, the back-and-forth between theory and empiricism create a sustainable body of knowledge. Get it? I hope so. Let's move on to defining some key terms and definitions...

Key Terms and Definitions (Bhattacherjee, 2012)

Inductive Research: When researchers aim to infer theoretical concepts and patterns from observed data (i.e., *theory-building research*).

Deductive Research: When the researchers aim to test concepts and patterns informed by theory using new empirical data (i.e., *theory-testing research*).

The Scientific Method: The standardized set of techniques that build scientific knowledge by informing how researchers make valid observations, interpret results, and generalize results (Bhattacherjee, 2012). The scientific method must meet the following four characteristics:

Replicability: If the same study is repeated by another team of researchers, the experiment should yield identical, or nearly identical results as the initial study.

Precision: Moving theoretical concepts from an abstract concept to a precise and operational definition, allowing for other researchers to measure the same terms in similar ways.

Falsifiability: Essentially, all theories must be discussed in ways that clearly identify a route for the theory to be disproven, or, falsified. For example, Bhattacherjee (2012) uses Freud's theory on psychoanalysis as an example of a practice that cannot be considered a theory of science given that the operating mechanics of Freud's definition of the unconscious cannot be proven, and therefore, cannot be disproven.

Parsimony: In the event that data produces multiple explanations for the same phenomenon, researchers must always accept and prioritize the least complex and most logically economical explanation.

Relative to Family Science, the scientific method actualizes through a variety of methods, tools, and techniques. Work through defining the following terms in preparation for the exam using Bhattacherjee's (2012) free resource or your materials from graduate school…

Construct:

Descriptive Research:

Epistemology:

Exploratory Research:

Ontology:

Operational Definitions:

Operationalization: Sampling:

Unit of Analysis:

Variable:

Key Attributes of a Research Design

The quality of research designs can be defined in terms of four key design attributes: internal validity, external validity, construct validity, and statistical conclusion validity (Bhattacherjee, 2012).

Internal Validity:

External Validity:

Construct Validity:

Statistical Conclusion Validity:

Types of Research Methods/Designs

Experimental Studies:

Field Surveys:

Secondary Data Analysis:

Case Research (Case Studies):

Focus Group Research:

Ethnography:

Survey Research:

Interview Survey:

Qualitative Analysis:

Quantitative Analysis:

Grounded Theory:

Terms from Statistics

Mean:

Median:

Mode:

Range:

Standard Deviation:

Correlation:

Inter-Rater Reliability:

Test-Retest Reliability:

Split-Half Reliability:

Internal Consistency Reliability:

Validity:

Ordinal Scales:

Interval Scales:

Nominal Scales:

Likert Scale:

Notes on Research Methods & Strategies

DSM-V

The new format of AMFTRB's National Exam has been updated to recognize changes in the DSM-V. Much like the other general concepts measured on the exam, there will likely only be a few questions related to your capacity to effectively diagnose individuals based upon presenting symptoms. Remember, we are systemically trained in ways that do not align with individual pathology, but the realities of managed care force us to adhere to individual diagnosis in order for insurance carriers to reimburse our services. As so, the National Exam will expect you to recognize symptoms of particular diagnoses as well as differentiate between similar diagnoses falling under the same category (e.g., Acute Stress Disorder vs. Posttraumatic Stress Disorder). It is up to you how much effort you choose to invest in your review of the DSM-V. Certain employers will expect a general competence in assessment and diagnosis, whereas others may adhere to the "everybody has an adjustment disorder" model. Unfortunately, this exam will not measure your finely tuned skills in justifying the diagnosis of an adjustment disorder with any given client complaint (which is a shame, as this is a very useful skill to have out in the field when practicing relational therapy).

If you don't have a DSM-V, and don't see yourself using it into the future, ask a supervisor or professor for a copy of the DSM-IV that they are currently using as a doorstop. To supplement the DSM-IV, use the following link to a free, on-line PDF document that nicely outlines the major changes in the DSM-V. For those of you more familiar with the DSM-V, this link will be helpful in guiding your review.

http://www.psych.uic.edu/docassist/changes-from-dsm-iv-tr--to-dsm-51.pdf

You will be best prepared for the questions on the exam informed by the DSM-V through establishing a working memory of the primary diagnostic categories, the various diagnoses within, and the particulars differentiating them from one another. It will be important to be aware of the significant changes from the DSM-IV to the DSM-V, as an update in the manual has significant implications for our profession's clinical practice.

The following link is another valuable resource for reviewing major changes in the DSM-V and is the other recommended resource for completing this section of your Independent Study Guide.

http://www.psychiatry.org/psychiatrists/practice/dsm/dsm-5

Remember, this focuses on the major changes and updates regarding the development of DSM-V, which informs the exam. It will still be worthwhile to review the diagnostic categories that went unchanged.

Conceptual Changes in DSM-V

Cultural Concepts

DSM-V and Diagnoses for Children

Integrated (Dimensional) Assessment Processes

Mixed Features Specifier

Changes in Diagnoses/New Diagnoses

Attention Deficit/Hyperactivity Disorder (ADHD)

Autism Spectrum Disorder

Conduct Disorder

Disruptive Mood Dysregulation Disorder

Eating Disorders

Gender Dysphoria

Intellectual Disability

Internet Gaming Disorder

Major Depressive Disorders and the Bereavement Exclusion

Mild Neurocognitive Disorder

Mild Neurocognitive Disorder

Obsessive-Compulsive and Related Disorders

Paraphilic Disorders

Personality Disorder

Posttraumatic Stress Disorder

Schizophrenia

Sleep-Wake Disorders

Specific Learning Disorder

Social Communication Disorder

Somatic Symptoms Disorder

Substance-Related and Addictive Disorders

Changes in Diagnostic Categories

Neurodevelopmental Disorders

Schizophrenia Spectrum & Other Psychotic Disorders

Bipolar and Related Disorders

Depressive Disorders

Anxiety Disorders

Obsessive-Compulsive and Related Disorders

Trauma- and Stress-Related Disorders

Dissociative Disorders

Somatic Symptom and Related Disorders

Feeding and Eating Disorders

Sleep-Wake Disorders

Notes on DSM-V

Notes on DSM-V

Part V

The Practice Exam

Practice Exam Questions

Now that you have reviewed the major theories, concepts, and clinical considerations involving the practice of Marital & Family Therapy, we will shift from retention to application. This is not meant to serve as a practice exam technically speaking, which would be an evaluative measure of your preparedness for the actual exam. This will serve as a learning experience as you work toward improving your preparedness for the actual exam. After providing your best answer to each question, the following segment will deconstruct the question and rationalize why the right answer was correct and why the rest were either wrong or less correct. Once you feel comfortable with the nature of the exam questions, it will be a good time to take your first practice test at **www.amftrb.org.** It will not show you which answers you got wrong, or provide the correct responses, but it will give you a score for each domain that the exam measures and an overall score that will demonstrate your preparedness. Aim for an 80% or better, but know that anything beyond a 75% means you are in good shape. Anything beyond a 70% means you are right where you need to be, but still a little too close for comfort. Below 70%? Keep reviewing this manual, consider other study approaches, or take a break from the exam and focus on growing as a therapist out in the field.

As you navigate these test questions keep in mind much of what was covered in Part I of this manual—particularly, the *Universal Family Therapist* and maintaining a *Systemic Perspective.* Also, always remain mindful of AAMFT's Code of Ethics as you deconstruct each question and potential answers. Be sure to pay attention to *qualifiers* as well as to *rule out* as many obvious incorrect answers as you can right off the bat.

If you find yourself frustrated with getting wrong answers, that is okay! That's what this portion of the study guide is about—working out your frustration now, better preparing you for the actual exam. Do not get caught up in your score of these questions, as they will not measure your readiness to pass the exam. Instead, use this as an opportunity to familiarize yourself with the language and expectations of what the exam will measure, preparing you to approach your AMFTRB practice exam and the actual exam with confidence.

Let's begin…

1. A family you have been working with report to you that their son's Case Manager is insisting that the child begin In-Home Family Skills Therapy to better help manage and regulate his behaviors. As their Family Therapist, you believe that the family is already getting their family needs met with outpatient therapy, and that redundant services may not benefit—and even, potentially harm—the son. What would be the best next step as a Family Therapist?
   a. Defer to your client's Case Manager as their specialty is in finding resources to meet the needs of their clients.
   b. Consult with the Case Manager in an effort to reach a collaborative decision between the two professionals involved in the case.
   c. Act within the best interests of your client.
   d. Provide your clinical opinion to the parents and let them decide which recommendation sounds more appropriate.

2. At the onset of a family intake interview, the mother of the family informs you that the husband decided to work late and will not be attending the first session. As a Family Therapist, you would be least likely to:
   a. Move along with the intake interview as scheduled and contact the father prior to the next meeting to let him know what was discussed, encouraging his future participation.
   b. Move along with the intake interview as scheduled but establish a rule that no one can talk about Dad given his absence in an effort to maintain neutrality.
   c. Inform the family that the intake interview must be rescheduled for a time that Dad can be present and send them home for the evening.
   d. Move along with the intake interview and assess for any potential metaphoric meaning behind Dad's absence.

3. During a family intake interview, the mother quickly begins to detail the issues of each member of the family and how the therapist should help them to change their "disappointing qualities." The rest of the family sat quietly as Mom continued. A Marital & Family Therapist would be least likely to:
   a. Validate Mom's frustrations through the use of reflective language and empathic understanding.
   b. Ask Dad how he thinks his son experienced and interpreted Mom's disclosures.
   c. Assess that Mom is reacting to Dad's authority over the family.
   d. Ask Mom to describe in greater detail how she suggests that the Family Therapist can best go about changing the behavior of everyone else in the family.

4. When meeting with a couple that has been in ongoing therapy, the husband begins processing in moderate frustration that his wife is too emotional, and that it is exhausting for him to keep up with her fluctuating moods and constant reactivity. He declares that everything in their relationship would be fine if she were only less emotional. The Family Therapist suggests that he gets his wife medicated, describing that a strong enough prescription has the potential to result in her experiencing virtually no range of affect what so ever. This intervention can be described as:
   a. An effective use of positioning.
   b. Unethical, as recommending prescription medication is beyond the scope of a Family Therapist's competency and training.
   c. A paradoxical intervention.
   d. The therapist intentionally aligning with the husband in an attempt to detriangulate the couple system.

5. When working with a couple in the earlier phases of treatment, the therapist recognizes that there is a profound difficulty for them to engage in non-reactive dialogue with one another. The Marital & Family Therapist instructs the couple that for the rest of the session, they may only talk directly to the therapist, and never directly to one another. This intervention best fits with the following theory of family therapy:
   a. Emotionally Focused Couple Therapy
   b. Haley & Madanes's Strategic Family Therapy
   c. Bowen's Multigenerational Family Therapy
   d. Contextual Family Therapy

6. When working with a family, the 20-year-old son reports that he has recently begun hearing voices inside of his head throughout the day, and cannot identify any triggers or make them stop. What would be the next best step for the Marital & Family Therapist to take?
   a. Diagnose the client with Schizophrenia.
   b. Refer the client for a psychological/neuropsychological evaluation.
   c. Instruct the client to schedule an appointment with his primary Physician so he can prescribe him anti-psychotic medication.
   d. Refer the client for a psychological/neuropsychological evaluation, and stop meeting with the family until it is completed to avoid any potential liability.

7. When working with a family, the 16-year-old son reports that he has recently begun hearing voices inside of his head throughout the day, and cannot identify any triggers or make them stop. You refer the client for a psychological/neuropsychological evaluation, which determines that the client has Schizophrenia. What would be the next best step for the Marital & Family Therapist to take?
    a. Discontinue working with the family and provide them with three referrals for Psychoeducation-Based Family Therapy.
    b. Discontinue working with the family due to not being trained to work with schizophrenia and provide them with three referrals to other mental health agencies in the area.
    c. Disregard the diagnosis as schizophrenia is most likely to onset when males are in their early 20s.
    d. Continue working with the family and revise the treatment plan to account for symptoms of schizophrenia.

8. You are a therapist trained in MRI Systemic Therapy and working out of the MRI Brief Therapy Center. After the 10th session of seeing a family, the presenting problem has yet to be resolved. A MRI Systemic Therapist would be most likely to:
    a. Consult with a team on why the family remains resistant to change.
    b. Discontinue therapy.
    c. Continue to restrain the progress of change.
    d. Prescribe the symptom.

9. A 16-year-old female client schedules an intake with you. Upon arrival, the adolescent shows up without a parent and discloses that she wishes to keep her involvement in therapy confidential from her parents, but wishes to use their family insurance plan. As a Marital & Family Therapist, the next best step would be to:
    a. Proceed with the intake given that the client is old enough to consent for her own medical treatment.
    b. Insist that the client inform her parents of treatment if she wishes to be seen.
    c. Agree to see the minor client privately while explaining to her the limits of privacy and confidentiality while using her parents' insurance plan.
    d. Refer to laws and regulations regarding minor consent for medical treatment within the State jurisdiction in which you are licensed.

10. A Master's Level Licensed Marriage & Family Therapist, Virginia Greenberg, is about to present on a topic in which she specializes in to a group of other mental health professionals. As a member of the organization that hosts the event announces her to the audience, he identifies her as Dr. Greenberg. As a Marital & Family Therapist, the next best step would be to:
    a. Not acknowledge the error of the introduction and proceed with the presentation.
    b. Before beginning the presentation, correct the error in your credentials to the audience at large.
    c. Make a mental note to let the individual who introduced you as Dr. Greenberg that you have not received a Doctorate Degree after your presentation.
    d. Begin the presentation just as you have prepared to do so to ensure the quality of instruction, and remember to correct the error to the audience prior to the conclusion of the presentation.

11. A family you have been working with for just two sessions comes in reporting significant changes they have noticed regarding the presenting problem. As a MRI Systemic therapist, you may respond to the family by:
    a. Reinforcing their growth and asking them to reflect upon what has been working for them.
    b. Ask them to scale how satisfied they are with the progress in relation to desired goals.
    c. Continue to align with the parental system to establish healthier relationships and boundaries.
    d. Instruct the family to slow down and caution them about changing too fast.

12. When working with a first-generation Asian-American family who is coming to therapy reporting a lack of connection from their adolescent son, a Caucasian Marital & Family Therapist would be mostly aware of:
    a. Differences in Western and Eastern views of mental illness.
    b. The triangle existing between the son and his two parents.
    c. The therapist's own comfort around working with clients of a different culture.
    d. The importance of creating a cultural-genogram.

13. You are working with a 16-year-old adolescent client. The parents request a copy of the client's file for them to keep in their own personal records. According to HIPAA, as a Marital & Family Therapist, you have the right to:
    a. Decline the parents access to the file since it is individual therapy for their daughter.
    b. Inform the client that you had to give her parents a copy of her record at their request due to them consenting to and paying for the treatment.
    c. Make a copy of the record as requested but withhold progress notes and black out any information contained in the file that you feel would be harmful to the client if another party were to read it.
    d. Inform the parents that their daughter must first provide written consent prior to you allowing access to the file.

14. A couple comes to therapy reporting a lack of physical intimacy and ongoing conflict. When the couple is asked about a history of physical abuse, the male discloses that he will at times become physically violent toward his partner, disclosing episodes of holding her against a wall, open-hand slapping her face, and forcefully pushing her to the ground. The male reported that the most recent episode was just last evening. The Family Therapist's best approach with this couple would be to:
    a. Assess for any history of physical violence in both partners' family of origin.
    b. Because the abuse is currently ongoing, stop the assessment and shift focus to deescalation techniques and anger-management skills to prevent the recurrence of physical abuse.
    c. Inform the couple that the male must engage in an anger-management program and the female must engage in a victim of domestic abuse program if they wish to continue couple therapy.
    d. Inform the couple that they both must engage in programming specific to domestic violence until the violence is no longer occurring before they can be seen for couple therapy.

15. When working with an adult client experiencing severe depression, your client discloses that they have been experiencing thoughts of suicidal ideation for the past several days. The best next step for the Marital & Family Therapist would be to:
    a. Explore the thoughts and feelings surrounding the suicidal ideation.
    b. Remind the client that you are a mandated reporter and that they must arrange transportation to a hospital for an emergency psychiatric evaluation or you will be bound to call 911.
    c. Perform a formal suicide assessment.
    d. Validate the client's pain and assure them that the thoughts will pass after engaging in an effective coping skill strategy.

16. A Marital & Family Therapist had an intake session scheduled with a notably wealthy and well-known individual. Upon intake, the client insists that he pay the therapist three times the top rate on the sliding fee scale. The Therapist accepts the client's request for payment. This therapist is:
    a. Ethical because they are respecting the wishes of their client in a critical joining phase of therapy.
    b. Ethical because it was at the request of the client, thereby not meeting criteria of exploitation.
    c. Unethical.
    d. Unethical because he is credentialed on the insurance panel that the client has, making it within the best interests of the client to use his insurance for reimbursement of treatment.

17. A client requests a copy of each session note documented by the therapist. According to HIPAA, the therapist should:
    a. Provide the client copies of his or her session notes as stated by law.
    b. Provide the client copies of his or her session notes and require the client to pay for appropriate fees associated with the costs to copy a client file.
    c. Decline the client access to his or her progress notes.
    d. Consider whether or not granting the client access to his or her progress notes has the potential to cause any harm.

18. A therapist has been seeing a client family for 14 weeks, and there appeared to be a healthy relationship and good signs of engagement and progress, although treatment goals have yet to be fully met. Come week 15, the family does not show up and calls the front desk to cancel any future appointments. A Symbolic-Experiential Therapist would interpret this event as:
    a. Bilateral Transference.
    b. A good sign that the family has experienced a flight toward health and no longer require therapy.
    c. Leaving therapy without a proper closing is a metaphor for continued emotional suppression.
    d. The need to call them and encourage their continued participation in therapy to ensure that treatment goals are met and progress can be maintained.

19. When performing a family therapy intake meeting, therapists often use a genogram as a primary assessment tool. A genogram provides rich information pertaining to the family system, including all of the following except:
   a. Presence of triangles.
   b. Conflict from past generations transmitting into current family system.
   c. The current presence of mental illness within the system.
   d. The prediction of future mental illness based on historical patterns.

20. A small town in Oklahoma was recently destroyed by a series of tornados. As some of the families struggled immensely and fell into a helpless despair, other families seemed to manage quite well and deeply engaged with their community. This phenomenon is an example of:
   a. Subjective-Resiliency
   b. Equipotentiality
   c. Macrosystemic Trauma
   d. Cultural Cohesion

21. A family is coming to therapy reporting that their 7th grade child has recently begun to withdrawal from the family and act out, no longer wanting to go on their weekly family Friday night outings or share in the details of her day every night at dinner. The parents are hoping that family therapy can get them their old daughter back. A Marital & Family Therapist would most likely interpret this dynamic as:
   a. The daughter has likely begun experimenting with drugs or alcohol.
   b. The daughter is the scapegoat for Mom and Dad to deny the problems within their marriage.
   c. The daughter has likely experienced a recent trauma around the time of the onset of these behaviors.
   d. The family system is failing to adjust to a new phase in the family life cycle.

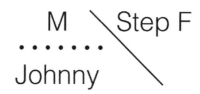

22. Upon intake with a family, a Structural Family Therapists creates a map of the family's hypothetical current structure. Based on the map shown above, a Structural Family Therapist would best interpret this as:
    a. Johnny is disengaged from his Mom due to her remarriage.
    b. Johnny is enmeshed with his Mom and unaccepting of her new husband.
    c. Mom, Step-Father, and Johnny are stuck in a triangle.
    d. Johnny's Mom has remarried.

23. A family you have been meeting with for 16 weeks has started to show some good progress. They are reporting that they have noticed a shift in how they communicate and connect, and are pleased that therapy has been effective. A Marital & Family Therapist should take which next step in treating this family?
    a. Tell the family to slow down and restrain their progress to change.
    b. Based on the positive results, invite the family to discharge at any time.
    c. Shift focus to maintaining the progress achieved as the family begins working toward discharge.
    d. Identify a new goal that they can start fresh with.

24. A Marital & Family Therapist is meeting with a couple for the third time. When the therapist checks in with the husband, he grumbles and says "Oh I'm doing great, I've been looking forward to another 55-minutes of getting ganged up on and chewed out, happy to be here!" Based on the husband's response, the therapist has made what mistake?
    a. Failed to have husband work through his "victim mentality" during the assessment phase of treatment.
    b. The therapist has not made a mistake and should be reluctant to enable the husband's sarcastic and rude behavior.
    c. Failed to establish a proper and balanced relationship with the husband.
    d. Failed to establish multidirectional partiality.

Questions 25-30 will be in relation to the following vignette:

The Beckers are a Caucasian, middle-class family pursuing therapy due to general family disconnection. Mom initiated the phone call stating that things are "out of control" and that "changes need to happen, and fast!" Mom further elaborated that she and her husband are very disconnected and have been for the past 11 years. She said he will work all day and come home to "decompress" in his workshop attached to the garage and spend most weekends with their two sons at various sporting activities and "guys-only outings." Mom reported that she and her husband have been sleeping in different bedrooms for the past three years. Mom said she will spend most days at her Mom's home—which is close in town—and as much time as she can with her daughter before she goes off to college in five months. Mom said she is very disconnected from her sons and her husband is very disconnected from his daughter. She reported the family being "split into two" and appeared quite desperate for change to occur. Mom requested that she, her husband, and her daughter come in as her two sons are refusing to attend family therapy.

25. A traditional Symbolic-Experiential Therapist would most likely respond to this referral by:
    a. Asking the family what a good time would be for them to come in as a means of joining via accommodating.
    b. Tell the mother that you will be happy to work with their family under the circumstances that the two sons come as well.
    c. Determine that the issue resides in the parental subsystem and recommend beginning with couple therapy.
    d. Agree to meeting with the family—whichever members care to come—for a maximum of 10 sessions.

26. Mom, Dad, and the daughter end up coming in for a family therapy session. After learning more about the problem, the therapist gives Dad the following directive: "Okay Dad, for the next week, every night when you get home from work, I want you to pull your car in the garage, walk right up to your bedroom, put your work clothes in the hamper, change into short/sweats and a t-shirt/sweatshirt, walk down to the kitchen, grab two beers, walk directly into your workshop, and stay there to decompress for no less than two hours, and no more than three hours. I am prescribing you to do just this, in the exact order, every single day, until we meet at this same time next week." This intervention can best be described as:
    a. Paradoxical intervention.
    b. Prescribing the symptom.
    c. Unethical as the therapist is promoting alcohol-use as a means of coping with relational distress.
    d. Unethical because the therapist may potentially cause harm to the clients by telling them to engage in the very unhealthy behaviors they are requesting to change.

27. The intervention used in question 26 would have most likely been done by:
    a. Milton Erickson
    b. Carl Whitaker
    c. Jay Haley
    d. Gregory Bateson

28. Mom, Dad, and the daughter show up for their third session. After the family describes their current situation in more depth, the therapist asks the daughter to leave the room, and instructs Mom and Dad to do the following: "This weekend, I am prescribing that the two of you arrange for a relative to come and watch the children, and without giving any great detail beyond the fact that you have a secret, discretely leave to go on a trip until Tuesday." This therapist was using the intervention referred to as:
    a. Instillation of Hope.
    b. Exoneration.
    c. Paradoxical Intervention.
    d. The invariant prescription.

29. The intervention used in question 28 would have most likely been done by:
    a. Luigi Boscollo
    b. Selvini Palazolli
    c. Gianfrano Cecchin
    d. Lynn Hoffman

30. After the eldest daughter had left for college, Mom and Dad reported an interest in continuing to work with you through Couples Therapy. After receiving consent from the rest of the family and renegotiating the terms of the therapeutic contract—now viewing the couple system as the primary client—therapy begins. In the third session, the father discloses that he has been hiding feelings of profound sadness, loss of interest in recreation, and has struggled with insomnia. He attributes many of these struggles to the distance between he and his wife. As a Family Therapist, the next best step would be to:
    a. Continue couple therapy to help relieve Dad's depression.
    b. Refer Dad to individual therapy that is more tailored to individuals with depressive disorders, and resume couple therapy once the depression is better managed.
    c. Discontinue therapy and refer Dad to arrange a meeting with his Primary Physician to prescribe medication.
    d. Refer Dad to individual therapy that is more tailored to individuals with depressive disorders while continuing to provide couple therapy.

31. I am going to pass the National Licensing Exam.
    a. True.
    b. True.
    c. True.
    d. True.

Practice Exam Answers

Now, go through and score your answers. Be sure to recognize the *qualifiers* in both **bold** and/or italics in the question body and the rationale in *italics* after each potential answer. Correct answer is **bolded.** Again, if you find yourself frustrated, that's what this exercise was meant for! Accept your frustration as a natural experience and make room to learn from the exercise.

1.   A family you have been working with report to you that their son's Case Manager is insisting that the child begin In-Home Family Skills Therapy to better help manage and regulate his behaviors at home. As their Family Therapist, you believe that the family is already getting their family needs met with outpatient therapy, and that redundant services may not benefit—and even, potentially harm—the son. What would be the **BEST next step** as a Family Therapist?
   a.   Defer to your client's Case Manager as their specialty is in finding resources to meet the needs of their clients. *The Case Manager may not be aware that the family is already receiving family therapy, and it is always best practice to coordinate care with all professionals involved when making treatment decisions.*
   b.   **Consult with the Case Manager in an effort to reach a collaborative decision between the two professionals involved in the case.** *This would be best practice given the options as it resolves the issue in answer A by consulting with the Case Manager and is more specific than answer C.*
   c.   Act within the best interests of your client. *This is an appropriate response, but is very vague and not AS CORRECT as answer B.*
   d.   Provide your clinical opinion to the parents and let them decide which recommendation sounds more appropriate. *As a professional, it is ethical to coordinate care. The family may not be able to articulate the clinical reasoning behind the inappropriateness of dual-services to the Case Manager as the therapist would be.*

2. At the onset of a family intake interview, the mother of the family informs you that the husband decided to work late and will not be attending the first session. As a Family Therapist, you would be *least* likely to:
   a. Move along with the intake interview as scheduled and contact the father prior to the next meeting to let him know what was discussed, encouraging his future participation. *It would be appropriate to make this decision.*
   b. **Move along with the intake interview as scheduled but establish a rule that no one can talk about Dad given his absence in an effort to maintain neutrality.** *It would not be a systemic assessment if the family was not able to discuss the role that a vital member plays in its functioning. This contradicts systems theory. Do not get tempted by the statement regarding maintaining neutrality. There are ways in which you could still meet with the family and maintaining neutrality moving forward.*
   c. Inform the family that the intake interview must be rescheduled for a time that Dad can be present and send them home for the evening. *It would be appropriate to make this decision, particularly if you are practicing from an experiential perspective.*
   d. Move along with the intake interview and assess for any potential metaphoric meaning behind Dad's absence. *This would also be an appropriate decision.*

3. During a family intake interview, the mother quickly begins to detail the issues of each member of the family and how the therapist should help them to change their "disappointing qualities." The rest of the family sat quietly as Mom continued. A Marital & Family Therapist would be *least* likely to:
   a. Validate Mom's frustrations through the use of reflective language and empathic understanding. *This would be very appropriate for a family therapist to do.*
   b. Ask Dad how he thinks his son experienced and interpreted Mom's disclosures. *This would be an example of circular questions via the Milan Systemic School.*
   c. **Assess that Mom is reacting to Dad's authority over the family.** *Based on the information provided, it suggests Dad has been passive throughout the interview. There is no evidence that would suggest Dad as having any authority over the family.*
   d. Ask Mom to describe in greater detail how she suggests that the Family Therapist can best go about changing the behavior of everyone else in the family. *This could be an appropriate intervention, and based on the delivery, could come off as either "collaborative" or "MRI Systemic."*

4. When meeting with a couple that has been in ongoing therapy, the husband begins processing in moderate frustration that his wife is too emotional, and that it is exhausting for him to keep up with her fluctuating moods and constant reactivity. He declares that everything in their relationship would be fine if she were only less emotional. The Family Therapist suggests that he gets his wife medicated, describing that a strong enough prescription has the potential to result in her experiencing virtually no range of affect what so ever. This intervention can be described as:

   a. **An effective use of positioning.** *This would be an appropriate intervention to use when practicing from a Strategic/MRI Systemic Orientation. It is pushing the husband deeper and deeper into the absurdity of his request. This is a fun one—I use it often when working with couples as this is a common complaint. Remember, positioning is most effective when there is a healthy therapeutic relationship.*

   b. Unethical, as recommending prescription medication is beyond the scope of a Family Therapist's competency and training. *It is not unethical for a Family Therapist to suggest that a client seek consultation with a Prescribing Physician.*

   c. A paradoxical intervention. *This answer is correct, but and A is more correct as it identifies the specific paradoxical intervention used. Positioning is described as an intervention that falls under the umbrella of paradoxical interventions.*

   d. The therapist intentionally aligning with the husband in an attempt to detriangulate the couple system. *Intentional alignment is not a method for detriangulating.*

5. When working with a couple in the earlier phases of treatment, the therapist recognizes that there is a profound difficulty for them to engage in non-reactive dialogue with one another. The Marital & Family Therapist instructs the couple that for the rest of the session, they may only talk directly to the therapist, and never directly to one another. This intervention **best fits** with the following theory of family therapy:

   a. Emotionally Focused Couple Therapy *This approach does focus on de-escalating the couple system, but does not identify with using this method in particular*

   b. Haley & Madanes's Strategic Family Therapy *Incorrect*

   c. **Bowen's Multigenerational Family Therapy** *A commonly used intervention by Bowen.*

   d. Contextual Family Therapy *Incorrect*

6. When working with a family, the 20-year-old son reports that he has recently begun hearing voices inside of his head throughout the day, and cannot identify any triggers or make them stop. What would be the ***next best step*** for the Marital & Family Therapist to take?

   a. Diagnose the client with Schizophrenia. *Technically, any Mental Health Provider can make this diagnosis, but it is best practice to have a psychological/neurological evaluation done when hypothesizing that a client may have a mental disorder of an organic nature. Differential diagnosis suggests other mental disorders that can account for the onset of auditory hallucinations, which a battery of assessments may better determine.*

   b. **Refer the client for a psychological/neuropsychological evaluation.** *This would be the next best step to either rule-in or rule-out schizophrenia or other mental disorders of an organic nature. The therapist will then make an informed decision based on the results of the evaluation, but the questions is specifically asking what the NEXT BEST STEP would be.*

   c. Instruct the client to schedule an appointment with his primary Physician so he can prescribe him anti-psychotic medication. *This is assuming that the client has schizophrenia or another organic mental disorder.*

   d. Refer the client for a psychological/neuropsychological evaluation, and stop meeting with the family until it is completed to avoid any potential liability. *This would be unethical and potentially viewed as client abandonment. There is no reason to suggest that the therapist should stop seeing the client family while the evaluation is conducted.*

7. When working with a family, the 16-year-old son reports that he has recently begun hearing voices inside of his head throughout the day, and cannot identify any triggers or make them stop. You refer the client for a psychological/neuropsychological evaluation, which determines that the client has Schizophrenia. What would be **the next best** step for the Marital & Family Therapist to take?

a. **Discontinue working with the family and provide them with three referrals for Psychoeducation-Based Family Therapy.** *The very diagnosis that fueled the development of family therapy was eventually deemed a disorder of organic nature, and as so, MFT's are encouraged to use Psychoeducation as the primary approach when dealing with Serious-and-Persistent-Mental-Illnesses (SPMI) such as schizophrenia*

b. Discontinue working with the family due to not being trained to work with schizophrenia and provide them with 3 referrals to other mental health agencies in the area. *Technically, you would be covering yourself ethically by taking these actions, but best practice would suggest providing them with a referral specific to Psychoeducation.*

c. Disregard the diagnosis as schizophrenia is most likely to onset when males are in their early 20s. *Although research suggests this as being true, it is still possible for schizophrenia to onset during adolescence—and in some documented cases, as early as the elementary years.*

d. Continue working with the family and revise the treatment plan to account for symptoms of schizophrenia. *As stated in answer A, MFT's are instructed to refer to Psychoeducation as the primary approach when working with schizophrenia. If this answer had stated, "knowing that you are trained in Psychoeducational Family Therapy in regard to schizophrenia, revise the treatment plan..." than it may have been the MOST right answer since you already have a relationship with the family and are competent to provide them with the necessary resources their situation demands.*

8. You are a therapist trained in MRI Systemic Therapy working out of the MRI Brief Therapy Center. After the 10th session of seeing a family, the presenting problem has yet to be resolved. A MRI Systemic Therapist would be **most likely to**:

a. Consult with a team on why the family remains resistant to change. *This is a part of MRI Brief Therapy, but would not occur after the 10th session and only during the earlier phases of treatment.*

b. **Discontinue therapy.** *Brief Therapies that are time-limited will disclose this to clients prior to treatment onset. It would be no surprise to the family that the therapist discontinued treatment as it was already discussed at intake.*

c. Continue to restrain the progress of change. *Again, another intervention used by this approach, but not at the 10th session.*

d. Prescribe the symptom. *Same rationale as discussed in answer C.*

9. A 16-year-old female client schedules an intake with you. Upon arrival, the adolescent shows up without a parent and discloses that she wishes to keep her involvement in therapy confidential from her parents, but wishes to use her family insurance plan. As a Marital & Family Therapist, ***the next best step*** would be to:

    a. Proceed with the intake given that the client is old enough to consent for her own medical treatment. *These laws are State-Driven and not bound by federal law. They will vary state-to-state. Remember, this is the NATIONAL EXAM, not the STATE LICENSING EXAM.*

    b. Insist that the client inform her parents of treatment if she wishes to be seen. *This would only be an appropriate response if the state in which the family therapist was practicing did not allow for minor clients to consent for their own mental health treatment.*

    c. Agree to see the minor client privately while explaining to her the limits of privacy and confidentiality while using her parents' insurance plan. *If the question read, "You are a Family Therapist practicing in the State of MN..." then this answer would be appropriate. However, the NATIONAL EXAM will not have any questions specific to State-Laws as they do not generalize.*

    d. **Refer to laws and regulations regarding minor consent for medical treatment within the State jurisdiction in which you are licensed.** *If any question relates to an ethical consideration that varies from state-to-state, this will be the likely answer. This is an issue that transcends Marriage and Family Therapy and governs Mental Health Professionals in general; as so, this will vary state-to-state.* **HOWEVER,** *if the question calls for an issue of ETHICS (e.g. dual relationships, exploiting clients) that is covered in the AAMFT Code of Ethics, answer these questions based off of what is delineated in the AAMFT Code of Ethics and NOT the Board of Marriage and Family Therapy for the State in which you will be licensed.*

10. A Master's Level Licensed Marriage & Family Therapist, Virginia Greenberg, is about to present on a topic in which she specializes in to a group of other mental health professionals. As a member of the organization that hosts the event announces her to the audience, he identifies her as Dr. Greenberg. As a Marital & Family Therapist, the **next best step** would be to:

   a. Not acknowledge the error of the introduction and proceed with the presentation. *Unethical. We must ALWAYS properly advertise our credentials and training, and in the event that some other entity misprints our credentials, it is our ethical obligation to correct the error ASAP.*

   b. **Before beginning the presentation, correct the error in your credentials to the audience at large.** *This would be best practice.*

   c. Make a mental note to let the individual who introduced you as Dr. Greenberg that you have not received a Doctorate Degree after your presentation. *Unethical as the audience would still be under the impression that you have a Doctoral-Degree.*

   d. Begin the presentation just as you have prepared to do so to ensure the quality of instruction, and remember to correct the error to the audience prior to the conclusion of the presentation. *This is better than answer C, but you are still delivering an entire presentation with the audience under the impression that you have a Doctoral-Degree. Still unethical and answer B is clearly a better choice.*

11. A family you have been working with for just two sessions comes in reporting significant changes they have noticed regarding the presenting problem. As a MRI Systemic therapist, **you may respond** to the family by:

   a. Reinforcing their growth and asking them to reflect upon what has been working for them. *This may be an appropriate response from an experiential or post-modern therapist, but would be a highly unlikely response from a MRI Systemic Therapist.*

   b. Ask them to scale how satisfied they are with the progress in relation to desired goals. *Scaling Questions are associated with Solution-Focused Therapy.*

   c. Continue to align with the parental system to establish healthier relationships and boundaries. *MRI Systemic Theory is not concerned with boundaries or structure. This would likely be an intervention used by a Structural or Strategic Therapist.*

   d. **Instruct the family to slow down and caution them about changing too fast.** *The above stated intervention is a paradoxical intervention originated by the MRI Group referred to as "Resisting the Progress of Change." This is another fun one to use.*

12. When working with a first-generation Asian-American family who is coming to therapy reporting a lack of connection from their adolescent son, a Caucasian Marital & Family Therapist would be ***mostly*** aware of:

    a. **Differences in Western and Eastern views of mental illness.** *The National Exam views Multicultural Therapies as having an understanding of general themes that may be assumed about particular cultures. Many questions related to Multiculturalism will ask specific questions about particular cultures, and the correct answer would be the "stereotyped" answer. This may be very incongruent with your training in Multicultural Therapies, as it was in mine. This is a testament to how important it will be to keep the right mindset throughout the exam as a "Systemic Therapist" and not "What would I do."*

    b. The triangle existing between the son and his two parents. *Since the question specifies the ethnicity of the therapist and clients as being different, it is likely wanting you to address that issue. Also, if the parents are reporting that the son is equally disconnected from both of them, a triangle MAY not even be an issue, let alone a primary concern.*

    c. The therapist's own comfort around working with clients of a different culture. *This is the NEXT BEST ANSWER and will be a good part of the process when working with families of a different culture, but answer A is more directly related to the here-and-now of the therapeutic encounter.*

    d. The importance of creating a cultural-genogram. *Again, not an incorrect answer, but also not THE BEST answer.*

13. You are working with a 16-year-old adolescent client. The parents request a copy of the client's file for them to keep in their own personal records. According to HIPAA, as a Marital & Family Therapist, you **have the right to**:

a. Decline the parents access to the file since it is individual therapy for their daughter. *Consenting Parents have the right to request access to the file of the minor client in w which they have consented treatment for.*

b. Inform the client that you had to give her parents a copy of her record at their request due to them consenting to and paying for the treatment. *This is correct in the sense that the therapist should inform the client that their parents have reviewed her file, but it fails to address the fact that progress notes would likely be withheld which would be an important piece of information for the adolescent to know, as progress notes are what contain the private details discussed within session.*

c. **Make a copy of the record as requested but withhold progress notes and black out any information contained in the file that you feel would be harmful to the client if another party were to read it.** *This is in the HIPAA Handbook. Know your HIPAA, People!*

d. Inform the parents that their daughter must first provide written consent prior to you allowing access to the file. *This is just a wrong answer. A minor client does not need to provide content for their parents to view their file, since the parents have consented for their treatment in the first place.*

14. A couple comes to therapy reporting a lack of physical intimacy and ongoing conflict. When the couple is asked about a history of physical abuse, the male discloses that he will at times become physically violent toward his partner, disclosing episodes of holding her against a wall, open-hand slapping her face, and forcefully pushing her to the ground. The male reported that the most recent episode was just last evening. The Family Therapist's **best approach** with this couple would be to:

   a. Assess for any history of physical violence in both partners's family of origin. *Incorrect because the abuse is currently ongoing. If the abuse was retroactive and in remission, this would be an appropriate assessment approach.*

   b. Because the abuse is currently ongoing, stop the assessment and shift focus to deescalation techniques and anger-management skills to prevent the recurrence of physical abuse. *This would be poor practice and is not a recommended approach in any of the MFT literature.*

   c. Inform the couple that the male must engage in an anger-management program and the female must engage in a victim of domestic abuse program if they wish to continue couple therapy. *Not an appropriate intervention, since you are agreeing to continue to do couple therapy that is concurrent with domestic violence programming prior to the violence ending.*

   d. **Inform the couple that they both must engage in programming specific to domestic violence until the violence is no longer occurring before they can be seen for couple therapy.** *Under the circumstance that the physical abuse is currently ongoing, it would be poor practice to work with the couple conjointly. Best practice would be to recommend separate services until the abuse is no longer occurring, and then conjoint couple therapy would be appropriate.*

15. When working with an adult client experiencing severe depression, your client discloses that they have been experiencing thoughts of suicidal ideation for the past several days. The ***best next step*** for the Marital & Family Therapist would be to:

a. Explore the thoughts and feelings surrounding the suicidal ideation. *Not the best response.*

b. Remind the client that you are a mandated reporter and that they must arrange transportation to a hospital for an emergency psychiatric evaluation or you will be bound to call 911. *A mandated report would be unethical at this point given that the client has not reported a plan and intent. Suicidal IDEATION does not warrant a mandated report and is a common part of the therapeutic process as clients work through mental health struggles.*

c. **Perform a formal suicide assessment.** *Whenever a client discloses the presence of suicidal ideation, crisis intervention would suggest that a formal (although, most likely brief) suicide assessment take place immediately to determine the level of threat of actual harm. If the assessment indicated presence of plan and intent, THEN a mandated report would be appropriate, but the question does not provide this information.*

d. Validate the client's pain and assure them that the thoughts will pass after engaging in an effective coping skill strategy. *Please, don't <u>ever</u> do this if a client reports the presence of suicidal ideation...*

16. A Marital & Family Therapist had an intake session scheduled with a notably wealthy and well-known individual. Upon intake, the client insists that he pay the therapist three times the top rate on the sliding fee scale. The Therapist accepts the client's request for payment. This therapist is:

a. Ethical because they are respecting the wishes of their client in a critical joining phase of therapy. *Incorrect. The therapist is potentially setting up an exploitative relationship, putting the client in a position where he may begin to expect more from the therapist than what a client paying the going-rate would receive. Essentially, if the therapist charges $100 per session, this client would be giving the therapist a "gift" of $200 each week.*

b. Ethical because it was at the request of the client, thereby not meeting criteria of exploitation. Incorrect. *See rationale for answer A.*

c. **Unethical**. *Despite being brief and lacking reasoning, it is the best answer given the options. This would be an example of a question that straddles the line of being a "trick question."*

d. Unethical because he is credentialed on the insurance panel that the client has, making it within the best interests of the client to use his insurance for reimbursement of treatment. *Just because you accept the insurance of a client does not necessarily mean that it is within the best interests of the client to use his or her insurance to reimburse for services rendered. Arguably, paying out-of-pocket ensures better privacy and is likely within the clients' best interests in situations where means of income is not a source of stress.*

17. A client requests a copy of each session note documented by the therapist. According to HIPAA, the therapist **should**:

a. Provide the client copies of his or her session notes as stated by law. *HIPAA actually states that progress notes are the only document in a client file that the professional may reserve the right to withhold.*

b. Provide the client copies of his or her session notes and require the client to pay for appropriate fees associated with the costs to copy a client file. *This answer may be correct if the question further stated that "After reviewing each session note, the therapist determined that no information contained within would cause any potential harm to the client if he or she were to read them."*

c. Decline the client access to his or her progress notes. *This answer may be correct if the question further read "After the therapist reviewed the case notes, he determined that the information recoded within would likely cause harm to the client if he or she were to read them." Best practice would suggest that you explain to the client why you are withholding his or her progress notes despite the request.*

d. **Consider whether or not granting the client access to his or her progress notes has the potential to cause any harm.** *Based on the rationales provided above, this is the best answer as HIPAA uses similar language in its manual.*

18. A therapist has been seeing a client family for 14 weeks, and there appeared to be a healthy relationship and good signs of engagement and progress, although treatment goals have yet to be fully met. Come week 15, the family does not show up and calls the front desk to cancel any future appointments. A **Symbolic-Experiential Therapist** would interpret this event as:

   a. Bilateral Transference. *This is a term used in Symbolic-Experiential Therapy, but does not apply to the vignette.*

   b. **A good sign that the family has experienced a flight toward health and no longer require therapy.** *This would be an example of the term "Flight Toward Health" as identified in the Symbolic-Experiential Therapy literature. Remember, this approach will always interpret family's dropping out of treatment or requesting early termination as a positive sign and be supportive of the family's decision.*

   c. Leaving therapy without a proper closing is a metaphor for continued emotional suppression. *This would actually contradict the concept of "Flight Toward Health" and such an interpretation is not suggested in any of the literature.*

   d. The need to call them and encourage their continued participation in therapy to ensure that treatment goals are met and progress can be maintained. *Whitaker actually advised against tracking clients down for skipping sessions, as doing so would grant the clients victory over the battle for structure and the therapist victory over the battle for initiative—something that Whitaker states should be avoided at all costs for there to be any hope of effective treatment outcomes.*

19. When performing a family therapy intake meeting, therapists often use a genogram as a primary assessment tool. A genogram provides rich information pertaining to the family system, including all of the following **except**:

   a. Presence of triangles. *A genogram does this.*

   b. Conflict from past generations transmitting into current family system. *A genogram does this.*

   c. The current presence of mental illness within the system. *A genogram does this.*

   d. **The prediction of future mental illness based on historical patterns.** *A genogram does not PREDICT future events or occurrences. It may give the family insight as to what cycles they wish to prevent from transmitting into the next generation, but do not CLAIM to PREDICT this.*

20. A small town in Oklahoma was recently destroyed by a series of tornados. As some of the families struggled immensely and fell into a helpless despair, other families seemed to manage quite well and deeply engaged with their community. This phenomenon *is* an example of:

   a. Subjective-Resiliency *Wrong Answer*

   b. **Equipotentiality** *This is the correct term and a concept from General Systems Theory. It states that multiple systems can experience the same event and have drastically different responses and outcomes. Its counterpart is EQUIFINALITY, which would suggest that various systems can experience remarkably different events, yet in the end, all things are the same.*

   c. Macrosystemic Trauma *Wrong Answer*

   d. Cultural Cohesion *Wrong Answer*

   KNOW YOUR TERMS PEOPLE. THIS IS AS CLOSE TO A FREEBIE AS YOU MAY GET ON THE EXAM!!!

21. A family is coming to therapy reporting that their 7th grade child has recently begun to withdrawal from the family and act out, no longer wanting to go on their weekly family Friday night outings or share in the details of her day every night at dinner. The parents are hoping that family therapy can get them their old daughter back. A Marital & Family Therapist **would most likely** interpret this dynamic as:

   a. The daughter has likely begun experimenting with drugs or alcohol. *Although this may be a reasonable hypothesis that calls for further assessment, there is not nearly enough evidence provided to make this the best answer and would be inappropriate for the therapist to assume or disclose to the family prior to gaining more information.*

   b. The daughter is the scapegoat for Mom and Dad to deny the problems within their marriage. *This may be a correct answer, particularly if the question called for "A Symbolic-Experiential Family Therapy," but answer D is more correct as family life cycle is more primary to the common factors of a systemic therapist than the concept of scapegoating.*

   c. The daughter has likely experienced a recent trauma around the time of these behaviors onsetting. *Again, it would be appropriate for the therapist to explore this further throughout the assessment as a potential cause of these behaviors, but is not the best answer at this point based on the information given.*

   d. **The family system is failing to adjust to a new phase in the family life cycle.** *The Family Life Cycle is an important part of the Universal Concepts of a Systemic Therapist. Adolescence is a difficult stage in the Family Life Cycle and often comeswith behavioral changes. It would be important for the Family Therapist to be aware of this dynamic.*

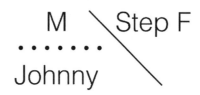

22. Upon intake with a family, a Structural Family Therapists creates a map of the family's hypothetical current structure. Based on the map shown above, a Structural Family Therapist would best interpret this as:
    a. Johnny is disengaged from his Mom due to her remarriage. *Incorrect*
    b. **Johnny is enmeshed with his Mom and unaccepting of her new husband.**
    c. Mom, Step-Father, and Johnny are stuck in a triangle. *Incorrect.*
    d. Johnny's Mom has remarried. *Incorrect. Although the map suggests this, it is not the best answer.*

    KNOW HOW TO INTERPRET YOUR STRUCTURAL FAMILY MAPS AND GENOGRAMS!

23. A family you have been meeting with for 16 weeks has started to show some good progress. They are reporting that they have noticed a shift in how they communicate and connect, and are pleased that therapy has been effective. A Marital & Family Therapist ***should*** take which next step in treating this family?
    a. Tell the family to slow down and restrain their progress to change. *This COULD be the correct answer if the question called for a MRI Systemic Therapist, but then it would be a poor question because a MRI Systemic Therapist would not be seeing a family for a 16th session.*
    b. Based on the positive results, invite the family to discharge at any time. *A SHIFT toward progress does not suggest that goals have been met. This question suggests the family being in the Mid-Phase of treatment, not Later-Phase.*
    c. **Shift focus to maintaining the progress achieved as the family begins working toward discharge.** *This is a good opportunity to build upon the progress made. This suggests that the family is in the Mid-Phase of treatment and can consider working toward discharge.*
    d. Identify a new goal that they can start fresh with. *There is nothing in the literature that would suggest this as being an appropriate action.*

24. A Marital & Family Therapist is meeting with a couple for the third time. When the therapist checks in with the husband, he grumbles and says "Oh I'm doing great, I've been looking forward to another 55-minutes of getting ganged up on and chewed out, happy to be here!" Based on the husband's response, the therapist has made what mistake?

    a. Failed to have husband work through his "victim mentality" during the assessment phase of treatment. *This is a judgment, and as MFTs, we know better* :-)

    b. The therapist has not made a mistake and should be reluctant to enable the husband's sarcastic and rude behavior. *This fails to acknowledge the pain and needs that the client is expressing behind the mask of sarcasm.*

    c. **Failed to establish a proper and balanced relationship with the husband.** *This comment suggests that the client does not feel that the therapist has maintained neutrality and instead has perhaps aligned with his partner. It would behoove the Family Therapist to explore these feelings as a means of joining with both parties. Even if the therapist has been intentional about maintaining neutrality, this is still the lived experience of the client and needs to be validated, explored, and repaired.*

    d. Failed to establish multidirectional partiality. *Although technically correct, this is a concept exclusive to Contextual Family Therapy and would not account for a Universal Concepts Family Therapist.*

Questions 25-29 will be in relation to the following vignette:

The Beckers are a Caucasian, middle-class family pursuing therapy as a result of general family disconnection. Mom initiated the phone call, stating that things are "out of control" and that "changes need to happen, and fast!" Mom further elaborated that she and her husband are very disconnected and have been for the past 11-years. She said he will either work all day and come home to "decompress" or head to his workshop attached to the garage. He will also spend most weekends with their two sons at various sporting activities and "guys-only outings." Mom reported that she and her husband have been sleeping in different bedrooms for the past 3-years. Mom said she will spend most days at her Mom's place—which is close in town—and as much time as she can with her daughter before she goes off to college in 5-months. Mom said she is very disconnected from her sons, and that her husband is very disconnected from his daughter. She reported the family being "split into two," and appeared quite desperate for change to occur. Mom requested that she, her husband, and her daughter come in as her two sons are refusing to attend family therapy.

25. A traditional **Symbolic-Experiential Therapist** would most likely respond to this referral by:
   a. Asking the family what a good time would be for them to come in as a means of joining via accommodating. *Incorrect, this would be losing the "Battle for Structure."*
   b. **Tell the mother that you will be happy to work with their family under the circumstances that the two sons come as well.** *This is what many traditional Symbolic-Experiential Therapists would do as a means of winning the Battle for Structure and test whether or not the family is ready to win the Battle for Initiative.*
   c. Determine that the issue resides in the parental subsystem and recommend beginning with couple therapy. *This would not fit with the Symbolic-Experiential Approach as they strived to have at the very least every nuclear family member present at each session.*
   d. Agree to meeting with the family—whichever members care to come—for a maximum of 10 sessions. *This would be an example of the MRI Systemic Approach.*

   *****Note:** Several questions on the exam will follow a similar format (i.e. 2-4 questions relating to the same vignette).

26. Mom, Dad, and the daughter end up coming in for a family therapy session. After learning more about the problem, the therapist gives Dad the following directive: "Okay Dad, for the next week, every night when you get home from work, I want you to pull your car in the garage, walk right up to your bedroom, put your work clothes in the hamper, change into short/sweats and a t-shirt/sweatshirt, walk down to the kitchen, grab two beers, walk directly into your workshop, and stay there to decompress for no less than two hours, and no more than two hours. I am prescribing you to do just this, in the exact order, every single day, until we meet at this same time next week." This intervention can **best** be described as:

a. Paradoxical intervention. *Correct, but answer B is MORE correct.*

b. **Prescribing the symptom.** *This is an example of prescribing the system, commonly used in Strategic and MRI Systemic Family Therapies. What this does is draw awareness around the freedom to choose by having the father be mindful of his DECISION to withdraw from the family. He may either comply with the therapist and come to this realization (and, thereby putting him in a position where he needs to choose whether or not he wishes to continue the behavioral sequence) or defy the therapist and stop spending time in his workshop (and, thereby disrupt the behavioral sequence).*

c. Unethical as the therapist is promoting alcohol-use as a means of coping with relational distress. *Not necessarily. This would be a poor interpretation of this intervention, and the family has not reported that having two-beers on occasion has been harmful to the father or family system.*

d. Unethical because the therapist may potentially cause harm to the clients by telling them to engage in the very unhealthy behaviors they are requesting to change. *This would be another poor interpretation, as it is instructing someone to just keep doing something they have already been doing for quite some time. It is not the act in and of itself that is harming the family, it is the ongoing repetition of its pattern that is harmful. This is a means to disrupting the pattern.*

27. The intervention used in question 26 would have **most likely** been done by:

a. Milton Erickson *Did not practice Family Therapy*

b. Carl Whitaker *Whitaker used Paradox, but this one reeks of Jay Haley*

c. **Jay Haley**

d. Gregory Bateson *Was a Theoretician, not Clinician*

28. Mom, Dad, and the daughter show up for their third session. After the family describes their current situation in more depth, the therapist asks the daughter to leave the room, and instructs Mom and Dad to do the following: "This weekend, I am prescribing that the two of you arrange for a relative to come and watch the children, and without giving any great detail beyond the fact that you have a secret, discretely leave to go on a trip until Tuesday." This therapist was using the intervention referred to as:
   a. Instillation of Hope. *This would not fit with Installing Hope.*
   b. Exoneration. *Incorrect, this is a Contextual Family Therapy Term and does not fit with the vignette.*
   c. Paradoxical Intervention. *Incorrect*
   d. **The Invariant Prescription.** *Landmark Intervention by the Later Milan Group.*

29. The intervention used in question 28 would have most likely been done by:
   a. Luigi Boscollo
   b. **Selvini Palazolli**
   c. Gianfrano Cecchin
   d. Lynn Hoffman

   BE ABLE TO DIFFERENTIATE BETWEEN EARLY-MILAN and LATER-MILAN, INCLUDING WHICH PRIMARY CONTRIBUTOR WENT WHERE

30. After the eldest daughter had left for college, Mom and Dad reported an interest in continuing to work with you through Couples Therapy. After receiving consent from the rest of the family and renegotiating the terms of the therapeutic contract—now viewing the couple system as the primary client—therapy begins. In the third session, the father discloses that he has been hiding feelings of profound sadness, loss of interest in recreation, and has struggled with insomnia. He attributes many of these struggles to the distance between he and his wife. As a Family Therapist, the next best step would be to:

   a. **Continue couple therapy to help relieve Dad's depression.** *Research endorses that Couple Therapy is an effective treatment approach for individual depression. Dual services would not be necessary at this point.*

   b. Refer Dad to individual therapy that is more tailored to individuals with depressive disorders, and resume couple therapy once the depression is better managed. *The literature does not suggest this, and instead, supports Couple Therapy as an effective treatment approach. Depression is not a symptom that would make couples therapy inappropriate like physical abuse and substance abuse would.*

   c. Discontinue therapy and refer Dad to arrange a meeting with his Primary Physician to prescribe medication. *You can refer Dad to his Physician to consider medication, but this would be both premature and discontinuing therapy when it is a proven intervention for depression would not make sense.*

   d. Refer Dad to individual therapy that is more tailored to individuals with depressive disorders while continuing to provide couple therapy. *This would result in dual-services that may not be necessary to burden the client with at this point in time.*

31. I will pass the National Licensing Exam. Is this statement:
   a. **True**
   b. **True**
   c. **True**
   d. **True**

That brings us to the end of the Independent Study Guide. I hope this manual addressed many of your curiosities and concerns regarding the National Licensing Exam for Marriage and Family Therapy. Hopefully by now you are feeling prepared to approach the practice exam offered on the AMFTRB website; that score will be a good predictor of your preparedness for the actual exam. If you do well, wonderful! You're in a great shape. If you find yourself struggling, review this manual a few more times in relation to the Domains in which you received a low score. If you continue to find yourself struggling, consider scheduling a web-based tutoring session through **www.mftlicensingexam.com** to better identify where the struggles are.

Based on your dedication to working through this manual, focus throughout the practice exam, and passion for the field of family therapy, let yourself feel confident and enthusiastic walking into this part of the licensing process. Self-assurance will come from being prepared. Being prepared will come through two domains: (1) a combination of memorizing key terms, comprehending concepts, and applying the two accordingly to real-life client encounters, and, (2) field experience. Experience with clients, experiences in supervision, and experiences in clinical case consultation will drastically contribute to your success on the exam. Fortunately, all of you are either currently in or recently completed a clinical practicum which will serve you well come test day. Again, if your state requires successful completion of the exam prior to your supervision hours counting toward licensure, that is fine. Your experiences in your clinical practicum at the end of graduate school on top of your rich knowledge for the field will suffice.

As stated earlier, slow down and enjoy the ride. Pre-licensure is an exciting and passionate time to grow and learn about your *self as a therapist*. Be creative. Be Daring. Move beyond the textbook. Your subjective approach to therapy will eventually become a unique blend of the various ideas, concepts, and theories that have always fit for you along the way as they emerge through a lens of your particular idiosyncrasies. Enjoy as you fully emerge yourself in this process. When people ask me what kind of therapist I am, I often respond that, "I'm a Nike Therapist; I just do it…" Most therapists I know would say the same for themselves, and you will too!

My last piece of advice…Pre-licensure is a great time to experiment with using paradox in session. Enjoy as your supervisor nearly explodes from anxiety while you casually reflect on instructing your client who hasn't left her home in three weeks—out of fear she will publicly wet herself—to go stand in the middle of Target and pee her pants…

Best of luck and I will look forward to having you as a colleague!

Glossary (Key Terms & Primary Interventions)

A Learning Process: Milan Family Therapists viewed the use of interventions as nothing more than a learning process in which the therapist tests hypotheses and interventions through trial and error as they learn about the family.
Milan Systemic

A System: A unit bounded by a set of interrelated elements and which exhibits coherent behaviors.
Cybernetics

Activating Constructive Anxiety: A Symbolic-Experiential Therapist's effort to reframe symptoms as efforts toward building competence by focusing on the positive attributes of anxiety as a means toward self-growth.
Symbolic-Experiential Therapy

Affective Confrontation: The therapist's intentional confrontation with the family where he or she will directly and openly share his or her subjective emotional experience of working with the family.
Symbolic-Experiential Therapy

Affective Intensity: Increasing the emotional intensity of the system to encourage structural change.
Structural Family Therapy

Aligning with Parental Generation: A technique directed at strengthening the parental hierarchy and reinforcing that parents are in charge of the children. The therapist will break neutrality and intentionally align with the parental subsystem.
Strategic & Structural Family Therapy

Amplifying or Positive Feedback Loops: These increase change in a family's homeostasis (*morphogenesis*). They attempt to change these systems from its steady state to a new steady state or balance.
Cybernetics

Analogic Communication: Has little structure, but is rich in content such as a child's kinetic family drawing.
Communications Theory

Analogical Message: A metaphorical or symbolic message (process).
Milan Systemic

Attachment: The individual's basic need for trust and security, significantly influenced and developed throughout infancy and early childhood per the child's relation to his or her primary caregiver. Attachment in early childhood influences relationship styles throughout adulthood.
Emotionally Focused Couples Therapy

Attenuating or Negative Feedback Loops: These reduce change in an existing homeostasis.
Cybernetics

Battle for Initiative: After the therapist wins the battle for structure, the family must win the battle for initiative—that is, realize and demonstrate that they are responsible for change, not the therapist.
Symbolic-Experiential Therapy

Battle for Structure: Whitaker stated that the therapist must first win the battle for structure if therapy is to be effective—this entails determining who attends the session, what time sessions are, how frequently sessions occur, and for how long. If the family is not willing to meet these expectations set by the therapist, then they are not prepared to invest in the growth process and change would be unlikely.
Symbolic-Experiential Therapy

Beginner's Mind: This concept refers to the therapist's stance in Solution-Focused Therapy. It is important that the therapist maintains an open mind which lends itself to possibilities, while being careful not to exert expertise which limits possibilities.
Solution-Focused Therapy

Bilateral Pseudo-Therapy: Occurs when family members attempt to play therapist to one another—this is avoided.
Symbolic-Experiential Therapy

Bilateral Transference: A therapist's intentional maneuver to adapt to the language, accent, rhythm, or posture of the family.
Symbolic-Experiential Therapy

Blamers: One of Satir's four dysfunctional communication styles. Often disagree with others and hold others responsible for things not going their way. Blamers often feel insecure and powerless, and feel that they must go to extreme measures—verbal and/or physical aggression—for anyone to really listen to them. Here, the self and the context are acknowledged, while the other is not.
Satir's Communications Approach

Body, Mind, and Feelings: Satir's belief that the mind, body, and feelings interact and influence communication processes at both the verbal and nonverbal level.
Satir's Communications Approach

Bonding: Attachment Theory's term for the process in which individuals form a connection in a relationship that satisfies the primary need for attachment.
Emotionally Focused Couples Therapy

Boundaries: Individuals, subsystems, and families are separated from one another by boundaries. A boundary is a hypothetical line of demarcation that serves to protect a family and its subsystems.
Structural Family Therapy

Boundaries: These are theoretical lines of demarcation in a family that define a system as an entity and separate the subsystems from one another and the system from its environment.
*Cybernetics

Boundary Interface: Regions between each subsystem of the family and between the family and the suprasystem.
*Cybernetics

Boundary Making: An intervention in which therapists reinforce appropriate boundaries and diffuse inappropriate boundaries by adapting the interactional patterns of the family's structure.
*Structural Family Therapy

Bridge Maneuver: This intervention calls for the manual stimulation of the female in an effort to produce orgasm. This would gradually decrease as treatment progresses as partners begin to fill that role.
*Sex Therapy

Case Research (Case Studies): An in-depth investigation of a problem in one or more real-life settings over an extended period of time.
*Research Methods & Techniques

Centrifugal: A measure on The Timberlawn Model suggesting that family members look to get their needs met outside of the family system.
*Assessment in Family Therapy

Centripetal: A measure on The Timberlawn Model suggesting that family members look to get their needs met within the family system.
*Assessment in Family Therapy

Challenging Family Assumptions: Offers the family alternative perspectives and views on how they interact with one another.
*Structural Family Therapy

Challenging the Symptom: Offers the family alternative ways of perceiving the role of the symptom in relation to the family's structure.
*Structural Family Therapy

Change is Constant: Solution-Focused Therapies view that change is inevitable and constant, that the client's situation is always in flux although these changes often go overlooked.
*Solution-Focused Therapy

Circular Causality: In determining the origins of problems, *General Systems Theory* departs radically from traditional, *linear causality*. This is different than *linear causality* and acknowledged that two things do, say, or feel mutually influence one another in a recursive, circular relationship.
*Cybernetics

Circular Questioning: The therapist asks one family member to comment on the interactions of two other family members to create circularity within the system and help the therapist build a more elaborate hypothesis.
Milan Systemic

The Circumplex Model: An objective assessment tool measuring levels of cohesion, flexibility, and communication within family systems.
Assessment in Family Therapy

Clear Boundary: A clear boundary between the parental subsystem and the children establishes the parents in leadership positions. It allows the parents and children to interact, but supports the couple in a separate relationship, with time to enjoy the mature activities of recreation and pleasure. Healthy families have clear generational, hierarchical boundaries that allow parents to maintain parental roles and children to maintain child roles.
Structural Family Therapy

Clients as Consultants: In Narrative Therapy, after clients had discharged the therapist would welcome them back to serve as consultants on current cases. This would reinforce their growth and maintain the collaborative stance of the therapist.
Narrative Family Therapy

Closed Systems: Are more isolated and resistant to interactions with the environment.
Cybernetics

Co-Therapist: Whitaker would always work with a co-therapist, as he believed this allowed him to be more crazy in session as he could rely on his co-therapist to ground him. In Symbolic-Experiential Therapy, the co-therapy team was used as a therapeutic tool.
Symbolic-Experiential Therapy

Coaching: Bowen used this term to identify what he believed his role to be with clients as he coached them through the process of differentiation of self. He used the metaphor of "coach" to exemplify that he is responsible for getting the process started, but that the actual work must be done by the client.
Bowen's Multigenerational Approach

Coalitions: When two family members join to create a coalition against one or several other family members.
Structural Family Therapy

Coital Alignment Technique (CAT): An intervention used to increase mutual stimulation through full body contact (male learns to position and maneuver on top of the woman).
Sex Therapy

Collaborative Case-Notes: In Narrative Therapy, the therapist may write case notes collaboratively with the client toward the end of each session to ensure that he or she was correctly capturing the essence of the client's experience of the session.
Narrative Family Therapy

Communication: In Satir's approach, all forms of behavior are considered communication and need to be tended to by the individual communicating as well as the recipient.
Satir's Communications Approach

Complainant: One of the three types of clients in Solution-Focused Therapy. Complainants are willing to acknowledge that there is a problem, but unwilling to acknowledge their role in it and instead keep focus on others.
Solution-Focused Therapy

Complementarity: A balanced relationship between two individuals that often results in effective teamwork. The relationship may not be symmetrical—that is, equal parts—but nonetheless balanced.
Structural Family Therapy

Complementary Relationships: Based on differences that fit together.
Communications Theory & MRI Systemic Approach

Compliments: Solution-Focused therapists will intentionally and consistently compliment and reflect upon client's efforts, strengths, and improvements throughout the entire discourse of therapy.
Solution-Focused Therapy

Computers: One of Satir's four dysfunctional communication styles. Computers are often overly-rational, level-headed, analytical, and speak in a matter-of-fact manner. Computers often fear the vulnerability associated with expressing their true feelings. Here, the context is acknowledged, but the self and other are not.
Satir's Communications Approach

Conflict Management: The family's capacity to resolve conflict and negotiate effective and balanced solutions.
Structural Family Therapy

Constitutionalist Self: The concept that the self is fluid, constantly constructed and deconstructed through interaction with others and the environment.
Narrative Family Therapy

Construct: An abstract concept that is specifically chosen (or "created") to explain a given phenomenon.
Research Methods & Techniques

Construct Validity: Examines how well a given measurement scale is measuring the theoretical construct that it is expected to measure.
Research Methods & Techniques

Contextual: Contextual refers to the systemic impact of all that are impacted by the therapeutic effort. Also refers to the social and political context within a family.
Contextual Family Therapy

Counterparadox: An intervention used to unravel a family's double-bind message by referring to their dysfunction as legitimate and necessary, and as so, instructing the family not to change.
Milan Systemic

Correlation: A number between -1 and +1 denoting the strength of the relationship between two variables.
Research Methods & Techniques

Countertransference: The therapist's tendency to attribute qualities that reflect unresolved grievances from a previous relationship onto a client.
Object-Relations Theory

Craziness: Falls into three categories of being driven crazy, going crazy, or acting crazy. Different orientations of craziness as exhibited in dysfunctional families.
Symbolic-Experiential Therapy

Customer: One of the three types of clients in Solution-Focused Therapy. Customers acknowledge that there is a problem, are willing to accept their role in it, and are engaged in putting forth effort toward change.
Solution-Focused Therapy

Debts or Filial Responsibility: As an account for the child's experience of the degrees of fairness and ethical consideration from their parents toward them, they will either be debts (resulting in destructive entitlement) or filial responsibility (resulting in loyalty).
Contextual Family Therapy

Deconstruction Questions: These questions help individuals to unravel their stories and see them from different perspectives, creating an opportunity for them to decide whether or not they choose to continue identifying with it.
Narrative Family Therapy

Deparentification Process: This is a two-part process. (1) The therapist becomes temporarily parentified to relieve the parentified child and then (2) addresses the larger spectrum of family dynamics to work toward systemic change.
Contextual Family Therapy

Descriptive Research: Research that is directed at making careful observations and detailed documentation of an identified phenomenon. Observations here are based on the scientific method.
Research Methods & Techniques

Destructive Entitlement: This results when individuals experience the denial of entitlement from their family of origin, and in turn, seek what they believed to be owed to them through a different relationship—typically, their family of creation.
Contextual Family Therapy

Detriangulate: Bowen believed that families will automatically attempt to triangulate the therapist into their conflict—and if they are successful in doing so, therapy will become ineffective. The therapist detriangulates the family's emotional process by remaining neutral and differentiated, thereby decreasing emotionality across the family and making room for constructively resolving conflict.
Bowen's Multigenerational Approach

Differentiation of Self: This concept refers to an individual's capacity to balance thinking with feeling—and thereby, balance individuality with togetherness. Highly differentiated individuals are able to act rationally in the midst of anxiety. Individual's with low levels of differentiation are highly reactive and easily driven to emotionality.
Bowen's Multigenerational Approach

Diffuse Boundary: Boundaries that are permeable and permit fluid contact with other subsystems. May be prone to enmeshment.
Structural Family Therapy

Digital Communication: Verbal communication that is perceived and interpreted based on meaning.
Communications Theory

Digital Message: The content of the message (objective).
Milan Systemic

Directed Masturbation Training: To treat anorgasmic women, this technique helps a woman to touch herself, and then her partner, in various ways to trigger her orgasm.
Sex Therapy

Directives: Specific, directed behavioral tasks for the family to engage in different behaviors in-session and then carried out into the home between sessions.
Strategic Family Therapy

The Dirty Game: When parents struggle for control, they triangulate a symptomatic child who then works to defeat the parents.
Milan Systemic

The Dirty Middle: The phrase used to describe when therapy reaches an impasse, in which Framo uses as leverage to gain the client's willingness to bring in his or her family of origin.
Object-Relations Theory

Disengaged Systems: May be independent or isolated.
Structural Family Therapy

Displacement Stories: Guerin's intervention meant to assist individuals in creating distance between themselves and their problems and encourage rationality by having them reflect on another couple's conflict as opposed to their own.
Bowen's Multigenerational Approach

Distractors: One of Satir's four dysfunctional communication styles. Distractors desperately avoid conflict and will often change the topic of focus or conversation in the midst of escalation. Distracters may also avoid conflict by taking on the role of a placater, blamer, or computer, but quickly shift out of the stance prior to another's reaction. Distracters often feel insignificant and scared inside. Here, the self, other, and context go **un**acknowledged.
Satir's Communications Approach

Dysfunctional Communication Styles (or, Survival Stances): Satir identified four primary dysfunctional communication styles within families: Placaters, Blamers, Computers, and Distractors. Levelers referred to the functional communication style.
Satir's Communications Approach

Emotional Cutoff: A problematic manner in which individuals deal with unresolved attachment issues through a process of separation, isolation, withdrawal, running away, or denying the importance of one's parental family.
Bowen's Multigenerational Approach

Enactments: Having the family experiment with new ways of behaving and interacting, as instructed by the therapist, in the here and now of the therapeutic encounter.
Structural Family Therapy

Enmeshed Systems: Receive affection and nurturance within the family system but may risk autonomy and outside relationships.
Structural Family Therapy

Entitlement: What individuals are inherently due from others in their family as well as what is earned from others based upon behavior toward them.
Contextual Family Therapy

Entropy: This refers to a system's tendency to break down which, over time, threatens the survival of the system.
Cybernetics

Epistemological Error: A set of beliefs that are incongruent with reality and become problematic, such as not believing that one is responsible for his or her own behaviors.
Milan Systemic

Epistemology: The manner in which individuals (families) make sense of the world, including their relationships to and with others.
Milan Systemic

Epistemology: Refers to our assumptions about the best way to study the world (e.g., should we use an objective or subjective approach to study social reality).
Research Methods & Techniques

Equifinality: This is the idea that an organism or system can reach a certain end state from a variety of different sources, conditions, and means or from different initial states. For example, Generalized Anxiety Disorder may stem from a biological imbalance, trauma, or free-will.
Cybernetics

Equipotentiality: This refers to the notion that different end states can occur from the same initial conditions. Similar events (e.g. natural disaster) can turn into depression or trauma as well as growth or happiness.
Cybernetics

Equitable Asymmetry: Refers to the concept that children are not able to care for themselves and are entirely dependent upon their parents—making them both incredibly vulnerable or delightfully entitled based upon the circumstances of their upbringing.
Contextual Family Therapy

Ethnography: An interpretive research design emphasizing that research phenomenon must be studied within the context of its native culture. The researcher is deeply immersed in a certain culture over an extended period of time (8 months to 2 years), and during that period, engages, observes, and records the daily life of the studied culture, and theorizes about the evolution and behaviors in that culture.
Research Methods & Techniques

Exception Questions: Questions that have clients reflect on times when the problem was not present, or when the problem was not a problem.
Solution-Focused Therapy

Existential Encounter: The therapist's willingness to both receive the family's reactions to him or her as well as disclose his or her own reactions toward the family.
Symbolic-Experiential Therapy

Exoneration: The process in which an individual restores balance within his or her ledger.
Contextual Family Therapy

Expanding Distress: This is a process of expanding the symptom to the system, that is, expanding the distress to include each member, shifting the nature of anxiety within the family and reducing blame and scapegoating.
Symbolic-Experiential Therapy

Experimental Studies: Studies that are intended to test cause-effect relationships (hypotheses) in a tightly controlled setting by separating the cause from the effect in time, administering the cause to one group of subjects (the "treatment group") but not to another group ("control group"), and observing how the mean effects vary between subjects in these two groups. For example, one group receives an intervention (i.e., the experimental group), the other group receives a placebo (i.e., the control group), and then responses from each group are measured against one another to determine whether or not the intervention was effective. In a true experimental design, subjects must be randomly assigned between each group. If random assignment is not followed, then the design becomes quasi-experimental.
Research Methods & Techniques

Exploratory Research: Research conducted in new areas of inquiry, where the goals of the research are: (1) to scope out the magnitude or extent of a particular phenomenon, problem, or behavior, (2) to generate some initial ideas (or "hunches") about that phenomenon, or (3) to test the feasibility of undertaking a more extensive study regarding that phenomenon.
Research Methods & Techniques

External Validity: Or, generalizability, refers to whether the observed associations can be generalized from the sample to the population, or to other people, organizations, contexts, or time.
Research Methods & Techniques

Externalizing Questions: Questions oriented toward helping the client to externalize the problem, thereby separating from them in an effort to feel less powerless. These questions usually entail shifting the use of language from identifying the problem as an adjective (i.e. feeling depressed) to a noun (i.e. recognizing the presence of depression).
Narrative Family Therapy

Externalizing the Problem: A process that separates the problem from the person, often personifying the problem into its own external entity. The manner in which the problem becomes externalized is based upon the client's use of language and expressed lived reality.
Narrative Family Therapy

FACES: The Family Adaptability and Cohesion Evaluation Scale, is the report coming out of the Circumflex Model that identifies a family's level of *cohesion* and *flexibility*.
Assessment in Family Therapy

Facts: One of the four dimensions of individual and relational psychology that interact with one another in Contextual Family Therapy. Facts refer to the stable and physical attributes that individuals are born with (i.e. gender, ethnicity, race, disabilities, cognitive functioning, etc.) and the contextual circumstances of their upbringing (i.e. divorce, moving, trauma, etc.).
Contextual Family Therapy

Familial Boundary: The term used to represent the concept of *Boundary Interface* mentioned above within the literature of family therapies.
Cybernetics

Family Interaction: Healthy family interaction in Experiential Therapy is traditionally characterized through flexibility and openness to life experiences.
Symbolic-Experiential Therapy

Family Models/Maps: Individuals and the system at large will *consciously* or *unconsciously* use models or maps meant to manage their boundaries and make sense of their individual and shared realities.
Cybernetics

Family Projection Process: This concept identifies that individuals with limited emotional resources are likely to project their needs onto others in the family. For example, a mother who was neglected as a child (too much individuality, not enough togetherness), and as a result, *emotionally cut-off* from her parents, may become over-involved (too much togetherness, not enough individuality) with her children.
Bowen's Multigenerational Approach

Family Reconstruction: A process in which an individual re-experiences the development of their primary triad across several generations.
Satir's Communications Approach

Family Sculpting: An in-session intervention where family members are asked to place other family members in positions symbolic of their role in the family from the perceptive of the sculptor. Family members will take turns going about this process while reflecting on the experiences and interpretations throughout.
Satir's Communications Approach

Fantasy Alternative: Discussing problematic or stressful situations in fantasy based, "what if" terms or deemphasizing stressful situations by suggesting absurd fantasy alternatives (e.g. maybe if you medicated your husband, he wouldn't be so emotional).
Symbolic-Experiential Therapy

Feedback Loops: These are at the core of the cybernetics model. They are the self-correcting mechanisms which serve to govern families' attempts to adjust or vary from customary patterns and maintain its organizational sameness (homeostasis).
Cybernetics

Field Surveys: Non-experimental designs that do not control for or manipulate independent variables or treatments, but measure these variables and test their effects using statistical methods. Field surveys capture snapshots of practices, beliefs, or situations from a random sample of subjects in field settings through a survey questionnaire or less frequently, through a structured interview.
Research Methods & Techniques

Filial Loyalty: This concept suggests that children are inherently loyal to their family of origin.
Contextual Family Therapy

First-Order Change: Change that occurs at the behavioral level only regarding family patterns of interaction.
MRI Systemic Approach

Flight Toward Health: When a family would abruptly stop showing up for treatment, Whitaker would take this as a positive sign that the family experienced sudden and profound growth and no longer requires therapeutic support. Whitaker would always be supportive of a family's request to terminate therapy regardless of the phase of treatment.
Symbolic-Experiential Therapy

Focus Group Research: A type of research that involves bringing in a small group of subjects (typically 6 to 10 people) at one location, and having them discuss a phenomenon of interest for a period of 1.5 to 2 hours.
Research Methods & Techniques

Formula First Session Task: In Solution-Focused Therapy, the therapist will use the first session to shift the attention of the individual or family toward the overlooked positive aspects of their situation. This occurs through illuminating upon times when the problem is not present as well as explores strengths and resources. This sets the stage for therapy being solution-focused as opposed to problem-focused.
Solution-Focused Therapy

Games: Unacknowledged strategies that result in destructive interactions within families—often, games are unspoken and used as attempts to control another's behavior.
Milan Systemic

Genogram (Guerin) / **Family Diagrams** (Bowen): These gather a rich family history through the creation of a diagram resembling a family tree with various symbols used to identify gender and the degree of conflict, fusion, emotional cut-off, or health between individuals. It identifies the multigenerational transmission process and triangles among many other dynamics.
Bowen's Multigenerational Approach

Going Home Again: This was an intervention used to encourage adult individual clients to go home and repair any conflicted relationships.
Bowen's Multigenerational Approach

Grounded Theory: An inductive technique of interpreting recorded data about a social phenomenon to build theories about that phenomenon.
Research Methods & Techniques

Haptic (or, symbolic) Communication: Includes touch.
Communications Theory

Hierarchy: The physical structure of the family as determined by the system's rules, boundaries, and interactional patterns.
Structural Family Therapy

Homeostasis: This refers to the tendency of a system to resist change and maintain dynamic equilibrium or a steady state. This is maintained by negative feedback and input loops.
Cybernetics

Hope: In Solution-Focused Therapy, the therapist is intentional about maintaining the presence of hope that things will improve and get better for the client.
Solution-Focused Therapy

Hypothesizing: Continual process of conceptualizing the nature of the family's behavior that guide questioning and interventions.
Milan Systemic

The "I" Position: This was an intervention used to encourage clients to learn more effective ways of expressing what/how they are feeling through ownership and not blame. For example, a client would be redirected from saying, "You're so cold-hearted," to, "I wish you would tend to my emotional pain more genuinely." This would break cycles of emotional reactivity and promote "person-to-person" relationships.
Bowen's Multigenerational Approach

Incongruous Hierarchies: Occurs when children create symptoms in an attempt to change their parents.
Strategic Family Therapy

Individuality & Togetherness: The two counterbalancing forces that drive human relationships. Bowen believed that each individual needs companionship and independence, and that anxiety is experienced when these two needs polarize the individual. Balance is achieved in relation to the extent that the individual has learned to manage emotionality—that is, the individual's level of *self-differentiation*.
Bowen's Multigenerational Approach

Individuation: A primary goal in growth-oriented therapies, encouraging each individual family member in becoming more and more of who they are.
Symbolic-Experiential Therapy

Insight: The process of raising unconscious forces to awareness, allowing clients to better understand how underlying dynamics impact their behavior and relationships.
Object-Relations Theory

Intensity: The therapist can achieve intensity by increasing the affective component of an interaction, by increasing the length of a dialogue or by repeating the same message in different interactions through the use of tone, volume, and pacing.
Structural Family Therapy

Interactional Patterns: Dichotomous patterns of relating such as the pursuer-distancer or attacker-blamer relationship pattern.
Emotionally Focused Couples Therapy

Interpretation: The therapist's hypotheses pertaining to the influence of a client's past experiences on their current behaviors and struggles.
Object-Relations Theory

Inter-Rater Reliability: Also called inter-observer reliability, is a measure of consistency between two or more independent raters (observers) of the same construct.
Research Methods & Techniques

Internal Consistency Reliability: A measure of consistency between different items of the same construct.
Research Methods & Techniques

Internal Validity: Also called causality, examines whether the observed change in a dependent variable is indeed caused by a corresponding change in hypothesized independent variable, and not by variables extraneous to the research context. Essentially, is the data congruent to the hypothesis and measured variables as opposed to other factors not accounted for.
Research Methods & Techniques

Intervening: Structural Family Therapists are continually stepping in and out of the family, raising intensity, and unbalancing the system through swift and strategic interventions.
Structural Family Therapy

Interval Scales: Scales where the values measured are not only rank-ordered, but are also equidistant from adjacent attributes. For example, the temperature scale (in Fahrenheit or Celsius), where the difference between 30 and 40 degree Fahrenheit is the same as that between 80 and 90 degree Fahrenheit.
Research Methods & Techniques

Interview Survey: Interviews are a more personalized form of data collection method than questionnaires, and are conducted by trained interviewers using the same research protocol as questionnaire surveys (i.e., a standardized set of questions).
Research Methods & Techniques

Introject: Internalized objects become introjects, and are split into being either all-good or all-bad.
Object-Relations Theory

The Invariant Prescription: Typically during the third session, the therapist(s) will instruct the mother and father to tell their family that they have a "secret," and to then take a trip together, away from the family, for a few days. They are cautioned not to tell the family anything more than the mere fact that they have a secret prior to leaving.
Milan Systemic

Isomorphism: This is a phenomenon in which two or more systems or subsystems exhibit similar or parallel structures. For example, a therapist seeing a family that starts showing up late to sessions will similarly begin showing up late to supervision to discuss the case.
Cybernetics

Joining & Accommodating: An intentional maneuver by the therapist to establish a therapeutic relationship with the family system. The therapist will adapt to the family's communication pattern and other mannerisms to create a comfortable therapeutic space.
Structural Family Therapy

Kinesthetic Communication: Refers to body motion.
Communications Theory

Landscape of Action Questions: Questions that explore specific situations and efforts that are congruent with the preferred narrative.
Narrative Family Therapy

Landscape of Meaning Questions: Once there is a clear understanding of the preferred narrative, these questions serve to explore the meanings within the preferred narrative. For instance, how does the client's preferred narrative of spending more quality time with family reflect upon them as a person.
Narrative Family Therapy

Language and Meaning: By attending to the language and meaning used by clients, therapists can gain an understanding of their lived reality and how they experience the meaning of situations, relationships, others, and self.
Solution-Focused Therapy

Ledger: The manner in which individuals within a family keep track of and balance debts and entitlements.
Contextual Family Therapy

Legacy: Certain attributes or qualities that are attributed to an individual as an account of being born to his or her parents.
Contextual Family Therapy

Levelers (congruence): Satir considered levelers to be those demonstrating functional and effective communication styles. They can be open and honest in their communication and display genuine receptiveness as they listen to others. Levels are able to acknowledge the self, the other, and the context throughout communicative interactions.
Satir's Communications Approach

Likert Scale: Designed by Rensis Likert, this is a very popular rating scale for measuring ordinal data in social science research. This scale includes Likert items that are simply-worded statements to which respondents can indicate their extent of agreement or disagreement on a five or seven-point scale ranging from "strongly disagree" to "strongly agree".
Research Methods & Techniques

Loyalty: Central to the theory of Contextual Family Therapy, loyalty refers to an individual's internalized expectations of and obligations to his or her family of origin. This concept is assumed to exert a powerful influence over the individual's functioning.
Contextual Family Therapy

Mapping the Influence of the Person: This process entails exploring the role that the person has had on the life of the problem.
Narrative Family Therapy

Mapping the Influence of the Problem: This process entails exploring the role that the problem has had on the individual's life.
Narrative Family Therapy

Marital Schism: The parents are overly focused on their own problems which harms the marriage, the individuals, and the children.
Theodore Lidz

Marital Skew: One parent dominates the family, and the other is dependent.
Theodore Lidz

Mean: The simple average of all values in a given distribution.
Research Methods & Techniques

Median: The middle value within a range of values in a distribution.
Research Methods & Techniques

Merit: Merit is earned when parents are responsible and ethical with the equitable asymmetry within the parent-child relationship. If they are ethical and fair, they earn merit, which rewards them with loyalty from their childhood as they mature into adults.
Contextual Family Therapy

Metacommunication: Communicating about communication—communication that modifies, qualifies or even disqualifies a communication (this is frequently occurring in family therapy). Essentially, this is referring to the non-verbals going on in the room that have a profound impact on what is being said at the auditory level. This is directly related to the emphasis of tracking content AND process in family therapy.
Communications Theory

Metacommunication: Refers to the *command* aspect of communication—the communication about communication in reference to the relationship. Typically, a non-verbal or implied message.
MRI Systemic Approach and Milan Systemic

Metaphor: This is a symbolic representation that captures the basic and essential features of an object or event by using a description of a different category of objects or events.
Cybernetics

Metaphoric Tasks: Prescribing a directive to a family that engages them in a conversation or activity that is easier or more accessible than talking about the problem directly. It is a metaphor that represents or resembles a family dynamic that is too difficult to talk about directly, but by discussing it through metaphor, it will indirectly contribute to resolving the actual problem.
Strategic Family Therapy

Metaphors: Satir considered metaphors as powerful tools for promoting change, often using them to communicate ideas that language cannot directly describe—this is particularly useful when introducing threatening material.
Satir's Communications Approach

Mimesis: An intentional maneuver by the therapist to join and accommodate with the family by replicating their body language, use of expressive language, mannerisms, and other observable behaviors to create a comfortable, trusting therapeutic space.
Structural Family Therapy

Miracle Question: In Solution-Focused Therapy, the therapist will ask the client to describe what their lives would look like without the problem, as well as define what would be different to the point that they would know the problem was resolved or no longer present. This question comprises components of assessment, goal setting, and intervention.
Solution-Focused Therapy

Mode: The most frequently occurring value in a distribution of values.
Research Methods & Techniques

Model Integration Analysis: The process in which a developing child begins to make sense of his parents' differences, internalizing various perceptions of their behavior toward one another which will ultimately serve as a road map for his or her relational behaviors toward others.
Satir's Communications Approach

Modeling Communication: A key component to Satir's approach to working with families was the therapist's capacity to effectively model functional, healthy communication.
Satir's Communications Approach

More of the Same: In MRI Systemic Therapy, this term refers to the problem in families being a failure to appropriately respond to normal life circumstancese, making the attempted solution to the problem the problem. Families falling into this pattern end up doing "more of the same" behavior, meaning that they do more of the failed solution as opposed to trying a different solution.
MRI Systemic Approach

Morphogenesis: Describes a system's tendency toward growth, creativity, change, and innovation.
Cybernetics

Morphostasis: This describes a system's tendency towards stability and staying the same.
Cybernetics

Multidirectional Partiality: This concept is similar to neutrality while expounding upon the importance that the therapist remains accountable for everyone whose well-being is potentially impacted by a therapeutic intervention. This concept elaborates that every intervention must serve the best interests of everyone involved.
Contextual Family Therapy

Multigenerational Transmission Process: This term refers to the emotional forces in families that continue over the years in interconnected patterns, transmitting down from one generation to the next.
Bowen's Multigenerational Approach

Narrative Metaphor: This describes the primary tool people use to make sense of their lived experiences—that is, story and narrative as a metaphor.
Narrative Family Therapy

Negative Entropy: A systemic state that emerges when a system is balanced between openness and closeness.
Cybernetics

Neutrality & Irreverence: The therapist's stance of being open to multiple hypotheses regarding the family's behavior.
Milan Systemic

Nominal Scales: Also called categorical scales, measure categorical data. These scales are used for variables or indicators that have mutually exclusive attributes. Examples include gender (two values: male or female) or religious affiliation (Christian, Muslim, Jew, etc.).
Research Methods & Techniques

Nonanxious Presence: Bowen emphasized the importance of the therapist remaining differentiated and providing a non-anxious presence throughout the session, influencing the family members to become less reactive and access rationality. This intervention served to promote higher levels of differentiation for each family member through modeling.
Bowen's Multigenerational Approach

Nuclear Family Emotional System: This concept refers to the emotional forces in a nuclear family that are expressed through recurrent patterns of individual behavior and interpersonal connectedness.
Bowen's Multigenerational Approach

Object: An individuals' collective distortions based upon his or her subjective experiences and perceptions of another person—typically, a primary care giver. The object is typically an internalized representation of a parent or primary caregiver based upon a series of repeated interactions throughout early childhood.
Object-Relations Theory

Ontology: Refers to our assumptions about how we see the world (e.g., does the world consist mostly of social order or constant change).
Research Methods & Techniques

Open Systems: Interact regularly with the environment with relatively no inhibition.
Cybernetics

Operational Definitions: Used to define constructs in terms of how they will be empirically measured.
Research Methods & Techniques

Operationalization: The process of designing precise measures for abstract theoretical constructs.
Research Methods & Techniques

Ordeal Therapy: A paradoxical directive that places a client in a situation where it creates more work for them to maintain problem symptoms or behavior than it would be to change it.
Strategic Family Therapy

Ordinal Scales: Scales that measure rank-ordered data, such as the ranking of students in a class as first, second, third, and so forth, based on their grade point average or test scores.
Research Methods & Techniques

Out-of-Session Directive: Paradoxical interventions were typically prescribed through out-of-session directives; that is, instructing the clients to engage in behavioral change outside of the session as opposed to in the here and now of the session.
MRI Systemic Approach

Paradoxical Intervention: Interventions used to address the concept that families are naturally resistant to change. They either involve instructing the family not to change, or to change in ways that contradict their desired change. Now, the family's natural resistance to change will promote them to rebel against the directive to not change, thereby experiencing the initial desired change.
MRI Systemic Approach

Paradoxical Prescription: Either prescribing the symptom or asking the family not to change.
Milan Systemic

Paralinguistic Communication: Includes tone, pace, and inflection.
Communications Theory

Parentification: This term is different from *parentified child* in Structural Family Therapy. Here, it refers to a process where a child attempts to earn love from their parent by acting as their caretaker. The child takes on the role of parent for the parent.
Contextual Family Therapy

Parts Party: An intervention where individuals will explore their various parts, both good and bad, to promote wholeness and integration in individual therapy. In family or group therapy, individuals will have others act out their various parts under their guidance and instruction.
Satir's Communications Approach

Person of the Therapist: Symbolic-Experiential Therapy attributes the psychological health and authenticity of the therapist as a person being a primary factor in effective therapeutic outcomes. The therapist is encouraged to be authentic and real with his or her clients, relying on the spontaneity of their emotional responses as they remain present with the family.
Symbolic-Experiential Therapy

Person-to-Person Relationships: This type of relationship defines two family members that are able to relate to one another openly and freely without the need to triangulate in a third party. Here, individuals tell each other how they are feeling—typically through the use of taking an "I" position—with a sense of wisdom and rationality.
Bowen's Multigenerational Approach

Placaters: One of Satir's four dysfunctional communication styles. Disregarding one's own feelings of worth and handing power over to another individual (e.g. pleasing everyone in the family except one's self). Here, the context and the other is acknowledged, but the self is not.
Satir's Communications Approach

Planning: The period of assessment in Structural Family Therapy when the therapist hypothesizes about the structure of the family while remaining curious about its actual structure.
Structural Family Therapy

Positioning: A paradoxical intervention of pushing a family member further into the absurdity of their initial position, thereby making them realize their own absurdity.
MRI Systemic Approach

Positive Connotation: The Hallmark of the early Milan Systemic School. Positive Connotation illuminates upon circularity by assigning a positive motive or value to each family member's behavior—whether it be a desirable or undesirable behavior.
Milan Systemic

Preference Questions: The manner in which the therapist checks in with the client to ensure that the discourse of therapy is congruent with the client's actual desires and hopes.
Narrative Family Therapy

Preferred Narrative: After the problem-saturated story has been deconstructed, clients reflect upon what sort of preferred narrative they may wish to construct moving forward.
Narrative Family Therapy

Prescribing the Symptom: A paradoxical intervention through instructing client's to intentionally engage in the behavior they wish to change. They may either rebel against the therapist's directive and experience desired change, or comply with the therapist's directive and become aware of their control over choosing to continually engage in the undesirable behavior.
MRI Systemic Approach

Presenting Symptom as Metaphor: The symptom was redefined as a metaphor of a larger problem. For example, a child wetting his bed was a metaphor for keeping focus on him so his father can maintain his addiction to marijuana.
Strategic Family Therapy

Pretend to Have Symptom: A form of paradoxical intervention where Madanes would instruct a child to have a symptom and instruct the parents to help the child through it.
Strategic Family Therapy

Primary Emotions: These referred to underlying emotions that drove relational behavior, but were hardly acknowledged or talked about directly. Primary emotions were the more fundamental emotional experiences such as powerlessness, fear, loneliness, etc..
Emotionally Focused Couples Therapy

Primary Needs: Needs that are related to attachment and experienced through primary emotions.
Emotionally Focused Couples Therapy

Primary Survival Triad: The triad consists of the child and both parents. These dynamics serve as the primary source of the infant's social interaction and only opportunity for a gratifying relationship—as so, it sets the stage for the developed internal sense of being within oneself and in relation to others. For example, a child will internalize how a woman treats a man based upon her perceptions of how her father treated her mother, and vise-versa with her mother toward her dad.
Satir's Communications Approach

Problem as Attempted Solution: In MRI Systemic Therapy, the therapist traditionally assesses that the problem is not the problem, but the attempted solutions to fix the problem reinforces the interactional behavioral sequence.
MRI Systemic Approach

Problem-Saturated Stories: When clients identify with a narrative that emphasizes a metaphoric problem throughout time, thereby influencing their perception of the past as well as their experience of the present and future. These are traditionally externally influenced and repress the subjugated story more congruent with the authentic reality of the individual.
Narrative Family Therapy

Process Questions: These questions aim to slow individuals down, thereby decreasing emotionality and increasing rationality as the individual becomes more aware of how stress and anxiety influence behavior.
Bowen's Multigenerational Approach

Process: This refers to dynamic aspects that are changing within the system. Often, family therapists make the distinction between process (how something is said) and content (what is being said).
Cybernetics

Projection: When a child is born, each parent projects the fragments of his or her repressed object relationships onto the child.
Object-Relations Theory

Projective Identification: When a child is born, each parent of the couple system projects the remnants of his or her repressed object relationships onto the child. The child then internalizes these projections into becoming significant components of his or her personality development.
Object-Relations Theory

Proxemics: Spatial relations between those in dialogue.
Communications Theory

Pseudohostility: A volatile and intense way of disguising and distorting both affection and splits.
Lyman Wynne

Pseudomutuality: Describes a systemic pretense of harmony and closeness that hides conflict and interferes with intimacy.
Lyman Wynne

Psychology: One of the four dimensions of individual and relational psychology that interact with one another in Contextual Family Therapy. Psychology refers to the person's internal experience of the world, including thoughts, desires, emotions, and meaning. As Facts occur externally to the individual, psychology develops internally within the individual.
Contextual Family Therapy

Punctuation (different than Milan): The therapist's intentional emphasizing of an individual's reaction (body language) or statement, allowing them to become aware of their responses and reflect upon their meanings.
Structural Family Therapy

Punctuation (different than Structural): The manner in which individuals attribute their behaviors as a result of another's behavior. For example, I only nag you cause you never offer to help.
Milan Systemic

Qualitative Analysis: The analysis of qualitative data such as text data from interview transcripts and heavily dependent on the researcher's analytic and integrative skills and personal knowledge of the social context where the data is collected.
Research Methods & Techniques

Quantitative Analysis: Statistics driven and largely independent of the researcher.
Research Methods & Techniques

Range: The difference between the highest and lowest values in a distribution.
Research Methods & Techniques

Recursiveness: This refers to reciprocal or circular causality. Rather than viewing an element in a vacuum devoid of interactions between its environment and its own system's levels or subsystems, recursiveness speaks to the mutual interaction and influence that occurs between people, events, and their ecosystem.
Cybernetics

Redefining Symptoms: Symbolic-Experiential Therapists will often redefine symptoms from pathological to efforts toward growth.
Symbolic-Experiential Therapy

Reframing: Presenting an alternative perspective on a family members view of another's problematic behavior.
Strategic & Structural Family Therapy

Relational Ethics: One of the four dimensions of individual and relational psychology that interact with one another in Contextual Family Therapy. Relational Ethics are the most significant component to Contextual Family Therapy, and refer to the responsibility each individual has for the impact that their behaviors have on others. Contextual Family Therapy endorses a consideration for the best interests of the other in your family.
Contextual Family Therapy

Relationship Experiments: These were used to help clients become aware of systemic processes within their relationship through understanding how their behaviors impact others. These were directive in nature and instructed clients to experiment with different ways of behaving and responding to one another.
Bowen's Multigenerational Approach

Relative Influencing Questioning: Assists the client in externalizing the problem through mapping the influence of the problem and mapping the influence of the person.
Narrative Family Therapy

Report and Command Functions: Every communication has two components, *report* (i.e. the content of the message) and *command* (a message about the relationship).
MRI Systemic Approach

Restraining the Progress of Change: A paradoxical intervention when clients come in reporting that therapy has been effective and that they are experiencing change, the therapist encourages them to slow down, and cautions them about the risk of changing too fast.
MRI Systemic Approach

Revolving Slate of Injustice: The multigenerational transmission of destructive entitlement in which one generation harms the next generation despite the fact that there was no wrong doing.
Contextual Family Therapy

Rigid Boundary: Overly restrictive boundaries that permit little contact with outside subsystems, often resulting in disengagement.
Structural Family Therapy

Ripple Effect: This refers to how a change that occurs at one level of a system will result in changes across other levels of the system.
Cybernetics

Rituals: An intervention presented by a therapy team that is described in great detail, instructing various individuals within the family to carry out specific behaviors at specific times of the day for a distinct period of time. They serve to provide consistency and clarity as to the hypothesized problem within the family.
Milan Systemic

Role of Therapist: Satir viewed the role of the therapist to be one of an equal; a unique individual serving to facilitate change through genuineness, empathy, curiosity, and transparency.
Satir's Communications Approach

Role-Function Discrepancy: The concept used to identify relationships comprised of inappropriate roles.
Satir's Communications Approach

Rubber-Fence Boundary: The families are seemingly yielding, but are in fact nearly impermeable to information from outside systems.
Lyman Wynne

Sampling: The target population from which they wish to collect data.
Research Methods & Techniques

Scaling Questions: Solution-Focused Therapists will often put questions in the form of a 10-point scale to measure progress. Emphasis is always drawn to the positivity associated with the number not being lower than it could be. For instance, if the client rates his depression as a 3, the therapist will celebrate that the depression is not at a 2.
Solution-Focused Therapy

Second-Order Change: Change that occurs at the level of family beliefs or rules that govern patterns of interaction.
MRI Systemic Approach

Secondary Data Analysis: An analysis of data that has previously been collected and tabulated by other sources.
Research Methods & Techniques

Secondary Emotions: These referred to the surface level emotions designed to protect the primary emotions and reflect more upon the interaction than the individual. Secondary emotions are usually reactive in nature and resemble defensiveness, frustration and anger.
Emotionally Focused Couples Therapy

Self-Mandala: This was an exercise where individuals would create a circle in the center of a page with the identifier "I am" along with eight other concentric circles labeled in the following order: physical, intellectual, emotional, sensual, interactional, nutritional, contextual, and spiritual. This illuminated upon an individual's strengths, resources, and interrelated nature of experience.
Satir's Communications Approach

Self-Worth: The degree to which an individual feels as if their existence has value, influenced both internally and interrelatedly. Satir believed that developing an individual's self-worth should always be a primary goal of growth-oriented therapy.
Satir's Communications Approach

Sensate Focus: This is an intervention that allows couples to ease into sex and overcome inhibition by becoming more familiar with one's body through a series of touch, identifying please responses and connecting mind and body.
Sex Therapy

Sexual Disorder: A <u>psychological</u> arousal or performance problem. *This can be treated by a Sex Therapist.*
Sex Therapy

Sexual Dysfunction: A <u>physiological</u> arousal or performance problem. *This requires a MEDICAL referral.*
Sex Therapy

Shaping Competence: This changes the direction of interactions. Therapists avoid telling families what they are doing wrong; rather, they point out what they are doing right and express confidence in the family's competence.
Structural Family Therapy

Sibling Position: Bowen endorsed that an individual's personality development will be highly influenced by his or her position in the sibling birth order. This also plays a role in how children are chosen as the object for the family projection process.
Bowen's Multigenerational Approach

Societal Emotional Process: This term refers to the impact of social influences on family functioning. Individuals (families) with higher levels of self-differentiation are less vulnerable to destructive societal influences, such as sexism and discrimination.
Bowen's Multigenerational Approach

Softening: This is displayed when a partner withdraws from defensiveness and/or aggressiveness, and begins to open up to the emotional experience of his or her partner as opposed to remaining exclusively focused on his or her own experience.
Emotionally Focused Couples Therapy

Solution and Future Focus: The concept that the therapist does not need to understand the problem in order to resolve it as the solution is often unrelated to the problem. Maintaining a future focus of what works is what will bring relief to the individual/family.
Solution-Focused Therapy

Spectatoring: When sexually active, one focuses all mental attention on his or her own sexual behavior (or, quality of performing that sexual behavior). This can either be a result of performance anxiety or result in experiencing performance anxiety.
Sex Therapy

Split Filial Loyalty: This concept arises when a child finds him or herself in a position where they have to choose loyalty toward one parent at the expense of being loyal to the other.
Contextual Family Therapy

Split-Half Reliability: A measure of consistency between two halves of a construct measure.
Research Methods & Techniques

Spontaneous Behavioral Sequences: Similar to enactments, except these behaviors are spontaneous as opposed to being directed by the therapist.
Structural Family Therapy

Squeeze Technique: This intervention is used to work through preejaculation. Prior to the male reaching orgasm, the partner squeezes the penis to disrupt the orgasmic process.
Sex Therapy

Standard Deviation: The second measure of dispersion. Corrects for such outliers by using a formula that takes into account how close or how far each value lies from the distribution mean.
Research Methods & Techniques

Statistical Conclusion Validity: Examines the extent to which conclusions derived using a statistical procedure is valid.
Research Methods & Techniques

Stop-Start Technique: To treat preejaculation in men. Preferred source of stimulation would occur until the male reaches premonitory sensations, then stimulation stops. This process is repeated, allowing the male to build a greater tolerance for pleasure as well as better control over his body. Also builds confidence by extending the duration of sexual interaction.
Sex Therapy

Strengths and Resources: During the assessment and throughout the ongoing process, the therapist maintains a focus on the client's strengths and resources, as these will likely serve as a component to resolving the presenting problem.
Solution-Focused Therapy

Streptic Communication: Sounds (e.g. claps, whistles).
Communications Theory

Structural Family Mapping: As a means of assessment, a therapist will create a Structural Family Map of the hypothesized family structure.
Structural Family Therapy

Structures: These are aspects of a system that are universal across systems, in that all systems have a structure to them. Structures can be adapted, changed, and influenced by a variety of events as well as intentionally through therapeutic intervention. Although all systems will have a structure, there is no one universal structure or set measure of the objective quality of structure. Structure is defined subjectively by the observer.
Cybernetics

Subjugated Story: The more positive, authentic, and congruent attributes of an individual that are vulnerable to suppression through a problem saturated or dominant cultural discourse. The subjugated story typically entails times in which the problem did not have power over the individual, or times that the individual was able to take control of the problem.
Narrative Family Therapy

Subsystems: Individuals, dyads, triads, and groups form subsystems or units within the family that perform certain functions.
Structural Family Therapy

Survey Research: A research method involving the use of standardized questionnaires or interviews to collect data about people and their preferences, thoughts, and behaviors in a systematic manner.
Research Methods & Techniques

Symmetrical Relationships: Based on equality; the behavior of one mirrors that of the other.
Communications Theory and MRI Systemic Approach

Team Approach: A team of therapists that strategically hypothesize and plan interventions regarding each particular family. Often, team members will watch therapy as it unfolds behind a one-way mirror as one or two therapists work directly with the family.
Milan Systemic

Teaming Roles: Healthy members of a family may be intentionally paired into teaming roles by the therapist to encourage further healthy behavior by other family members.
Symbolic-Experiential Therapy

Temperature Reading: An intervention that explores thoughts and feelings while improving communication and self-worth. Clients are encouraged to share particular experiences of their appreciations and excitements, complaints and possible solutions, hopes and wishes, etc..
Satir's Communications Approach

Test-Retest Reliability: A measure of consistency between two measurements (tests) of the same construct administered to the same sample at two different points in time.
Research Methods & Techniques

Therapeutic Certificates: After clients discharge, Narrative Therapists will present them with a Therapeutic Certificate for them to keep, honoring the effort and growth of their engagement in therapy.
Narrative Family Therapy

Therapeutic Double Bind: When asked about a possible diagnosis, Whitaker would initiate a therapeutic double bind—that is, a relational diagnosis that is unlikely to ever change.
Symbolic-Experiential Therapy

Therapeutic Letters: After clients would discharge, a Narrative Therapist may write them a therapeutic letter that reflects upon the nature of their work and the growth they achieved, helping to maintain the growth into the future.
Narrative Family Therapy

Therapy of the Absurd: Symbolic-Experiential Therapy may be referred to as absurd given its unrecognizable structure, spontaneous process, and therapist transparency.
Symbolic-Experiential Therapy

Tickling the Defenses: This denoted Ackerman's famous phrase for teasing, provoking, and stimulating members of the family to open up and say what is really on their minds.
Nathan Ackerman

The Timberlawn Model: An objective assessment tool measuring two types of family patterns: *Family Competence* and *Family Style*.
Assessment in Family Therapy

Time: Suggesting that a family's historic perception of a problem influences their current perspective on the problem, affecting their view of the past and present behavior. For example, if I perceive my mother as cold, I will only recall times in the past where my mother was cold and ignore current instances of my mother demonstrating warmth or compassion.
Milan Systemic

Transactions: One of the four dimensions of individual and relational psychology that interact with one another in Contextual Family Therapy. Transactions refer to the patterns of organization and dynamics within the individual's family system.
Contextual Family Therapy

Transference: The tendency of individuals to attribute qualities to other individuals—partners, family members, or the therapist—that reflect unresolved grievances from a previous relationship.
Object-Relations Theory

Triangles: Triangles are created when an individual in a relationship pulls in a third party (i.e. another person, a hobby, a substance, etc.) to create the illusion of emotional closeness that they are not receiving from the other individual in the relationship. The third party then creates a triangle, decreasing the anxiety between the two individuals by spreading it across a third.
Bowen's Multigenerational Approach

Triphasic Sexual Response: Kaplan included *sexual desire, excitement,* and *orgasm* to better explain sexual intercourse.
Sex Therapy

Unbalancing: An intervention where the therapist intentionally sides with one family member over the other, meant to disrupt homeostasis and encourage change at the behavioral and structural level.
Strategic & Structural Family Therapy

Undifferentiated Family Ego Mass (now referred to as the Nuclear Family Emotional System): This term is used to identify an excess of emotional reactivity, anxiety, and fusion within a family system.
Bowen's Multigenerational Approach

Unique Outcomes (Sparkling Events): These are types of questions aimed at exploring times when the problem did not have control over the individual's or family's life.
Narrative Family Therapy

Unit of Analysis: Refers to the person, collective group, or object that is the target of the investigation.
Research Methods & Techniques

Validity: Refers to the extent to which a measure adequately represents the underlying construct that it is supposed to measure.
Research Methods & Techniques

Variable: A measurable representation of an abstract construct.
Research Methods & Techniques

Vehicles of Change: Instead of relying on predetermined techniques, Satir endorsed a model of using vehicles of change with clients that were more adaptable.
Satir's Communications Approach

Visitor: One of the three types of clients in Solution-Focused Therapy. Visitors are agreeable to attend therapy, but are not willing to put forth effort to change.
Solution-Focused Therapy

Working Through: After insight is achieved, the working through process entails translating insight into more desirable and constructive ways of being.
Object-Relations Theory

Bowen's Family Systems Approach

When working with this family through this particular approach, the therapist will want to first assess for patterns of *togetherness* and *individuality* by exploring individual's *family of origin,* the presence of *triangles,* and begin recognizing the varying *levels of differentiation.* This approach also emphasizes the importance of the therapeutic relationship, which is done through maintaining *neutrality* and *remaining differentiated* from the *family's emotional system;* thereby providing a n*onanxious presence* throughout session.

> *Also be sure to attend to issues of early countertransference in reaction to your own family of origin issues, remembering that this approach is largely informed by *psychoanalytic thinking.*

A genogram will help in drawing attention to patterns of the *Nuclear Family Emotional Process, Family Projection Process,* and *Undifferentiated Family Ego Mass.* The insights gained through the co-creation of the *Genogram* can then be applied to identifying and addressing sources of anxiety, initiating the *working through* process of *decreasing anxiety within the family system.* Techniques in this phase will include *Process Questions, "I" Statements,"* and *Encouraging Differentiation.*

As the aim will be to *decrease anxiety* within the family system and encourage more *rational communication* (individuality) *and connection* (togetherness), you will eventually want to work toward facilitating change in the family process by *increasing the levels of differentiation* in each family member. Interventions in this phase may include *Coaching* members to communicate more effectively, assigning *Relationship Experiments* outside of the session, using *Displacement Stories* to draw awareness to the interrelated nature of family systems, and/or encouraging *"Going Home Again"* visits to relevant family members who may be experiencing *emotional cutoff.*

Areas to Explore

- The role that gender norms are playing in the division of family dynamics, and how these may have been *Transmitted Across a Multitude of Generations.*
- The many triangles within the family system (Dad and his two sons; Mom, Maternal-Grandmother, and Daughter; Dad, Mom, and Maternal-Grandmother; etc.).
- *Emotional Cutoff* from Dad and Paternal Grandmother.
- Dad's *fusion* to his deceased father.
- The *Hostile Fusion* between Dad and Mom.
- Considering how these patterns may influence the future spousal relationships of the children.
- The *levels of differentiation* and *mismanaged anxiety*

It will be important to work with Mom and Dad, helping them establish higher levels of differentiation which will positively impact their marriage. This will likely be done through Dad exploring how his experiences from his *family of origin* continue to impact his capacity to engage in balanced relationships (insight) and begin learning new ways of relating to others (working through). This will likely improve the marriage and *detriangulate* Dad from his two sons, making space for Mom to establish healthier relationships with her sons, Dad to establish a healthier relationship with his daughter, and for the siblings to improve their relationships as well.

Here, the therapist would maintain awareness of any transference and countertransference present in the therapeutic encounter, and therapy would be long term.

Contextual Family Therapy

After completing a thorough assessment during the early phase of therapy (as outlined in the Contextual Family Therapy chapter in this manual), the therapist may have likely discovered many dynamics congruent with the literature of this approach.

For instance, Dad's withdrawal from his wife and daughter and exclusive focus on parenting his two sons may be the source of a *destructive entitlement* developed from early childhood experiences. It would be important to explore the manner in which dad experienced being parented as a child and the role they played in developing his current parenting and spousal style.

Further, there is evidence of *split familial loyalties* organized by gender spreading across all three generations as the two sons are *loyal* to their father at the expense of their mother, the daughter being *loyal* to her mother at the expense of her father, and the father being *loyal* to his father at the expense of the relationship with his own mother. The manner in which these patterns have transmitted across generations suggests the present dynamic of a *revolving slate of injustice* that would need to be addressed in therapy to prevent it from transmitting through the next generation.

Although the vignette does not present this information in detail, it may be worthwhile to assess for any *parentification processes*. There is evidence of over involvement between dad and his two sons and mom and her daughter, suggesting the possibility that some of the children may have been put in a position where they are expected to parent and care for their parent. If so, the middle-phase of therapy would require working through the *deparentification process*.

There is evidence of behaviors suggesting a lack of *fairness* throughout the family, as Dad spends much time withdrawn from the family outside of work and exclusively with his two sons. This may be the source of *destructive entitlements* which prevent Dad from taking responsibility for how his behaviors affect others in the family. A therapy goal would be to have each family member take responsibility for their actions after gaining insight into its impact on the system.

As these themes develop throughout the therapist's continued assessment for each individual's experience of these many dynamics—thereby executing *multidirectional partiality*—therapy becomes a process of gaining mutual insight, shared accountability, and paves way for *exoneration*.

In the later-phases of therapy, Dad will become more aware of his behaviors and their impact on the family resulting in him taking accountability and acting more *ethically* and *fair* toward others. Similarly, Mom will recognize her role in becoming overly involved with her own mother and daughter. As Mom and Dad begin to act more *ethically* toward one another, this will transmit down to the sibling generation and encourage similar behaviors between one another. The siblings will no longer be put in a position of *splitting* their *familial loyalty* and open themselves to join *fairly* with all members in the family. *Exoneration* will be achieved, levels of *trustworthiness* and *reliability* will be sustained, and the family will reach higher levels of relational health.

Here, the therapist would maintain awareness of any transference and countertransference present in the therapeutic encounter and therapy would be long-term.

Object-Relations Theory

Here, therapy would be more so based on developing insight toward the underlying, internal conflicts fueling behavior than symptom relief. As so, therapy would be long term and emphasize the importance of working with the family of origin of each parent.

The early-phase of therapy would entail an in depth assessment attending to dynamics in the family of origin being transmitted into the sibling generation. It may include the use of a genogram and likely span across several sessions. Attention would be given to Mom and Dad's early childhood experiences and ways in which they related to their parents throughout the past and into the present. Some themes that we may hypothesize from the genogram include:

- The father feeling split from his mother and *projecting* those resentments onto his wife and daughter, which may influence them to act in ways similar to dad's mother through the process of *projective identification.*
- The *objects* and *introjects* that may be fueling the gender divisions within the nuclear family (e.g. women are all bad and men are all good).
- The degree to which the siblings are sacrificing their own healthy ego development due to craving acceptance from their mother or father (i.e. the boys sacrificing learning how to have healthy relationships with women in order to sustain the approval of their father, and vice-versa for the daughter and her mom).

As these dynamics suggest patterns within the family as a whole, the Object-Relations therapist may exclusively focus on working with just the mother or just the father and their family of origin. For instance, **Framo** would encourage the dad to bring in his mother for several sessions to work through the disconnection and resentment currently characterizing their relationship. If Dad is able to work through this directly with his mom, he will no longer *project* that resentment onto his family of creation and gain the *insight* necessary to understand how those experiences drive his current behaviors. He would then begin *working through* these insights as he explores new ways of behaving and relating to others in his family. This would create space for each member of the family to begin developing a healthy, *central ego.*

Here, the therapist would maintain awareness of any transference and countertransference present in the therapeutic encounter, and therapy would be long term.

MRI Systemic Approach

Here, therapy would be brief and problem focused. The family would identify one problem that the therapy team would aim to relieve by interrupting the behavioral cycle that is maintaining it. If the mom reported that the problem was Dad feeling disconnected from his daughter and wife, then therapy would invite only the mom, dad, and daughter into session.

The team would identify any *more-of-the-same behaviors* that have turned into the problem and *estimate the solution*. Here, we may assume that the father has *denied that a problem exists*, suggesting that he needs to *start acting* toward its potential resolution. After the first session has clearly identified the problem, given the estimation that the problem does not exist, the therapy team may likely instruct the family *not to change* as changing too fast could be harmful to the family (this would be the first use of paradoxical intervention by *restraining the progress of change*).

At the next session, it would be determined whether or not Dad *complied* with the directive to *not change*, *defied* the directive, or became more open to considering that a problem exists. Let us say Dad *defied* the directive and spent time with his daughter that next weekend. Here, therapy could either be terminated or attention can shift to Dad spending more time with Mom. A MRI Systemic therapist may likely give the directive that the problem between Dad and the daughter is relieved, so only Mom and Dad need to continue treatment. As the dynamic shifts to Dad withdrawing from Mom and spending most time with his sons or in his workshop, the therapy team may direct the father again to *not change* too quickly, and instead, continue to go into his work shop each night to decompress (i.e. *prescribing the symptom*). This directive will likely be specific and provide the client with an outline of specific steps to effectively decompress each night. For instance, the team may direct dad to come home each night after five pm, park his car in the garage, go right upstairs without acknowledging anyone in his family, change out of his work clothes and into more comfortable clothes, walk down stairs to grab two beers from the fridge—still without acknowledging anyone in his family—and enter his work shop for no less than two hours and no more than three hours.

The next session, the therapy team would assess whether or not Dad *complied, defied*, or *learned something new* based on the intervention. Let's say Dad *complied* the first night, but *defied* the directive every night after that and began spending time with his family. It would be hypothesized that the paradoxical intervention made Dad aware that he was *choosing* to engage in a behavior that was maintaining the problem, freeing him to *choose* to engage in a *different behavior* that would resolve the problem. As so, therapy could be terminated.

If the symptoms were still present after 10 sessions, the therapy team would discontinue treatment regardless of progress given the time-limited nature of this approach. Keep in mind, as we saw in this conceptualization, therapy will terminate the moment the symptom is relieved even if that occurs after the first session.

Strategic Family Therapy

Here, therapy would be similar to MRI Systemic given its problem-focused and brief-treatment approach, but differ in the sense that it will not be time limited and gives an additional focus to the importance of strengthening the parental hierarchy and the role of the family life cycle. Again, only members directly related to the problem would be introduced to treatment. Let's say the problem was Mom feeling disconnected from her two sons who are only interested in spending time with Dad. Since the two boys refuse to come to treatment, Mom and Dad would be invited to work with the therapist as a couple. After working through the *Four-Stage First Session,* the early treatment goal would likely have Mom and Dad find ways of working together to help Mom better join with the two sons. This act in and of itself will break the *interactional behavioral cycle* of Dad being disconnected from Mom, which influences the two sons being disconnected as well. It will also begin to *strengthen the parental hierarchy* by first being *child focused* prior to working on the relationship directly.

After the couple is able to work through this problem and Mom reports feeling more connected to her sons with Dad's encouragement and support, therapy can shift to strengthening the parental hierarchy directly. As this groundwork has already been paved indirectly by the first intervention noted above, Mom and Dad will be more open to this process considering that their relationship was not included in the presenting complaint. Now, the therapy team may intervene by the use of a *paradoxical intervention, a metaphoric task, ordeal therapy,* and / or the use of a *reframe.* Let us say the therapist decides to go with *ordeal therapy.* Here, the therapist may direct the dad to write down a list of 20 reasons why he needs to decompress away from his family that day, and share it with his wife prior to going into his workshop. Another example would be to direct the couple to prepare the workshop together each evening prior to Dad beginning his decompression process—knowing that clutter is anxiety-provoking for Dad yet the workshop is the only space that his wife does not maintain on a daily basis. An additional task would direct his wife to pour him each beer into a pint glass. This will introduce a sense of mindfulness and intentionality into the behavioral cycle, likely interfering with its maintenance by (1) introducing mom into Dad's routine while still allowing private decompression and (2) putting Dad in a position of questioning whether or not he wishes to continue detaching from his wife.

Again, the couple may *comply, defy,* or learn from the intervention. Once the symptom is relieved through strengthening the parental hierarchy, therapy is terminated.

Milan-Systemic Therapy

Milan Systemic would see the family for up to 10 sessions spaced 4-6 weeks apart. The focus here would be on changing the rules that govern family interactions which are best interrupted through the use of paradoxical interventions. Here, the family would be seen by a male-female therapy dyad while being observed behind a one-way mirror by a team of therapists. Before the first session—after the phone call—and after each following session, the team would meet to review the hypothesis and make changes according to new information presented in the session as well as collaborate on the paradoxical intervention.

The first session would likely include Mom, Dad, and the daughter given the resistance of the two sons to attend. After further assessment was done to clearly understand the presenting problem—which, in this case is the divisions between genders—the team would reconvene to devise an intervention. Throughout, the therapists may use *positive connotation* to begin introducing new ways of viewing the problem, such as referring to Dad decompressing each night as demonstrating impressive means of self-care or the daughter being split from dad as her selflessly sacrificing her relationship with dad to ensure her mom does not feel completely left out.

The next session may include the prescription of the paradoxical intervention, which in this case, may be a *positive connotation* combined with a *ritual* through the form of a letter that the therapy team wrote for the family to take home. The letter may read as follows:

> Dear Franklin and Mikey,
>
> After meeting with your mother, father, and sister, we wanted to personally thank the two of you for refusing to come to family therapy. Your absence continues to allow your sister to be your mother's saving grace, illuminating her dedication to pleasing her and relieving her of having to put any energy into her relationship with either of you. This will continue to allow Dad to isolate himself in the workshop as your mother's relationship with your sister relieves any guilt he would feel knowing that she was left all alone. Also, we fear that if the two of you were to come to family therapy you may witness your father becoming emotional as he shares the sadness he must sit with each evening as he isolates himself in his workshop, thereby shattering your illusions of masculinity and forcing the men in your family to consider how to have a healthy relationship with a female. We fear that this would be too much change too fast for the individuals in your family. Your continued absence will allow Dad to resume his impressive job of self-care each evening, prevent any interference within the relationship between your mom and sister, and allow the two of you to continue relishing in your masculinity each weekend with Dad, thereby preventing the prevalence of any felt-emotion.
>
> -The Milan Associates

The team may then prescribe a *ritual* that the mother, father, and daughter read this letter aloud to the two sons prior to leaving for each therapy session while personally thanking them. This dynamic would draw awareness to the problem maintaining patterns of interaction throughout the family by introducing a new *epistemology* to understanding the systemic problem.

The later Milan split may include the following:
Palazzoli & Prata may intervene with the *invariant prescription* and **Boscolo & Cecchin** would engage in an ongoing process of circular questioning as a means of introducing new information into the family system that will eventually result in symptom relief.

Structural Family Therapy

This approach would focus on the current structure of the family and identify any dynamics within that are likely causing the ongoing symptoms of the individuals and conflicts between one another. After effectively *joining* with the family, the therapist may assess by devising a *family map*, identifying the *coalitions* between Dad with the two sons and Mom with her daughter. The therapist may also assess for the *diffuse boundaries* (enmeshment) between Mom and her mother, Mom and her daughter, and Dad with his two sons.

The therapist may likely request that the two sons be present for all sessions moving forward, as this approach relies upon in-session directives as an agent for change. After the two sons begin attending therapy, the therapist would strengthen the parental subsystem and create clear boundaries between Mom and Dad and the sibling subsystem. This will strengthen the relationship between Mom and Dad while creating opportunities for the siblings to grow as individuals as well as build a stronger relationship between the two sons and daughter.

In-session directives would include *unbalancing, challenging family assumptions, reframing, shopping competences,* and *boundary making.* The therapist may likely join with the parental subsystem as a means of creating clearer boundaries between the parental subsystem and sibling subsystem. This would be an example of *unbalancing* and *boundary making.* Once a functional spousal subsystem and clear boundaries between all individuals within the nuclear family is achieved, therapy is terminated.

Symbolic-Experiential Family Therapy

Upon the first phone call, the therapist would require that the entire family be present for the first session of therapy if they wish to be seen. If the family complied, the therapist has won *the battle for structure* and the family has begun to win *the battle for initiative.* The goal here would be to facilitate sessions spontaneously and freely in a way that encourages emotional expression and healthy individuation and development of each family member. Therapy was not time limited and will vary between each family seen.

Here, the family would be seen by a co-therapy team that was transparent and present with the family, often using self-disclosure and sharing their personal emotional responses throughout the session. Some interventions may include the following:

- *Redefining Symptoms*: Dad spending time isolating is a good demonstration of self-care after working hard to financially provide for his family all day.

- *Fantasy Alternative*: After Mom reports that Dad spend so much time in his workshop, the therapist may say "well at least he is not having an affair."

- *Affective Confrontation*: The therapist may support Dad in identifying how it is for him to sit in the workshop each evening by himself, confronting the fact that his workbench does a better job of taking care of his emotional needs than his wife does.

These interventions are meant to *expand the symptom to the family system* and begin identifying the nature between the individual and the system. This not only helps individuals to become more emotionally expressive with themselves, but also with one another—two processes that will contribute to both individual and relational growth simultaneously. As family members begin to express what they are actually *feeling* with one another, the relational ties will strengthen and the family will begin to experience more connection and independence.

Satir's Human Validation Process Model

The nature of this treatment would be to draw attention to the inherent goodness within each family member and create an environment where everyone feels comfortable to explore their inner selves and grow in ways congruent to who they are. It would emphasize the patterns and styles of communication and help individuals develop more sensitive and compassionate ways of speaking with one another.

The therapist may explore the *primary survival triad* of each parent, having them reflect upon what their parents' marriage and parenting style taught them about being a spouse and a parent. Parents would consider how they recognize these similar or different patterns in their family of creation as well as how it influenced their *self-worth*. Also, the therapist may use an experiential intervention such as *family sculpting*, where each member would position the family in ways he or she experiences them creating space for deeper reflection at the emotional level.

After *communication style and patterns* are identified, the therapist would improve effective means of communication through modeling and exploration, improve the *self-esteem* of each individual in the family, and help each member to *actualize his or her potential for growth*. The therapist may effectively demonstrate the use of touch as healing throughout therapy and as well as empathic communication and connection through his or her relationship with each family member.

Emotionally Focused Couples Therapy

This approach would work exclusively with Mom and Dad in an attempt to strengthen family connection through the growth of the spousal relationship.

This therapy would identify the role that attachment has played in each partner's development and its impact on the relationship. Ernest and Carol would learn to identify the primary emotions that are present within their relational patterns, growing as individuals while their partner bears witness and gains compassion and empathy (i.e. a deeper understanding of their partner's pain).

This will *deescalate the problematic interactional cycle* and *promote identification with disowned attachment needs.* For example, instead of Ernest identifying that he isolates in the garage because he is exhausted from work, he may discover that he isolates in the garage because he is fearful that his wife will reject and disappoint his emotional needs. This fear is not only present in the spousal relationship, but as Ernest discovers is tied to ways in which his mother disappointed and rejected him throughout his early childhood and into his adult life (attachment wounds). Carol may identify that she is permissive of Ernest's withdrawal out of a fear that her attempts to soothe him will not be good enough and met with anger and disappointment, so she instead invests in relationships where she feels valued. As a result, she has learned to suppress her pain as much of her value in relationships has been her tendency to take care of others, realizing that she never learned how to let another take care of her in return.

Once Ernest and Carol work individually with the therapist, emotionally processing their experiences, therapy will direct them to *turn toward* one another and begin practicing constructive communication. With a deeper level of understanding and insight, the couple can learn to sensitively care for one another's attachment needs. This will create an *emotional engagement* between the two and make way for the *emergence of new solutions to old problematic behaviors*, thereby creating a new cycle of positive attachment.

Therapy here is somewhat brief, typically 12-20 sessions.

A Shift to Post-Modernism

Here, the therapist would take a dramatic shift from the *problem-focused* nature of the approaches reviewed thus far, and instead maintain an interest on the family's *strengths* and things they are already doing well. For instance, up until now I would assume you have not noticed the many positive dynamics suggested in the family's vignette and genogram. Let's review what the family is already doing well:

- Each member of the family has at least one healthy relationship, so everyone in the family has a capacity to relate well to another.

- Both Mom and Dad have displayed a capacity to join with a sibling and develop a strong relationship with children.

- Dad has a positive relationship with his mother-in-law, so he has demonstrated a capacity to have a healthy relationship with an adult woman in his life.

- Dad has a close relationship with his deceased father, suggesting some areas of exploration.

- Mom has a close relationship with both of her parents, suggesting a capacity to have a healthy relationship with an adult male.

- The family is still together! There is no report of desired divorce, no history of affairs, and the daughter is off to college. With this, we can assume that the family is doing some things right and remaining committed to one another.

- The two brothers have a positive relationship, suggesting a capacity to have a healthy sibling relationship.

- The boys are very outgoing and family oriented, spending almost every weekend going on outings with their father.

- Three out of the five of them are willing to come to family therapy! That glass is definitely more than half full.

I don't know about you guys, but all of the sudden I find myself feeling much more optimistic about working with this family. If you did experience a shift at the experiential level, that, my friends, is what the Post-Modern wave is all about. Overly focusing on what is not working in a family—which, assessment has traditionally been all about—can result in an overwhelming and detrimental distraction away from the things that *are* working. This would be the guiding philosophy of a Solution-Focused Therapist as well as many other Post-Modern approaches.

Solution-Focused Family Therapy

Here, the therapist would begin with the *Formula First-Session Task*, that is, quickly shifting the focus away from the problem and toward the *family's strengths and resources*, setting the stage for a *future-focused* therapeutic discourse. The problem is only explored to the point where the family feels validated and the therapist feels that he or she has a good sense of what is causing the family distress. The therapist will be under the impression that the solution will likely have little to do with the problem, and instead, lie within constructive behaviors and actions the family is already engaging in.

Interventions may include:

The miracle question: Ask Mom to visualize waking up tomorrow and realizing that all of the sudden there are no more divisions within the family and that the problems have been resolved. How would she know? What would be different?

Exception questions: Ask the family about times when Mom has connected with her sons, when Dad has connected with his daughter, when the three siblings have connected, and when Mom and Dad have connected with one another. Then, engage in a curious dialogue around what was going on those times that allowed that to happen while wondering about the family intentionally recreating those experiences.

Scaling questions: Have the family scale where they are at each week as far as feelings of connectedness and happiness. Always celebrate even the slightest improvement in the scale or acknowledge that things are not worse (e.g., if a family reports feelings of connectedness at a three, celebrate that is not a two!).

Compliments: A Solution-Focused Therapist will always *compliment* each client throughout every session—every little improvement, every insight, or just for showing up to therapy!

As the family begins to do more of what is working and less of what was not working, symptoms will naturally dissipate and the family will begin experiencing one another in more rewarding ways. Once these patterns have maintained themselves to some degree, therapy is terminated.

Narrative Family Therapy

Here, the therapist will begin to explore the narratives of each individual through the creation of a collaborative and supportive dialogue. Most therapeutic encounters will begin searching for a *unique outcome*, already orienting the clients to take control over their problems. For instance, the therapist may suggest that there must be some time that Mom and Dad were able to connect and illuminate upon that experience. Mom and Dad may report that just a few months ago they went to a wedding of a family friend, an evening that they spent dancing and laughing prior to returning to their hotel room where they made love for the first time in over a year.

Here, Mom and Dad were able to overcome *disconnection* (the externalized problem). The therapist would ask them how they were able to overcome *disconnection* (*landscape of action questions*) prior to moving into asking them what that says about them as individuals given their capacity and desire to *connect* (*landscape of meaning questions*). Mom and Dad may mention that they were able to overcome disconnection by planning an event, arranging for childcare, and spending the evening out of the home.

Here, the therapist has the opportunity to engage in *relative influence questioning,* further assisting the family to *externalize the problem.* The therapist may ask, "Mom, how does *disconnection* impact your emotional world," or, "Dad, how has *disconnection* impacted your relationships at work" (*mapping the influence of the problem*). Now, the *problem* is not personalized to any one individual or relationship, but is instead *externalized* as an outside entity. Next, the therapist may ask, "Dad, can you recall another time when you did not give in to *disconnection,* and instead acted against it to *connect* with your wife or daughter (*mapping the influence of the persons*).

Mom and Dad will begin to identify as people who crave connection with their partner (*subjugated self*) as opposed to people who *are* disconnected from their partner and cannot effectively achieve intimacy (*problem saturated narrative*). If connecting more with one another falls in line with their preferred narrative, *landscape of action* and *landscape of meaning* questions will help them to develop a *new, preferred narrative* congruent to what they are wanting. As they change their narrative, they change the manner in which they interact with themselves and the world.

Once clients report experiencing their *preferred narrative* as more of their everyday lives, therapy will work toward termination by *extending the narrative into the future.* Once the family and therapist collaboratively agree that they are pleased with the levels of connection within the family, therapy may be terminated.

References & Recommended Readings

American Association for Marriage and Family Therapy. (2013). *User's guide to the aamft code of ethics.* Alexandria, VA: AAMFT.

Association of Marital and Family Therapy Regulatory Boards (AMFTRB). (2015). retrieved from: www.amftrb.org

Bale, L. S. (1995). Gregory bateson, cybernetics, and the social/behavioral sciences. *Cybernetics & Human Knowing, 3*(1), 27-45.

Barbato, A., & D'Avanzo, B. (2008). Efficacy of couples therapy as a treatment for depression: A meta-analysis. *Psychiatric Quartlery, 79*(2), 121-132.

Bateson, G. (1979). *Mind and nature: A necessary unity.* New York, NY: Dutton.

Bateson, G. (1979). *Steps to an ecology of mind.* SanFrancisco, CA: Chandler.

Beavers, W. B. & Hampson, R. B. (1990). *Successful families: Assessment and function.* New York, NY: Norton Press.

Bhattacherjee, A. (2012). *Social science research: Principles, methods, and practices.* University of South Florida, Scholar Commons. *USF Tampa Library Open Access Collections.*

Boscolo, L., Cecchin, G., Hoffman, L., & Penn, P. (1987). *Milan systemic family therapy.* New York, NY: Basic Books.

Boszormenyi-Nagy, I., & Krasner, B. (1986). *Between give and take: A clinical guide to contextual therapy.* New York, NY: Brunner/Mazel.

Bowen, M. (1966). *The use of family theory in clinical practice.* In *Family therapy in clinical practice.* (2004). Oxford, UK: Rowman & Littlefield.

Bowen, M. (1974). *Toward the differentiation of self in one's family of origin.* In *Family therapy in clinical practice* (2004). Lanham, MD: Rowman & Littlefield.

Bowlby, J. (1988). *A secure base: Clinical applications of attachment theory.* London, UK: Routledge.

Broderick, C. B., & Schrader, S. S. (1981). *The history of professional marriage and family counseling.* In A. S. Gurman & D. P. Kniskern (Eds.), *Handbook of family therapy* (Vol. II, pp. 5–38). New York, NY: Brunner/Mazel.

Carr, A. (2000). Evidence-based practice in family therapy and systemic consultation: Child focused problems. *Journal of Family Therapy, 22*(1), 29-60.

Cecchin, G. (1987). Hypothesizing, circularity, and neutrality revisited: An invitation to curiosity. *Family Process, 26*(4), 405-413.

Chaffin, M., Funderburk, B., Bard, D., Valle, L.A., & Gurwitch, R. (2011). A combined motivation and parent-child interaction therapy package reduces child welfare recidivism in a randomized dismantling field trial. *American Psychological Association, 79*(1), 84-95.

De Jong, P., & Berg, I. K. (2000). *Interviewing for solutions* (2nd ed.). New York, NY: Brooks/Cole.

de Shazer, S. (1985). *Keys to solution in brief therapy.* New York, NY: Norton.

Forisha, B. (2013). *Advanced systemic theory and practice.* Argosy University. Eagan, MN.

Forisha, B., & Volini, L. A. (2014). *Wisdom and creativity: Revisiting the art of psychotherapy.* Headway Emotional Health Services All-Staff In-Service Training. Edina, MN.

Framo, J. L. (1992). *Family-of-origin therapy: An intergenerational approach.* New York, NY: Brunner/Mazel.

Gehart, D. R., & Tuttle, A. R. (2003). *Theory-based treatment planning for marriage and family therapists.* Belmont, CA: Brooks/Cole.

Goldenberg, H. & Goldenberg, I. (2013). *Family therapy: An overview* (8th ed.). Belmont, CA: Brooks & Cole.

Goldner, V. (2004). The treatment of violence and victimization in intimate relationships. *Family Process, 37,* 263-286.

Guerin, P. J. (1976). *Family therapy: Theory and practice.* London, UK: Gardner PR.

Haley, J. (1963). *Strategies for psychotherapy.* New York, NY: Grune & Stratton.

Haley, J. (1973). *Uncommon therapy: The psyhiatric techniques of Milton H. Erickson, M.D..* New York, NY: Norton.

Johnson, S. M. (2004). *Creating connection: The practice of emotionally focused marital therapy.* New York, NY: Brunner/Routledge.

Johnson, S. M., & Greenberg, L. S. (1988). *Emotionally focused therapy for couples.* New York, NY: Guilford Press.

Liddle, H. A. (2010). Multidimensional family therapy: A science-based treatment system for adolescent drug abuse. *SUCHT, 56*(1), 43-50.

Lieblum, S. R. (2007). *Principles and practice of sex therapy*. New York, NY: The Guilford Press.
Littlejohn, S. W. (2002). *Theories of human communication* (7th ed.). Belmont, CA: Wadsworth.

Madanes, C. (1990). *Sex, love, and violence: Strategies for transformation*. New York, NY: Norton.

Madanes, C. (1993). Strategic humanism. *Journal of Systemic Therapies, 12*(4), 69-75.

Mangen A, Velay JL. Digitizing Literacy: Reflections on the Haptics of Writing. Intech. 2011.

McGoldrick, M., Giordano, J., & Preto, N. G. (2005). *Ethnicity and family therapy* (3rd ed.). New York, NY: The Guilford Press.

Miller, S. D., Duncan, B. L., & Hubble, M. A. (Eds.), (1996). *Handbook of solution-focused brief therapy*. San Francisco, CA: Jossey-Bass.

Minuchin, S. (1974). *Families and family therapy*. Cambridge, MA: Harvard University Press.

Minuchin, S., & Fishman, H. C. (1981). *Family therapy techniques*. Cambridge, MA: Harvard University Press.

Napier, A. Y., & Whitaker, C. A. (1988). *The family crucible*. New York, NY: Harper & Row.

Nichols, M. P. (2012). *Family therapy: Concepts and methods* (10th ed.). Belmont, CA: Brooks & Cole.

O'Farrell, T.L. & Fals-Stewart, W. (2003). Alcohol abuse. *Journal of Marital and Family Therapy, 29*(1), 121-146.

Olson, D.H., Russell, C.S. & Sprenkle, D.H. (1989). Circumplex Model: Systemic assessment and treatment of families. New York: Haworth Press.

Piercy, F. P., Sprenkle, D. H., & Wetchler, J. L. (1996). *Family therapy sourcebook: Second edition*. New York, NY: The Guilford Press.

Rasheed, J. M., Rasheed, M. N., & Marley, J. A. (2011). *Family therapy: Models and techniques*. Thousand Oaks, CA: SAGE Publications.

Reuvini, U. (1979). *Networking families in crisis*. New York, NY. Human Sciences Press.

Roberto, L. G. (1991). *Symbolic-experiential family therapy*. In Gurman, A. S. & Kniskern, D. P. (Eds.) (1991). *Handbook of family therapy*. Philadelphia, PA: Brunner/Mazel.

Satir, V. (1987). *The therapist story: The use of self in therapy*. Binghamton, NY: Haworth Press.

Satir, V., Banmen, J., Gerber, J., & Gomori, M. (1991). *The satir model: Family therapy and beyond.* Palo Alto, CA: Science and Behavior Books.

Selvini Palazzoli, M. S., Cirillo, S., Selvini, M., & Sorrentino, A. M. (1989). *Family games: General modes of psychotic processes in the family.* New York, NY: Norton.

Selvini Palazzoli, M., Boscolo, L., Cecchin, G., & Prata, G. (1980). Hypothesizing-circularity-neutrality: Three guidelines for the conductor of the session. *Family Process, 19*(1), 3-12.

Sexton, T. L. (2011). *Functional family therapy in clinical practice: An evidenced based treatment model for working with troubled adolescents.* New York, NY: Brunner/Routledge.

Watzlawick, P., Beavin, J., & Jackson, D. (1967). *Pragmatics of human communication.* New York, NY: Norton.

Weakland, J., Fisch, R., Watzlawick, P., & Bodin, A. (1974). Brief therapy: Focused problem resolution. *Family Process, 13,* 141-168.

Whitaker, C. A. (1976). *The technique of family therapy.* In Sholevar, G. P. (Ed.) (1977). *Changing sexual values and the family.* Springfield, IL: Charles & Thomas.

Whitaker, C. A. (1989). *Midnight musings of a family therapist.* New York, NY: W.W. Norton.

Whitaker, C. A., & Bumberry, W. A. (1988). *Dancing with the family: A symbolic-experiential approach.* New York, NY: Brunner/Mazel.

Whitaker, C. A., & Keith, D. V. (1981). Play therapy: A paradigm for work with families. *Journal of Marital and Family Therapy, 7*(3), 243-254.

White, M., & Epston, D. (1990). *Narrative means to therapeutic ends.* New York, NY: Norton Press.

Wray Herbert. Ink on Paper: Some Notes On Note Taking*. Association for Psychological Science. 2014.

Acknowledgments

I could not rightfully acknowledge the support of any individual in the publication of this book prior to my wife, Lauren. The love and support you show me each day is with me in everything I do, and for that I will forever be grateful.

As I like to say, I have been spoiled rotten with the quality of mentors I have been privileged to encounter along the way.

To the Undergraduate Psychology Department Faculty at Saint Mary's University in lovely Winona, MN—it was under your guidance that I fell in love with learning through the field of psychology. In every progressive phase of my professional development I remain mindful of the foundation you helped me build and how well it has served me. I know some of you had your doubts, that I gave you good reason for (Dr. Bucknam), but you still gave me the space to grow into the professional I am now humbled to be. This is my unrelenting thank you to Dr. Elizabeth Seebach, Dr. Larry Luttmers, Dr. Daniel Bucknam, Dr. Jay Mutter, and Dr. Marilyn Frost.

To my many wonderful clinical supervisors that helped me develop as a clinician (in the order we first worked together): Dr. Steve Peltier, Dr. Sara Wright, Sarah Leitschuh, Jen Gustafson (Keep it real, Jen!), Dr. Kenneth Stewart, Char Forcier, and most recently, Beth Fagin. Your wisdom and curiosity has demonstrated the very qualities that make this field what it is, and for that, I thank you all.

To the educators who have exposed me to larger ways of thinking...

Dr. Bill Forisha, I mean, Bill...Being a part of your doctoral program has satisfied every curious bone in my body. I already find myself feeling the void in its absence of my weekly schedule. You have challenged me deeply and exposed me to a manner of thinking that transcends the textbook. Your commitment to this field is beyond inspirational and your knowledge base is arguably inhuman. I will forever be grateful for our relationship, and presenting you with the *Distinguished Services Award* will always be one of my greatest honors... All biological limitations and finitude aside, you'll forever be immortal in my book...

Dr. Sara Wright. As I've said many times before, there is a certain mysticism to you that oozes wisdom, compassion and humility in ways unlike anyone else I've known. You're a wonderful gift to not only our field, but our world.

Larry Tucker. there are few educational experiences I am more grateful for than your course on Multiculturalism. You are a valuable asset to our profession at large and an exceptional treasure within the Minnesota Association for Marriage & Family Therapy. Keep doin' it!

Dr. Rachelle Reinisch. It's been a treat connecting with you—for whatever reason, our modes of thinking have always complemented each other with such precision. I look very forward to what we come up with together moving forward.

Bruce Minor. I heard much about you prior to our first engagement after my master's program, and I must say, your reputation most certainly precedes you. Unlike any other professor, you have this ability to completely soothe my every lasting symptom of AD-HD. I have always been fascinated by the concept of wisdom, and as my definition of it is always changing, you remain as the constant. In the supervision course you taught, you had discussed the supervisors task of initiating the *fall from grace*, a necessary step in the supervisee working toward autonomy. I am not sure whether or not this was your intention, but in doing so, you created a paradoxical dilemma. You see, I am convinced that with you, there will be no *fall from grace*. SO convinced, in fact, that if you were ever able to prove me wrong, it would paradoxically add an additional level to the pedestal I've placed you on. Good luck…

What do you get when a Priest, a preacher's daughter turned Atheist, a Navy Sailor, a Lawyer, Shelley, and a 26-year-old pot stirrer walk into a Marriage & Family Therapy Doctoral Program?

Answer: My Cohort…

Those four semesters were a wonderful treat and I am grateful for my encounter with all of you. I look forward to sharing in our next steps and could not have asked for a better group to learn and grow with.

Thank you Dana (The Phenix), Marni, Father Rick, Barbara, and Shelley. And Herb!

I must also send a special acknowledgment out to my favorite co-therapist, Char, for spending the last four weeks independently maintaining all operations at Anicca while I was locked away in my cave finishing this book. Trust me, I got just as tired of telling you I was *almost done* as you did hearing it…

Don't worry, Mom, I did not leave you out…Your support and dedication in the lives of your three boys has been endless. Phillip, Brett and I were blessed in more ways than one to grow up with such loving and invested parents. The adoration and commitment that you and Dad showed us throughout our lives will serve us well in our families of creation as we raise children of our own. I am fortunate that my children, nieces and nephews will know the same unconditional love as they receive it from their Nana. Hang in there and stay strong, we all feel the void and miss him dearly with every day…

Pops, the next book goes out to you!

About the Author

Dr. Lucas Volini is a licensed marriage and family therapist in the state of Minnesota. Currently, Dr. Volini is the Clinical Director and core faculty for the Master of Science in Marriage and Family Therapy program at St. Cloud State University with a primary responsibility to oversee the clinical training requirements of the program, teach core courses, and advance his body of research. Holding a doctorate degree in Marriage and Family Therapy from Argosy University and master of arts degree in Marriage and Family Therapy from Saint Mary's University, he maintains professional membership in the American Family Therapy Academy, American Association for Marriage and Family Therapy, and the National Council on Family Relations. Dr. Volini is also a board member for the Minnesota Association for Marriage and Family Therapy.

Dr. Volini's research focuses on the development of Global Systems Theory to inform Global Family Therapy, an emerging approach of individual, couple, and family therapy that focuses on the interactional dynamics of cultural worldviews and self-esteem within and between family and social systems. Ultimately, Dr. Volini hopes to use this approach in reconciling conflict between opposing cultural groups. His research has been published in *The American Journal of Family Therapy* and presented at national conferences. Dr. Volini is also the author of a study guide and narrator of an audio review disc set that prepares professionals in marriage and family therapy to pass the national licensing exam.

Clinically, Dr. Volini has developed and directed a trauma-focused adolescent day treatment program, served as an outpatient therapist at a community mental health clinic, a school-based therapist, and an in-home family therapist. Currently, Dr. Volini practices through the Lorenz Clinic of Family Psychology (Victoria, MN), a Family Psychology training clinic where he sees individuals, couples, and families.

Most importantly, he is a fortunate and grateful husband to his wife, Lauren, and a loving father to his two children, Jackson James and Antonia AnnMarie.

Dr. Volini may be contacted at:
lucas@mftlicensingexam.com

VISIT
www.mftlicensingexam.com
for the following resources

Audio Review Disc Set
Put your commute time to good use by engaging in auditory learning as you listen to the author walk you through the primary theories covered throughout this manual, comparing and contrasting one another and applying them to the vignette!

MFT Exam App (Android/iOS)
Find the link to purchase the coordinating app for your smartphone or tablet. Easily and accessibly review the primary contributors and key terms/interventions of each theory.

Web-Based Tutoring
Schedule a 1-hour web-conference of personalized instruction with the author of this manual.

Training Courses
Register for the two-part training session scheduled throughout the year in the Twin Cities Metropolitan area.

Notes

Notes

Notes

Notes

Notes

Notes

Notes

Notes

Notes

Notes

Made in the USA
Columbia, SC
31 July 2021